Knight Errant

Knight Errant

A BIOGRAPHY OF

Douglas Fairbanks, Jr.

BY BRIAN CONNELL

Doubleday & Company, Inc., Garden City, New York, 1955

Library of Congress Catalog Card Number 55–5497
Copyright ©, 1955, by Brian Connell
All Rights Reserved
Printed in the United States
At the Country Life Press, Garden City, N.Y.
Designed by Diana Klemin

For Esmée,
who shared the enjoyment of our first
visit to the United States.

Foreword

IT TOOK ME three months to persuade Douglas Fairbanks to let me write this biography, a point I would like to stress in order to avoid any suggestion that he sponsored it for personal publicity purposes. It is published with his full permission, and he has given me countless hours of his time and unrestricted access to his personal files. All comments, deductions, and imputations of motive are my own. I hope I have not abused his prodigal co-operation.

The original idea of this book was conceived by my agent, Mr. Peter Lewin, who felt that there should be put on record the very real effort which men and women of good will in this country and the U.S.A. have been making to further amicable relations between their two nations. It was made possible, in the first instance, through the good offices of Mr. Julius Holmes, who was at the time American Minister in London and who, as a mutual acquaintance of Mr. Fairbanks and Mr. Lewin, was able to set the wheels in motion.

The chief outside documentary sources of Fairbanks' public work have been the archives of the Franklin D. Roosevelt Memorial Library, the U. S. Department of State, the U. S. Department of the Navy, the Committee to Defend America by Aiding the Allies, and the Co-operative for American Remittances to Europe (CARE). I am particularly grateful to Mr. Herman Kahn, Mr. John Cabot, the Public

Relations Division of the U. S. Navy, Mr. Clark Eichelberger and Mr. Richard Reuter for their kindness and co-operation in placing this material at my disposal.

All quotes other than extracts of documents and personal letters come from wire recordings of conversations with his family, friends, and associates in Britain and during the course of an extensive tour of the United States. I owe all the following personalities my warmest thanks for their friendly and forthcoming assistance:

Mrs. Eleanor Roosevelt, Representative Franklin D. Roosevelt, Jr., the Hon. Cordell Hull, the Hon. Sumner Welles, Messrs. Robert Sherwood, Lewis Douglas, Paul Warburg, James Dunn, Eugene Dooman, and Sir John Balfour. Admiral Sidney Souers, Messrs. Paul Hoffman, Paul Comly French, Henry Sell, Ed Flynn, Harold K. Whitford, William Griffin, Arthur Krock, Dr. Ralph Bunche, and Lord Tweedsmuir.

Admirals Earl Mountbatten of Burma, Lewis Strauss, H. Kent Hewitt, Charles Andrews, Neil Dietrich, Paul Foster, and Felix Johnson.

Messrs. Samuel Goldwyn, David O. Selznick, Darryl F. Zanuck, Jesse L. Lasky, Maurice Bergman, Alfred E. Green, Mervyn LeRoy, Mike Levee, Harry Crocker, and Mike Romanoff. Miss Loretta Young, Miss Irene Dunne, Miss Sally Eilers, Miss Virginia Bruce, Miss Janet Gaynor, and Mr. Gilbert Adrian. Messrs. Gilbert Miller, Cole Porter, Richard Barthelmess and Walter Pidgeon and Miss Clemence Dane.

Messrs. H. Alexander MacDonald, Irving Rubine, Peter Marriott, Harold Huth, Lance Comfort, Mrs. Christine de Lima, and Mrs. G. Hughes.

Miss Genie Chester, Dr. Mason Hicks, and the late Mrs. Henriette Patten. Messrs. Charles Chaplin, Gene Markey, Irving Asher, John McClain, Air Commodore Constantine and Lady Morvyth Benson, Colonel Rex Benson and Colonel Philip Astley.

Mrs. Jack Whiting (mother), Miss Mary Pickford (stepmother), Miss Joan Crawford (first wife), his first cousins Mrs. Letitia Fairbanks-Milner and Mrs. Flobelle Burden and her husband Shirley.

I must also render my humble duty to Mrs. Mary Lee Fairbanks, who has borne this intrusion into their lives with the utmost good humor.

Illustrations

1

THE SHALLOW ELLIPSE of grass and plane trees known as The Boltons, on the borders of Chelsea and Kensington in London, is a totally intact survival of later Victorian days. The tall, square, solid, detached houses, suggestive of the rhododendron and the laurel bush, wear a look of bland regret that no shining brougham and pair stands before the door to convey some top-hatted city magnate to his office. Many of them have been converted into flats and maisonettes of the more spacious kind, still preserved from the grinding brawl of the city's traffic. This quiet backwater harbors one notable exception to the prevailing air of diffident anonymity.

At the south-west corner, where the two looping carriageways join, leaving their continuation to degenerate in the smut and dirt broadcast by the Thames-side power stations, stands the acre plot of No. 28, with its secluded garden. Here it was, on a dripping November evening in 1952, that Elizabeth II and the Duke of Edinburgh came to dine with their good friends Douglas and Mary Lee Fairbanks, an event which fluttered the dowagers' dovecots of a hemisphere and focused attention on the remarkable position the hosts have come to hold in the world of affairs on both sides of the Atlantic.

Their guest list reads like a Who's Who of those who influence events in America, Britain, and half the countries of Europe. In one of the few salons to survive into the second half of the twentieth century, the Fairbanks provide a setting where minds can meet on neutral ground in an atmosphere of easy hospitality. Sir Anthony Eden, a friend of many years' standing, is a frequent guest. Adlai Stevenson, during his world tour, spent the only uncluttered hour of his London visit talking to Fairbanks in the summer sunshine of his garden. Winthrop Aldrich, on his arrival as Ambassador to the Court of St. James's, made dinner with the Fairbanks his first private engagement. King Paul of Greece, Prince Bernhard of the Netherlands, the Duchess of Kent, royalty, diplomats, politicians, personalities of stage and screen, come to dinner, cocktails, or just for a cup of tea. The list is endless.

All this happens in the home of a man aged forty-five, and has been happening in his other homes in London, California, and Virginia for years. He has won the personal regard of three American presidents and been accepted for more than two decades into the circle of the British royal family. Men of mark confide in him and listen to his views, in the knowledge that their trust in his discretion will not be misplaced and that his quiet advocacy has served many a good cause.

This is a privileged position in any context, all the more remarkable in someone who has combined its attainment with the apparent paradox of a long career as matinee idol and film star. Even now, the antic background associated with Hollywood prevents a great many people from taking him entirely seriously. Fellow Americans in particular, while grudgingly acknowledging his social success, are apt to dismiss it as a triumph of calculated snobbery. Popular gossip imputes to him an exaggerated liking for decorations and a weakness for appearing in overelaborate array on the wrong occasions. His forays into public affairs are dismissed as a by-product of purblind Anglophilia. Yet something more than this list of deficiencies is required as qualification for the many honors Fairbanks has received from a dozen governments, including his own.

Fairbanks keeps in his London and California homes signed and dedicated photographs of the hundreds of people whom he knows and with whom he has worked. The fact that this penchant for tangible evidence of his activities has led him to write and ask for some of these portraits does not detract from the warmth of many of the superscriptions.

"To Douglas Fairbanks with best wishes and warm regard to a distinguished American from his friend Dwight Eisenhower" can be read in one large frame at The Boltons. Another says simply: "To Douglas Fairbanks, Jr., from his friend Franklin D. Roosevelt"; while other rooms contain signed portraits of almost every member of the British royal family.

In his California home, Westridge, at Pacific Palisades, the facsimile British pub called the "Rose and Crown," which forms an incongruous part of the Spanish-colonial style of the whole, is literally lined from floor to ceiling with such photographs. "Fellow workers in the vineyard where the grapes of wrath are stored," writes Robert Sherwood, the playwright and a doughty ally in the days when they were campaigning for aid to beleaguered Britain and American participation in the war. Not far from a warm dedication from President Harry S. Truman there is a typically barbed comment from George Bernard Shaw: "To Douglas Fairbanks, the second, from one who remembers the first."

The paneled library at Westridge contains innumerable books with similar comments. He has a complete signed collection of the works of Sir Winston Churchill, while the author of the definitive lives of George Washington and General Robert E. Lee has signed the set: "For Douglas Fairbanks (who does not read history in vain)—Douglas Southall Freeman." Here again a jester has his say. Robert Benchley, author of *The Treasurer's Report, and Other Aspects of Community Singing*, poked sly fun at the recipient back in 1930 with the dedication: "For Young Doug, without whose co-operation this book was written."

The gay ambivalence of his personality has earned him friends in every walk of life. His popularity as an actor gave him a running start in the outside activities to which he has devoted so much of his time, and his success in them has given him a standing perhaps never enjoyed by a member of his profession. One of the most appealing aspects of his character is that however serious-minded his interests, he never takes himself too seriously. In a place of honor in his library he keeps a copy of Logan Pearsall Smith's *All Trivia,* a present from Veda Buckland, wife of the stage designer who mounted his father's *Robin Hood.* In it she marked the following passage with the comment, "A bit like you, Doug, what?":

I sometimes feel a little uneasy about that imagined self of mine—the Me of my daydreams—who leads a melodramatic life of his own, out of all relation with my real existence. So one day I shadowed him down the street. He loitered along for a while, and then stood at a shop window and dressed himself out in a gaudy tie and yellow waistcoat. Then he bought a great sponge and two stuffed birds and took them to lodgings, where he led a shady existence. Next he moved to a big house in Mayfair, and gave grand dinner-parties, with splendid service and costly wines. His amorous adventures among the High-up Ones of this Earth I pass over. He soon sold his house and horses, gave up his motors, dismissed his retinue of servants, and went—saving two young ladies from being run over on the way—to live a life of heroic self-sacrifice among the poor.

I was beginning to feel encouraged about him, when in passing a fishmonger's he pointed at a great salmon and said, "I caught that fish."

Above the fireplace in the Westridge library hangs an oil painting of his father. The light which illuminates it is kept on day and night. The artist, T. Costa, had never met his subject, and painted the picture, after Senior's death, from photographs. So uncannily perfect is the reproduction that former friends are apt to break off their conversation in mid-sentence as it catches their eye, as if they had seen a ghost. It is the sad, baffled, bemused face of a man in advanced middle age. During the years their lives overlapped, Douglas Fairbanks, Sr., was both bane and lodestar of his son's existence.

What manner of man was this who was a hero to a whole generation of filmgoers and lived to see the work which had been the very essence and expression of his life crumble into intangible memories?

Charles Chaplin, in one of his rare moments of quiet, grave detachment, says of him: "Of all my host of acquaintances, I think he was one of the few real friends I ever had." Yet Fairbanks himself remarked to one of his intimates, Frank Case, when speaking of his only son: "You know, I have no more paternal feeling than a tiger in the jungle for his cub."

Fairbanks Senior boosted the limited talents of a Broadway juvenile lead into one of the most resounding reputations in the history of the motion-picture industry. During the fifteen years of his marriage to Mary Pickford, they were the acknowledged leaders of the film colony. During the twenties, the years of his greatest acclaim, his films were an annual event, eagerly awaited by millions. He spent fifty years triumphantly surmounting every obstacle in his path, only to find in his last decade that he had not equipped himself with the qualities of character to sustain success when the energies which had provided it began to flag.

To all outward appearances the elder Fairbanks was a man of dynamic simplicity, his personal and professional personality so interwoven that it became impossible to tell where one ended and the other began. A man of self-centered pride in his achievements, his character had its dark side. Only his very close intimates knew that behind the ebullient, extrovert façade there were moments of black despair and a capacity for corroding, all-consuming jealousies. His wives and his son, each in their turn, were to feel the full savage lash of it. During the intervening periods he was gentle, considerate, and courteous, and that was the only side of him most people saw.

Behind his driving momentum and the almost violent strength of his personality, he was a man of hidden paradoxes. Maintaining in many ways throughout his life the strict Victorian outlook of his upbringing, he nevertheless married three times, leaving two wives in circumstances which did him little credit. Having given his own name to his only son, he seemed to spend most of his life regretting it.

Even their nicknames for each other were part of the pattern of wary acquaintance which characterized all but two periods of their relationship. It irked the father to be called by any name which denoted paternity, and one day his son asked him how he would have wished to be christened if he had had the choice. "Pete" was the answer, and "Pete" it was in the family from that time on. "Douglas" came equally hard as a method of addressing his son, who from his teens onward was known as "Jayar," a phonetic form of the Jr., which he bore as a suffix to his name for most of his own acting career.

For the first dozen years of his life young Douglas was subjected to his father's indifference; for most of the second decade to almost pathological opposition to his development as a screen personality; and in his third decade fought an uphill battle to win the confidence and friendship of a parent whose social and professional reputation decreased as his own grew.

Senior cast an almost hypnotic spell over those who shared his life. Mary Pickford, happily married for many years now to Buddy Rogers, still speaks of him with pent-up nostalgia. Quite recently his son's wife was shopping with her mother-in-law in a big New York department store when someone behind them called out: "Oh! Mrs. Fairbanks." It was the older woman, two marriages and thirty years later, who turned round to answer the cry.

It is not easy to carry the weight of a famous father's name, especially when circumstances have pitchforked the son into the same profession. Douglas Junior labored during most of his early life under a compulsion to win his father's regard and break down the barrier of disinterest. He tried not only to emulate him as an actor but was fired with an ambition to follow in his footsteps as a producer. Being perhaps more intelligent, more sensitive, and less single-minded, he failed to succeed and found outlets in spheres of activity where his father was no rival.

The two Fairbanks provide the only example in the—admittedly brief—history of Hollywood of a successful theatrical "dynasty." Other sons have made pathetic efforts to perpetuate, or merely cash in on, a father's fame, but in almost every case they have disappeared into oblivion after one tentative film. Douglas Fairbanks, Jr., is a unique exception. During his difficult early years he sought deliberately to interpret roles as far removed from the style of his father as possible, only to find that he was most popular in those that were identical. Their characters were very different, even if some of the outward mannerisms are similar. Until he was a grown man, the younger Fairbanks lay constantly in Senior's shadow without sharing his life. It is to the elder Fairbanks we must first look for the factors that formed the younger.

2

FAIRBANKS SENIOR was born in Denver, Colorado, on May 23, 1883, and baptized a month later, by a Catholic bishop, with the names of Douglas Elton. His father, H. Charles Ulman, had been a distinguished lawyer in New York, who moved west to the foothills of the Rockies in an attempt to make a fortune during the silver boom. The venture, financially disastrous, contributed to the never fully explained abandonment of the family five years after his young son was born.

During and just after the Civil War days H. Charles, as his descendants still call him, was a man of some substance and influence. There was Jewish blood in his veins. His father had been one of the principal millowners in the central part of Pennsylvania. H. Charles studied law with a leading barrister and political figure, the Hon. James T. Brady, and established a successful practice in Philadelphia.

When the War between the States broke out in 1861, he enlisted a company on the Union side, the Jersey Shore Rifles, and became its captain. Wounded in a skirmish after the first battle of Bull Run, he was then assigned to guard duties in the White House grounds, where he became closely acquainted with President Lincoln and Stanton, the Secretary of War. His grandson still possesses a statement of services drawn up for a pension application, with a short biography from which these details are taken. Pinned to the first page is a daguerreotype of its subject, the face of a man so strikingly handsome that he was often mistaken during his lifetime for the great actor, Edwin Booth, whom he closely resembled.

Ulman's by no means inconsiderable claim to notice is described in the following passage from this family document: "It was while at Philadelphia that the necessity of such an organization as the United States Law Association first suggested itself to his mind. He felt the want of a reliable source from which to obtain the name of trustworthy lawyers in different sections of the United States to whom he could entrust business with safety. That he did in the spring of 1866, and in January 1867 removed to New York as president of the United States Law Association, conducting the same until 1883, when he went to Colorado and engaged in mining."

The name of Fairbanks borne by his descendants results from the somewhat complicated marital misfortunes of H. Charles's wife. She was born Ella Adelaide Marsh, the beautiful and spirited daughter of a well-to-do Massachusetts family, whose first husband was John Fairbanks, a New Orleans plantation owner of considerable means. When he died of tuberculosis not long after the birth of their son John, a business partner absconded with his fortune. Ella turned in despair to the trusted lawyer and family friend, H. Charles Ulman, but she never saw a penny of it back. Her second marriage, to Edward Wilcox, broke up when her husband took to drink. Although she belonged to a staunchly Catholic family, she turned again to Ulman to obtain a divorce.

Still young and attractive, her third marriage was to her lawyer, an alliance consummated so soon after the divorce that the outraged Victorian propriety of his partners demanded his resignation. A letter from a friend opened a vista of quick riches in Denver, and H. Charles moved there with his wife and family.

Accustomed to the comfortable opulence of the Old South, Ella had to accommodate herself to the raw air of a frontier boom town. Within a few years her husband had lost all his money, and he traveled east again to become Republican campaign manager for Benjamin Harrison in the Presidential elections of 1888. His few modest remittances soon dried up, but as a result of one chance encounter in Denver a few months later, he exercised a lasting influence in at least one respect on his younger son. Adjourning to a bar, with sarsaparilla for the boy and a succession of something stronger for his father, the interlude gave his parent sufficient courage to agree to the little boy's excited pleadings that they should visit his mother. She nearly fainted from the shock, and the next day took Douglas to the local temperance league headquarters to sign the pledge. He remained an abstainer until he was nearly fifty.

This meeting brought no reconciliation, and the family never saw H. Charles again. He died practically destitute in 1915, the year in which the name of Douglas Fairbanks first became part of the Hollywood scene.

Ella Ulman moved into a smaller house and took in boarders. Her eldest son, John, went to work with a wholesale grocery business. Somehow she scraped a living, maintained her standards, and gave her two small boys a decent education. A couple of years after her husband's disappearance she obtained a divorce on the grounds of desertion, resuming the name of her first husband, Fairbanks. Both Robert and Douglas came to be known by it, and in 1900 legalized it as their own.

After a curious early period when he seemed to lead a withdrawn, glum little life of his own, her youngest child became the tartar of the family. Sunny-tempered, indulging in endless practical jokes and schoolboy pranks, forever bounding, climbing, and leaping out of sheer animal spirits, he nevertheless retained in after years the streak of morbidity he had shown so young.

Brilliant but inattentive at school, he soon developed a passion for the stage. His teachers found that one way to curb his restlessness was to give him long passages of Shakespeare to memorize. In the callow days of his first appearance in the theater he refreshed his acquaintance with the great plays, and it was always a source of astonishment to the friends who knew him in the swashbuckling years of his success that he could break into word-perfect renderings of the famous speeches.

From the slim family resources his mother managed to pay for dramatic lessons with Margaret Fealy, a member of a well-known American theatrical family who had settled in Denver. Through her he was introduced to Frederick Warde, a very good actor of the old school, who barnstormed his way through fifty years of one-night stands the length and breadth of the United States. On the strength of a half-serious promise to engage the eager young man with his company in

New York, Douglas left Denver in the spring of 1900, accompanied by his mother.

Warde was as good as his word, and the career of Douglas Fairbanks, actor, commenced at the Academy of Music in Richmond, Virginia, on September 10, 1900, when he appeared as Florio, a lackey, in *The Duke's Jester*. He was not given his first important speaking part until several weeks later at Duluth, when the illness of another member of the cast obliged him to take over the role of Laertes. An appalling attack of stage fright was probably not the only reason for the terse comment in the next morning's review: "Mr. Warde's supporting company was bad, but worst of all was Douglas Fairbanks."

It should not be supposed that he did not develop as an actor, and it is quite untrue to suggest that he emerged from nowhere to become one of the great stars of the films. For most of the next fifteen years he slowly fought his way up in the theater on the strength of an indefinable but very positive quality of personality, which made him one of the busiest and most popular juvenile leads on the New York stage. His first film contract resulted from this reputation and for no other reason.

The beginnings were sketchy enough. Frederick Warde's gentle suggestion that he would become a better actor with greater experience of the world was followed by a short excursion to Harvard University, where he enrolled for what he later called a "special course," although no one can suggest how it was paid for. His search for knowledge ended with a decision to travel with two friends he had made there to Europe, working their passage in a cattle boat. During this modest prelude to the triumphant world tours of his later years, he worked in the London docks and as a day laborer in Paris, where he picked up a remarkable collection of French expletives in the original *argot* which used to convulse such friends of his heyday as Maurice Chevalier.

On his return he essayed a last fling at orthodoxy by becoming a stockbroker's clerk. Within six months he was back on the stage. Soon after, he attracted the attention of the theatrical impresario William A. Brady, who divined in him a talent for juvenile comedy leads and in whose productions he made his name.

On December 4, 1906, he appeared in a leading role in George Broadhurst's *The Man of the Hour*. During its run of 479 performances, Fairbanks was introduced to a great admirer of his acting, a stage-struck debutante named Beth Sully, the pretty, vivacious daughter of Daniel J. Sully, the "Cotton King" and "Savior of the South," one of the great business tycoons of the turn of the century. They were married on July 11, 1907.

Ella Fairbanks was delighted. Douglas had allied himself with all the lost splendor of her own youth. Dan Sully was a lavish and resplendent figure, a reputed multimillionaire, with a handsome New York town house and a country estate called Kenneth Ridge at the fashionable summer resort of Watch Hill, near Providence, Rhode Island. It was here that Beth had grown up, the belle of that rich, turn-of-the-century society. There was much Scottish blood in her veins. Her mother's name was Thompson, and she claimed kinship with the Campbell clan, while the Sullys traced their line back to Scottish Jacobites, some of whom emigrated to France, where their descendants bear the name of Béthune-Sully, with a château on the Loire. Beth Sully owed her Christian name to this connection.

Grandfather Thompson was a model employer who had introduced the cotton gin into New England and owned a number of mills in Connecticut and Massachusetts. Daniel J. Sully went to work for him as an up-and-coming, bright young man, and married the boss's daughter. He became a power in the cotton world, built up a colossal business, and in the early 1900s cornered the world market. Kenneth Ridge was kept up in tremendous style. Their daughter had her own carriage and horses, and her coming-out party was the event of the year.

Dan Sully was a great admirer of the Emperor Napoleon, and amassed a considerable collection of relics and books about him. But he met his own Waterloo at the hands of a business rival named Theodore Price. A year or two before Beth Sully married Douglas Fairbanks, Sr., her father owned every bale of cotton in the world. Then Price outmaneuvered him, and he was practically ruined. Through friends in Wall Street he made something of a comeback and became associated with a big soap company, but the old buccaneering spirit had gone out of him and he had slowly to liquidate all his assets. There are those who say that if he had conserved his fortune, his daughter's marriage would probably never have broken up.

He had insisted that his son-in-law should leave the stage and become a respectable businessman, and he set him up as managing director of the company he formed, Buchan's Soap Corporation. It was one of the old man's last financial operations. The soap business failed, and Fairbanks turned, not unwillingly, back to Broadway. William Brady had a new play ready, *All for a Girl,* and made him its star. That was followed by one of Fairbanks' best parts in *A Gentleman from Mississippi.* During its run his son, Douglas Elton Fairbanks, Jr., was born on December 9, 1909.

Fairbanks Senior was always a man for keeping up a bold front, while with Beth the maintenance of at least the outward appearance of her social contacts and position became almost an obsession. For the arrival of their son, they borrowed enough money to rent a luxurious suite in the Apthorp Apartments on the corner of 79th Street and Broadway in New York.

For most of the next five years, while his father consolidated his position on the stage, the family lived at the Algonquin Hotel on 44th Street, the highly characterful establishment run by Frank Case. It had a bustling, sophisticated atmosphere, redolent of grease paint, newsprint, and heady artistic chatter. Case was a great friend of all the actors of his day and used to extend them almost endless credit. They always paid up in the end, even John Barrymore, who at one time was said to owe five years' rent.

Some residents have described young Douglas as rather a fat and unattractive child, very spoiled, always in and out of the lift and all over the place. Once he was caught roller skating through the lobby. This his mother denies with some heat, saying that she would never have permitted such a thing, nor would his nurse, "Dedie" Dowd, a stern disciplinarian of the old school. Douglas ruefully admits the incident because he cannoned into the half-blind actor John Drew and frightened him out of his wits. Normally the boy was kept under very strict control, and these lapses from the firm nursery discipline his mother considered essential probably resulted from the difficulty of applying her country-mansion standards to life in a hotel.

"Dedie" Dowd—her full name was Delia O'Dowd—was indeed a character. She was engaged during a family visit to England when Douglas was five months old. "We had a house on the Thames at Bourne End," his mother recalls. "In those days one used to land at Holyhead, and I was up all the night before because we had to get off in a tender. His father was terribly embarrassed about carrying a baby, but he had started down with some milk pails, and all the other things one has for infants, until he saw someone coming and just dropped them. Then we found it was not a corridor train, and as we had nothing to heat the milk with Senior lit matches under it until we got it a little warm.

"Dedie was absolutely marvelous, but sometimes I felt she was one of the most disagreeable human beings that ever lived," Douglas' mother recollects. "I used to fire her about four times a year, but she was a wonderful nurse and Douglas adored her. She had straight, lank hair, and Douglas would look at her and say to my mother, who was a beautiful woman with naturally wavy white hair, 'Why don't you fix your hair like Dedie?'"

She stayed with mother and son for years, and kept Douglas firmly in hand. "I'll have to ask The Lady Who Lives With Us," he used to tell young friends who wanted him to go out and play with them. He was a little embarrassed to admit that he still had a nurse, and that was the name by which she became known. As Douglas grew up, she retired on a pension from her former charge to a little cottage in County Sligo, and died only in 1954.

The earliest record of his contact with two of the interests in life with which he is now identified came at the age of four. His mother had taken him to London again, where they lived at the Goring Hotel. There it was his supreme delight to march up and down with the sentries outside Buckingham Palace. He claims to have received a charming smile from King George V when the monarch rode out in an open landau and Douglas shouted in a piercing treble, "Hallo, King."

His first visit to the theater was in New York, when he was taken to a box to see one of his father's performances. He spent most of his time looking at the audience, but then turned to watch the actors in a love scene. His clear, childish voice brought down the house with the remark: "Look, Mummy. Daddy's kissing that woman."

The boy's chief joy was the holidays he spent at his grandfather's Kenneth Ridge estate. This big Victorian pile was the last tangible evidence of old man Sully's vanished fortune. One way and another, chiefly with the help of his son-in-law, a semblance of the old pomp was still maintained. Even so, Douglas' childhood mind must have received the imprint of a factor which was to loom large as he grew up —his father felt absolutely no paternal affection for him. Beth saw it only too clearly and grieved. "Senior was perfectly tender and nice, he just did not have the instinct of being a father. All through Douglas' youth he paid no attention to him. He used to come into the house, day in, day out, and he wouldn't know the child was there. Unless I asked if he was going up to say good night to Douglas or somebody wanted to see the child, Senior displayed no interest in him—he didn't care; he was just bored."

By 1915 Senior had become well known on Broadway as a successful light comedian, appearing in a number of stage hits in which his easy ebullience, quick charm, and flashing smile made him a popular and acceptable figure. But he was already thirty-one and beginning to wonder whether he could make the transition from juvenile lead to more mature character actor.

At this juncture he was approached by Harry E. Aitken, sent by the newly combined "Big Three" of the still barely respectable film industry, D. W. Griffith, Thomas Ince, and Mack Sennett, to engage Broadway stars for their new program of production. Griffith's *Birth of a Nation* had by now induced polite society to visit the cinema, and more than sixty actors, including Sir Herbert Beerbohm Tree, Mary Anderson, and Billie Burke, took the tempting dollar bait offered by the three producers' Triangle Film Corporation. Douglas Fairbanks was well down the list, but his contract provided for a weekly salary of two thousand dollars, an enormous sum in those days, and far more than he had ever earned on the legitimate stage. Taking his wife and small son with him, he left for Hollywood.

After nearly four days and nights on the transcontinental train, they arrived in Los Angeles. For the first three days it poured with rain. Junior, in his childish fancies, expected to find cowboys and Red Indians, cattle stampedes and stagecoach robberies. There was neither wigwam nor hitching post in sight. Instead of bald prairie, Los Angeles was just another large American city, with tram tracks and policemen on corners directing traffic. He probably did not hide his disappointment too well, because his father, in unexpected genial mood, would not rest until he had produced the necessary local color.

"The first day I visited my father at his studio," Douglas remembers, "he introduced me, shy and tongue-tied, to my first Indian. He was as dirty and scruffy an Indian as you could ever imagine. But that was a later recollection. Then, he was *my* Indian, and when he let me wear his war bonnet I let out a triumphant whoop.

"At home, when I told my mother about wearing the Indian's feathers, she was more than somewhat disturbed. She could imagine me crawling with every form of bug. Rushing me into the bathroom, she seized the scissors and 'scalped' me. She was speechless with anger, but my father just laughed. 'It's good for him. It will toughen him up,' he said."

The film industry when the Fairbanks went West was still centered in New York. Griffith's Triangle Film Corporation and the Cecil B. de Mille—Sam Goldwyn—Jesse Lasky combination of Famous Players-Lasky Corporation, were among the first in California. Their studios were barns in a citrus estate called Hollywood Ranch. As more film people came in, the woman owner leased more land. The farm became a village, the village a town, and the town Hollywood.

Soon young Douglas was being introduced to his father's new friends. Charles Chaplin, who used to meet Senior at corner drugstores after the day's shooting was over, was one of the first visitors to the Fairbanks' home. "I was taken upstairs to meet the son of the house, and my chief recollection is that he had no top front teeth," Charlie recounts. "Junior was so sleepy that when his father said, 'This is Charles Chaplin,' the child said, 'Oh yes,' and went off to sleep again."

Anita Loos, his father's scenarist, a tiny woman, used to play with young Douglas, who at the age of six was very nearly as tall as she was. He seemed to think that she was about his own age. While being undressed one night, he asked: "Anita, who undresses you?"

At first he was sent to a girls' school, which accepted half a dozen young boys, and for years afterward was teased about it. Even now it is a private joke between him and Paul Hoffman, later the administrator of the Marshall Plan, an earlier alumnus.

Senior's first film, *The Lamb,* was an adaptation of one of his Broadway successes, *The New Henrietta,* and only the fact that it took the public fancy at its first showing saved Fairbanks from premature oblivion. His extrovert ways and seemingly shallow talents struck no spark of personal enthusiasm in the aloof, demanding, and intense Griffith, who supervised the production. Moreover, the camera crew and technicians had made Fairbanks the butt of their accumulated resentment against the importation of so many extraneous stage personalities in an industry which had largely manufactured its own talent.

Fairbanks would have been shunted into Mack Sennett comedies if his original sponsor, Aitken, and Griffith's production manager, Frank Woods, had not paused long enough to give him a second chance. They sensed in him a personal quality which might find enduring expression in the new medium. Turning to the man-and-wife director-writer team, John Emerson and Anita Loos, also just making their mark, the two men suggested a collaboration with their problem star. The future authoress of *Gentlemen Prefer Blondes* was the first to realize that the way to present Fairbanks was to devise situations in which he could play himself, and her husband had the skill to transfer them to celluloid.

Fairbanks embodied in his own life and in his stories a philosophical outlook which, to the battered generation enduring and emerging from the Great War, seemed to provide a simple answer to their problems. To a world beset with social neuroses he offered the creed that there was nothing which could not be accomplished by sheer enthu-

siasm. This he expressed in his own words as meaning "that uncon-
querable spirit of enterprise that laughs at reverses, knowing that they
are part of the game, takes obstacles as something to whet the appetite
for further endeavor, and fights for what it wants for the pure joy of
fighting."

The enormous popularity he soon acquired enabled him to emerge
as the successful author of a series of superficial, largely ghost-written
books on the same theme. Their titles are sufficient explanation of their
contents: *Laugh and Live, Making Life Worth-while, Initiative and
Self-reliance, Taking Stock of Ourselves, Whistle and Hoe—Sing as
We Go, Assuming Responsibilities,* and *Profiting by Experience.*
"Speed's the keynote of this age and this land," he said once. "It's the
principal ingredient in the success formula. Action—the straight line
of direct motion between the man and the objective—explains the top-
notch fellow in any line of life." The public lapped it up and flocked to
his pictures.

Twenty-nine pictures in three years, more than two thirds of his
entire life's work, with Fairbanks playing the sane, triumphant hero in
a world of villains and crackpots, made him the idol of America. They
also made him extravagantly rich. He had very soon discovered that
even a salary of one hundred thousand dollars a year was only a
minute proportion of the net cash profits contributed by an adoring
public. Calling his considerably older half brother, John, from his
wholesale grocery office in Denver, and his year-older brother, Robert,
an engineer, from prospecting in Utah, he formed his own family
company.

By 1918 he was worth well over a million dollars, but his private life
had gone awry. Before he left New York he had been introduced to
the woman star whose fame rivaled his own, Mary Pickford, and he
had seen her with increasing frequency since. Soon they were deeply
in love. Four lives were affected, as Mary was married to Owen
Moore, an actor; but human nature being what it is, nothing could
now stop the inevitable.

"Senior always used to say I should have been his sister and not his
wife, and I think it's true," Beth muses. When the crisis came she was

on a visit to New York, where Senior had asked her to look into some business matter for him, and was awaiting his arrival at the Algonquin. Instead, he booked in at another hotel, leaving instructions that his wife should be told that he was out. When it was clear that the situation was beyond repair, she instituted divorce proceedings.

Young Douglas was still only nine years old, and although he had been vaguely aware of family difficulties, the news that his father and mother were going to part was only broken to him gradually. His recollections of the period were not happy: "My cousin Flobelle, who was the elder of two daughters of John Fairbanks, was my chief playmate at this time, but we were not overly popular, because we did put up a rather fat appearance and were not as trim as my father would have preferred. However, he was always very kind to me, and I can never remember any gesture of meanness or disagreeableness. At the same time, I do not remember any particular display of affection or consideration either.

"I remember once, however, on a visit to Watch Hill, a trusted old dog bit me under the chin rather severely, and my father nearly killed the dog in revenge for having hurt me. He had somehow felt that because I was relatively reticent and shy, easily embarrassed, that I was somehow not basically aggressive, adventurous, and daring. He frequently complained to my mother that he did not feel in the least paternal toward me and although I was a 'nice kid,' I was being brought up as a mother's boy. On another occasion, during some rumbustious eight- or nine-year-old sport, I fell down and very severely cut my knee. The bone was exposed and they poured, rather than applied, a bottle of iodine into the hole. I remember his admiration for my refusal to weep or to show any sign of pain. It was one of the proudest moments of my youth, as this behavior was remarked on by him for some weeks afterward.

"Up until the time my mother and father separated, I always associated him with a pleasant, energetic, and agreeable 'atmosphere' about the house, to which I was somehow attached but which was not attached to me. He also seemed to be someone I did not know very well."

3

BETH AND HER SON moved to New York. The only stipulation she had made in the divorce was that Douglas should remain under her control. There was one strained meeting between his parents, at which it was arranged that Senior should continue to see his son. But Beth was under no illusions: "I knew he would never care whether he saw him from one year's end to another" was her thought.

It was a difficult period for young Douglas. He was sent to a bewildering variety of schools, and it is perhaps no wonder that he was a poor scholar. First came Bovee School, a select preparatory establishment, where every ounce of the almost vanished Sully social prestige had to be invoked to obtain his entrance. It was run on old-fashioned lines, and his chief memory is of being soundly and consistently caned. He then went for a short period to the Collegiate Military School. His mother also wanted him to join the Knickerbocker Greys, another exclusive society where little boys marched up and down in Civil War uniforms every afternoon. Douglas was at first turned down because he was an actor's son, but after furious lobbying was finally accepted. Twenty-five years later, when he went to a New York tailor to order a naval uniform, the cutter sighed reminiscently: "The last time I fitted you, Lieutenant, was for a uniform of the Knickerbocker Greys. I still have your picture, and I wonder if it would be presumptuous to ask you for a new one?" Douglas sent it by the next mail, with the inscription: "From the Greys to the Blues, 1918–1943."

His mother soon married Mr. James Evans, a Pittsburgh stockbroker. A hypersensitive woman, she had been badly hurt and took this step too hastily, perhaps seeking to prove to herself and her friends and family that she was not, after all, unwanted. The marriage lasted little more than a year and brought financial disaster. Through bad advice and unwise speculation most of her generous divorce settlement was lost. "Senior settled one hundred thousand dollars on Douglas and four hundred thousand dollars on me, at least on paper," says Beth.

"The actual value was less than that because I had to take securities. Douglas got about eighty thousand dollars, which was in trust, and I got about three hundred and fifty thousand dollars. People have said I was a spendthrift and just spent it. I wish I had, because I would have had some fun, but I lost it. I tried to make more."

This arrangement had cost Senior another three hundred thousand dollars in taxes, and he had to borrow part of the money, which it took him two years to pay off. He did not learn until many years later that the settlement had been mishandled.

For a period the Evanses moved back to Los Angeles, where Douglas was sent to Harvard Military School. There he failed to pass a single examination and incurred a record amount of "extra duty." Every infraction of the rules involved these small boys in an hour's drill carrying a full-sized pack on their shoulders. By the time Douglas was taken away, he had a backlog of forty-five hours.

His next school, the Polytechnic, a co-educational establishment at Pasadena, may be said to have opened another chapter in his life. His mother recounts that he developed a crush for a little girl named Agnes Hawkins and came home in high glee one day to say that he had kissed her in an orange grove.

"Why, that's wonderful, Douglas," she said. "But why did you have to take her out in the orange grove?"

"Well, that's where my arithmetic teacher took my geography teacher," he explained.

One facility he did have, a portent of things to come, was his success in the school plays. He was a dunce at mathematics and algebra, but by the time he was twelve he had memorized the whole of *Richard III,* everybody's part, and could recite the complete play from beginning to end. But economic pressure was beginning to tell. He had made a couple of further trips to Europe with his mother during the school holidays, and then, with her second marriage breaking up, she decided they would go and live in Paris, where life was much cheaper. They took an apartment at the Hôtel des Champs Elysées on the rue Balzac. There, from being a rather delicate child, subject to more than his share of ill-health, Douglas suddenly shot up about five inches. His mother remembers him growing out of his clothes three times in eighteen months. He had a tutor, learned French and Italian, and started to develop the precocious talents that marked his teen-age years. He showed more than promise at drawing and painting, studied sculpture and had one plaster model of a baby's head accepted at a second-rate exhibition.

It was shown under another name. Even at this young age the sharp remarks of many of his elders had bitten home. Too plump and not very bright at school, he had heard only too often: "He'll never be the man his father is"; "You'd never think he was old man Sully's grandson." Almost his whole life had been spent in an adult world, and if there was precocity there was sensitiveness and a maturity of intelligence far beyond his years. He knew his mother was in straitened circumstances and felt obliged to help her and prove himself.

His father's fame was now resounding round the world. Quite apart from a childish wish to emulate him, there was the subtle atmosphere of living with a mother whose two marriages had now failed and who saw in these first awakenings of talent in her child a new justification in life. When suggestions reached her from Hollywood that Douglas should make a film, the thought that she might be the mother of a prodigy probably outweighed maternal qualms about the suitability of such a step.

It is not surprising that so important a turning point should remain vivid in Douglas' mind: "My mother and I were loath to ask my father for any more money after his liberal settlement; furthermore, my mother was determined not to impose on his life any more than was necessary. I am sure also that pride had a great deal to do with it. In any case, it was decided that some move must be made, and when an offer came that I should enter films as an actor and cut off my formal studies, continuing in California with a tutor, my mother hesitatingly accepted on my behalf. Being young and seeing a means of finding a new outlet for energies without surrendering my studies, and at the same time having a youthful pride in being a responsible breadwinner, I jumped at the whole opportunity."

Few boys of his age have been involved in a situation so complicated by ulterior motives and personal resentments. At this moment of decision his father and Mary were also visiting Paris. Douglas sought him out, was delighted to see him, but had great trouble in summoning up the courage necessary to tell him the news of his decision to begin work in films. Finally, the big moment took place in his father's suite at the Crillon Hotel. Senior hit the roof. He asked if money was the decisive reason, but this his son stoutly denied.

The discussion went on for several days. It reached quite serious proportions, and the boy was terrified that his father would discover that it was really money which was the deciding factor. Although he was only thirteen, he stood up to his parent as if he were over twenty-one, staunchly defending his right to earn his own living and lead his own life. Almost on the verge of impertinence, while respectfully hinting at Senior's past neglect and lack of interest, a number of other pent-up emotions and frustrations found release.

It was certainly not the most admirable behavior for someone of his age, but Douglas had, although idealizing his father and adoring him as a hero, been severely hurt by his lack of attention to anything Douglas had done until it was something of which Senior disapproved. Senior, in a rage, said that as a punishment he would cut his son out of his will, give him no help whatsoever, and oppose his every professional move. This he did, but his opposition was kept away from the public press because the resultant publicity would have been extremely disagreeable.

When the transcontinental train pulled into Los Angeles on June 18, 1923, it was met by an honor guard of Boy Scouts in full regalia. The platform was crowded with reporters, press agents, photographers, cameramen, station personnel, and a couple of hundred gawping bystanders with nothing better to do. They converged on a plump, handsome woman and her good-looking young son as they descended from their compartment. The boy was Douglas Fairbanks, Jr. He was thirteen and a half years old.

His father had just reached the peak of his career. Audiences the world over had flocked to *The Mark of Zorro, The Three Musketeers,* and *Robin Hood*—three of the most popular films he ever made. Lavish romances produced at his own expense, they had earned him a fortune.

The tumultuous success of such productions and the growing might of the United Artists Corporation, which Fairbanks had formed with Mary Pickford, Charles Chaplin, and D. W. Griffith, was highly disconcerting to another original moving-picture giant, Jesse L. Lasky, whose Famous Players-Lasky Corporation was feeling the draft of such strenuous competition. Something had to be done to steal the thunder of this triumphant quadrumvirate. The shrewd publicity stunt he devised has him chuckling reminiscently to this day.

Word had reached him from Paris that Douglas Fairbanks' first wife was living with her son in a modest hotel in the French capital in circumstances unduly straitened. Lasky's informant was an actor-manager named William Elliott, an old acquaintance of the Fairbanks' family and a former son-in-law of David Belasco, the famous New York theatrical impresario. Elliott also indicated that Mrs. Evans was by no means averse to the idea of Douglas Junior following in his father's footsteps.

Lasky, a splendid buccaneer, round whom the fur had always flown thick in the endless dogfight of moving-picture production, began to see the possibilities of a diversionary operation of heroic magnitude. He announced, with suitable fanfare, that he had signed up Douglas Fairbanks, Jr., at a salary of a thousand dollars a week to make his first film. "My motives?" the septuagenarian Lasky recalls. "Douglas Fairbanks was the greatest name in picture business. This was a commercial proposition to capitalize on his name."

A contemporary account had this to say:

"It may be that the thirteen-year-old son of the great Douglas has been engaged in order to furnish his employers with a weapon against his father, perhaps merely a thorn to irritate the Fairbanks' flesh, perhaps even a club to bruise and dent. Simultaneous publicity campaigns would be disastrous to the father, and even the fact that Fairbanks *Père* is undoubtedly at the top of his profession would not prevent the incidental annoyance of having the son starring in rival productions. The sudden flashing of Fairbanks *Fils* as a full-fledged star would foster the notion that Fairbanks *Père* is much older than he really is, certainly not a thing one would care to have thought. Then, too, it might revive the story of his divorce, it would serve as a constant reminder of his first marriage, and the scandal that attended its breaking up before his marriage to Mary Pickford. That particular skeleton has lain moldering in its closet for so long that it was pretty well forgotten. The appearance of the boy brings it out in rattling panoply, and that hurts."

To say that his father was annoyed is a massive understatement. "He's too young and doesn't really know what he's doing," he said for the record. "I wanted him to have the best education possible, but I don't think that's possible now. You can't work in pictures and attend a university at the same time. He should have been permitted to wait until his education was completed before he took up a career. The boy's management is in his mother's hands though, and she ought to know what's best for him. . . ."

The full blast of a Hollywood publicity campaign whistled round young Fairbanks' ears for the first time. "The first instance of the second generation in filmdom," the headlines proclaimed. In an effort to imitate the bounding acrobatics which had made his father famous, slightly pathetic pictures were circulated of him standing shakily astride an iron railing on the roof of his Paris hotel and hanging at ungainly arm's length from an overhead ring. "He is the clean, healthy, breezy all-boy, American Boy!" the sickening blurbs announced. The only reaction the victim himself can recall now is that he was delighted to have so much attention paid to him, and that a thousand dollars a week sounded like a handsome contribution to a strained exchequer.

In his first press interview, bolstered by the presence of Noah Beery, Lois Wilson, Richard Dix, and Ernest Torrence, he produced one remark which the friends of his later years regard as one of the most wildly inaccurate forecasts ever made: "Girls are all right, but they are kind of silly. If I ever have to make love to one in a scene, I'll use a double."

The film was made in the Famous Players-Lasky studio on Vine

Street, at that time lined with pepper trees, occupied today by the N.B.C. television studio. Every effort was made to produce a success. A good director, Joseph Henabery, who had directed his father in *The Man from Painted Post, Say Young Fellow,* and *His Majesty the American,* was engaged, and three top-flight actors, Theodore Roberts, Noah Beery, and Harry Myers, had leading parts. The story was an adaptation of the Richard Harding Davis story *The Grand Cross of the Crescent,* and the film version was called *Stephen Steps Out.* It was a topically angled story of a son who confounds his father's opinion of him as stupid after flunking in Turkish history, who then goes to Turkey, rescues a Sultan's son, and obtains a decoration for his teacher, whom the father, a rich man, had caused to be fired. "What we really meant was 'Young Doug Steps Out,'" says Lasky. "The idea of Stephen was that of an aggressive boy, like his father. Although he was physically mature for his age—he looked and was playing a boy of about sixteen—he was quiet and shy. He lacked a quality which he later developed. He showed no particular talent beyond the average young man, and there was no reason at that time to think that he'd ever become an important actor on his own."

Douglas' chief memory of it today is of one scene in which Noah Beery was supposed to slap him and succeeded in knocking him clean out. But he did get one piece of professional training. Harry Myers told him how to steal a scene from Theodore Roberts. Nobody thought it could be done because Roberts always smoked a cigar. Whenever he wanted to grab a scene he just rolled the cigar from one corner of his mouth to the other and any other actor on the set was a dead pigeon. Myers told Douglas to take out his handkerchief and move it from one pocket to another. He was scared to death to do it, but the crew kept urging him on, and when Roberts looked down Douglas smiled right into the camera. Myers and everyone on the set started laughing, and Roberts thought they were amused by something funny he had done. When he saw the rushes a couple of days later he was furious, but by that time the set had been dismantled so they could not take the scene over again.

The film was an unqualified flop. The reviewers were fairly amiable, but Jesse Lasky was well aware that his gamble had failed. It was made quite clear to the young victim and his mother that the whole idea had been premature and that there would be no repetition. But Douglas had had his horizons broadened and his appetite whetted. He had discovered a wholly delightful way of earning a living and was puffed up with pride at the contribution he had made to the family finances. Taken East again by his mother, he at least was determined to return.

4

MOMENTARILY CHASTENED, Douglas and his mother returned to the same Paris hotel. They traveled across the Atlantic with the United States team to the 1924 Olympic Games. On the boat, Charley Paddock, the great sprinter, befriended young Douglas, who more or less became the team's mascot and was allowed to train with them. Among the distinguished visitors to the French capital during the games were Mary Pickford and his father, who, to his mother's secret delight, was unable with all his influence to obtain a pass to join Douglas with the athletes. But father and son did meet, a little formally, and there was something of a reconciliation. There was no more talk from Senior about cutting Douglas out of his will, although he had some curt comments to make when he found that his son was still enthusiastic at the idea of making a career in films.

Although he was still only fourteen, the boy looked seventeen or eighteen. He was always in the company of older people, and often played tennis with Georges Carpentier and Maurice Chevalier, who found him a very acceptable doubles partner. While spending a holiday in the South of France he took tennis lessons from Suzanne Lenglen, and played in one game with an elderly gentleman who turned out to be the King of Sweden.

Douglas' mother, ever grand in her manner, asked a young university graduate friend of the family named Carlton Hoekstra to join them as companion-cum-tutor. Douglas was already developing the voracious appetite for knowledge that marked his next few years, but he was still hoping that someone would give him another chance in Hollywood.

The opportunity arrived just when economic necessity became most pressing. Grandfather Sully now had practically nothing left, Kenneth Ridge was gone, and his daughter and her relations were slowly starting to sell some of their family jewels, heirlooms, and furniture to make ends meet. Toward the end of the year word came that Jesse Lasky was prepared to give Douglas a contract in the Paramount stock company at an infinitesimal salary.

Mother and son made their way back to Hollywood, this time arriving unheralded and unnoticed, to begin Douglas' long struggle for recognition. "For a couple of years I played in anything and everything that came along," he says. "I worked every single week, sometimes had a nice part, sometimes a lesser one, and sometimes no part at all, just walked on. My salary was cut in half after six months, but I still kept on working."

They rented a frame house, substantial but not pretentious, on Franklyn Avenue, from which in due course they moved to 912 Beverly Drive, not far from the Beverly Hills Hotel. Beth always tried to keep up some approximation to the large existence she had known since her girlhood. She entertained, the conversation was on a high level, there were musical evenings and serious discussions. To her the maintenance of outward appearance was paramount. Only the dwindling stock of valuable furniture and jewelry measured the cost.

The proud Sully clan had fallen on sad days. The former "Cotton King" came to live in a tiny house in Los Angeles and remained dependent on his grandson's earnings until he died. Aunts and sundry cousins, unable to accommodate themselves to the demands of a harsher world, all had to be helped. At an age when he should have been going to school, Douglas found himself the only family breadwinner, at a time when his employers, having once boosted him as a prodigy, now went to the other extreme and detected no talent in him at all. "What the boy needed was opportunity and training," Jesse Lasky recalls.

"We had decided he must make his own way and that we would not capitalize on his name."

It was a grueling apprenticeship. Sometimes Douglas would act as assistant cameraman, lug cases of film weighing nine pounds apiece all over the countryside when on location, and help edit the rough cut. This was long before the trade-union days of three men for each job, and everyone except the star had to do his share of the manual labor. Very often the company would work until one in the morning and report back on the set again at seven. In addition, the boy had to spend a certain number of hours a day with his tutor.

It is a labor of love to track down the titles of these productions nowadays, and even then they are not very edifying. There was *The Air Mail, The Texas Steer, Wild Horse Mesa,* and one, almost too near the truth for comfort, called *Broken Hearts of Hollywood.*

As it was, the boy, eager, cheerful, and well liked, enjoyed every minute of it. *The Air Mail,* with Warner Baxter and Billie Dove, was made at a mining ghost town called Ryolite, abandoned after the gold rush like some terrestrial *Marie Celeste.* For *Wild Horse Mesa,* with Jack Holt, made on location in Arizona, the company had to find five thousand head of wild horses. It was like the old frontier days come to life again, with Indians stripped to a loincloth, their long hair down, galloping across the desert bareback holding on to the horses' manes.

The Texas Steer, with Will Rogers, was shot in Washington, D.C. Normally, in order to conform to California State law concerning the employment of minors in films, Douglas was accompanied everywhere by his mother. However, she took advantage of the occasion to visit relations in New York, and Douglas decided that he would cater to his thirst for experience by spending the night on a park bench. His only reward was a sound thwack from a policeman's truncheon across the soles of his feet in the small hours.

His first break came toward the end of 1925, when Samuel Goldwyn gave him a part in *Stella Dallas,* with Ronald Colman, Jean Hersholt, Belle Bennett, and Lois Moran. "Douglas Fairbanks was a complete, almost overwhelming success as Richard Grosvenor, the young lover," said one heart-warming critique. Douglas was sixteen, looked twenty-one, but to his chagrin had to stick on the mustache called for in the part. The somewhat inadequate adornment which characterizes his lips these days was a later development.

Charles Chaplin is one of the people who liked his performance in *Stella Dallas*. "It was a very competent effort," says Charlie. And to Douglas' delight he gave a very warm account of it to his father.

"He was breathlessly bound-up with himself and his profession at the time," Charlie remembers. "There was one evening, I cannot recall where it was, when he made me sit on a curb with him until about one in the morning, pumping me with questions about life and art and everything under the sun. I doubt if the advice I gave him was very good.

"He was an extremely intelligent young man, and among his gifts he was a remarkable mimic. I remember he had one party turn of portraying various film actors coming out of the sea after a bathe. His version of Ronald Colman was a riot."

Douglas' imitations of his father, John Gilbert, and John Barrymore were equally good. It is a gift he retains to this day, and his powers of observation are so acute and the results so hilarious that it is difficult to meet the subject without breaking into an appreciative and reminiscent chuckle.

Relations with his father were resumed on a level of strained formality. Very occasionally Douglas would be invited with his girl cousins to swim in the pool at Pickfair. Every few weeks or so he might be asked to dinner. Three times over a period of years he remained to watch a film and stay the night. These visits were extremely irregular, and he often found himself embarrassed in front of other people, who took it for granted that he was there most of the time. The handsome mansion was the most impregnable social fortress in the West and invitations to it were as coveted as those to the White House. Junior found Hollywood stars and executives constantly hovering round him, darting here and there to do favors, pressing kindnesses upon him, all in the mistaken hope that his friendship could win them social recognition.

"An invitation to Pickfair was an event, issued some days ahead of time, worked up to, involving special combing of the hair and very careful selection of what I was to wear, like a child going off to a party," says Douglas. He would frequently try to persuade his uncle Robert to suggest to Senior that he be allowed to spend a Sunday there. Then he would stall around hoping to be asked to dine. Often he would tell his mother that he was expected for dinner, knowing full well that he had not been invited, in the hope that during the day he would be able to drop a broad enough hint. Usually the hint was not taken up and, rather than lose face at home, he would go back and tell Beth that he was tired and as it had looked as though it was going to be a long evening, he had asked his father to excuse him.

During this difficult period his mother and stepmother, Mary Pickford, did everything they could to foster Douglas' frustrated admiration for his father. Mary Pickford let it be known that he was always welcome at Pickfair, and indeed ties of the warmest affection bind the two to this day. Whenever it looked as if Senior and Junior were engaged in friendly conversation, she would retire to the upstairs sitting room to knit or read a book and leave the two together. But for a long time it was all of no avail.

Mary, who has a soft heart, took a more charitable view of the prickly relationship between the two. "There's an impression about that doesn't do Douglas Senior credit," she says, "that he didn't love his son. That is not true, he loved him very dearly. But Senior was so much of a little boy himself, I don't think he felt like a father. He was a very shy person, he didn't like to show affection or emotion. That's not unique in men, even in women. But toward the end they were very, very close, probably closer than he was to any man, including his own brother Robert. There was this sense of misunderstanding between them, augmented undoubtedly by the greed of certain people that forced his son into a position that he didn't think was right. He felt at the time that the boy was being exploited, to his injury and hurt and the detriment of his father. When that was over, I know positively he was very proud of him."

Many of the older stars, conscious of young Douglas' difficulties, went out of their way to be kind to him and invite him to their houses. Gloria Swanson was one. She and Douglas still delight in the anecdote of the evening he spent at one of her parties disguised as a footman. Still a little young to attend as a guest, she let him dress in knee breeches and a wig and wait at table. It was all done very seriously, and he made an excellent servant, without anyone guessing his identity.

Junior developed a certain proficiency in such sports as wrestling, boxing, swimming, and fencing, and began to appear more frequently at his father's studio, with its nearby swimming pool and gymnasium, to exercise with him. Each afternoon Senior held court to a constant sequence of internationally famous faces—distinguished writers, visiting royalty, nobility, politicians, and artists. Senior enjoyed a range of acquaintance which provided Douglas with many of his introductions into the larger world. The same friendships appear in both generations: the Prince of Wales, the Duke of Kent, the Mountbattens, the Duke of Alba, and many American political figures. Senior and Mary Pickford were world celebrities and met others in different walks of life on terms of equality.

Senior not only enjoyed the company of the great, he had a curious facility for seeking out people of accomplishment in other fields. He delighted in acting as host to prominent athletes, and even as late as 1932, when he was forty-nine, his studio and home became a mecca for those taking part in the Los Angeles Olympic Games. He was a fanatic in matters of physical fitness and managed to give a good account of himself against champions in the hurdles and the decathlon. He maintained a pensioned coterie of eccentrics and was especially proud of the friendship of a seventy-five-year-old relic of the old West, who had been a mail robber with a string of convictions and ten notches on his gun.

Like many men who have made a fetish of success, Senior expected to excel in all things. The film legend was projected into his private life. Gilbert Miller, the theatrical impresario, recalls inviting him one day to take part in a clay-pigeon shoot on his estate. When he saw a crowd of onlookers Senior refused to try his luck. "I don't think I'll shoot with all these people here," he said. "What does it matter?" queried Miller. "No; in the movies the legend is I never miss," was the reply.

On the occasions when Junior and his young friends were invited to take part in Senior's private sports, the trainer would always warn them that they must be very careful not to beat him at anything. Charles Chaplin was one of the few people who had managed to ignore this rule. He and Senior had been attending a meeting of the United Artists Corporation directors at the Bank of America in Los Angeles. When it was over it was suggested that they should walk back to the studio, a couple of miles away.

"Why don't we run?" Charlie said, and before anyone could stop them they agreed to race. They took off their coats and started to trot back through the streets of Beverly Hills toward Hollywood. Fairbanks shot into the lead, but what no one suspected was that Chaplin had been a devotee of cross-country running in his youth. He eventually passed Fairbanks and got to the studio first. The great athlete could never bring himself to talk about it.

The two Fairbanks were still very shy of each other. When Senior returned from one of his long trips abroad, young Douglas would become so excited with anticipation that he could hardly contain himself for days before they were due to meet again. When the big moment came the old veil descended, and they could do little more than nod to each other and say some sort of mumbled hallo.

"My father's hesitancy at demonstrating paternal interest was a source of much youthful regret to me," Douglas says. "When he forgot my seventeenth birthday, and Christmas too, and then repeated that performance the following year, I was frankly hurt and embarrassed. But I would not admit it. When asked what he'd given me, I pointed to something and said 'that.' Then he suddenly gave me my first car, which of course more than made up for all past oversights. And that's what they were, because my father could never be consciously unkind to anyone."

One concession his father did permit, after much lobbying by Douglas through his uncle Robert and the brothers' trusted business manager, Clarence Ericksen, to whom the boy would turn as go-betweens, was the use of his magnificent beach property at Laguna—when Senior was not there himself.

This was a quarter-mile crescent of private beach, hemmed in by cliffs, not far from San Diego. Fairbanks Senior had erected a mock Arab sheik's encampment, with luxuriously fitted-out tents, where he used to entertain the great of the world in idyllic surroundings. Two summers running Douglas was allowed to take a group of about ten friends to stay, living like South Sea islanders, falling out of bed and straight into the ocean.

At home most of his companions were older men, like Rod La Rocque, John Charles Thomas, and Ramon Navarro, a great favorite of his mother's, who always used to come and sing at her musical evenings.

Douglas himself continued to exhibit a considerable precocity of talent, drawing, painting, and playing the piano. "Somebody would give me a banjo, and I wouldn't know one string from another. Inside three days I could play it. Consequently I can't play a single thing now, because I never applied myself," he says.

Then he started to worry about his missing education. How was he to catch up on all the knowledge he should have been acquiring, instead of trying to earn a precarious living? Veda Buckland, wife of one of his father's associates, thought she knew just the right person, and introduced him to an immensely erudite old gentleman named Thomas G. Patten.

Patten had been an intimate friend of President Wilson, a member of the American delegation to Versailles and, during the war, at the President's express request, had become postmaster-general of New York, an appointment which included all the confidential work involved in wartime censorship.

The old gentleman was not a tutor in the normal sense of the word, but he had just accepted another pupil whom Douglas already knew. Her name was Genie Chester, daughter of Colby Chester, an extremely wealthy businessman who for years was head of the General Foods Corporation. The deep and close friendship between the two is a touching and happy affair which has lasted since Douglas was a boy. They first met at Watch Hill when she was staying at a nearby hotel. Genie was playing clock golf with her brother when Douglas came up and challenged the winner. Before they could start she was tired, so they sat down to talk, and in a minute had started a lifelong friendship. Genie Chester is two years older than Douglas, a highly intelligent woman with a lovely head and face. But when she was five she was stricken with polio, which has condemned her to the cruel tyranny of steel braces and a wheel chair ever since. During every phase of Douglas' life she has always been one of his closest confidantes and correspondents.

Patten liked the two eager young things who had been placed in his care, and from 1926, for three years, he taught them all he knew. Every morning they would meet in the little bookroom at the back of his brown shingle bungalow on the upper part of Vine Street, with its painted pine shelves and the etching of Thomas Jefferson, or on the back porch under the eucalyptus tree, looking out over the brown and purple Pasadena Hills. It was just what was needed for Douglas' untrained, vacuum-cleaner mind. With his fine library— which Douglas bought when he died and which formed the nucleus of his collection of books at Westridge—and his encyclopedic knowledge of matters historical and topical, Patten used to sit and answer their questions. There was no subject they did not roam over; literature, philosophy, politics, economics, everything. By the time he was of the age when other young men go to universities, Douglas had a first-class grounding in the humanities and international affairs, and gives his mentor most of the credit for his present interest in them. Patten in his turn was immensely proud of his young protégé. "My husband used to say he had never known anybody with such a mind at that age," recalled his widow, Mrs. Henriette Patten, who maintained a sprightly correspondence with Fairbanks until she died, at the age of eighty-five, in the autumn of 1954. In her declining years she had been one of the regular recipients of his quiet philanthropy.

Douglas could never read enough, absorbing every kind of book on every possible subject, cultivating people from ballet dancers to

Chinese poets, scientists, politicians to military men. The world was not big enough to supply him with enough things to satisfy his interest. How could he possibly live long enough to take it all in? How could he walk through a library, press a button, and read every book and absorb everything they had to say—he used to feel. He developed a desire to visit every country and find out what made its inhabitants tick.

Curiously enough, Mr. Patten was an uncle by marriage of John Barrymore, another of Douglas' idols at the time. Their first contact had been back in the Algonquin Hotel days, when the great actor was playing in *Dr. Jekyll and Mr. Hyde*. Douglas cornered him in the lobby and asked him to show how he managed to change his face for the part. Barrymore bent down low so that no one else could see and went through his villainous facial contortions, to the boy's squeals of fascinated delight.

In the "Rose and Crown" at Westridge today there hangs a photograph of him signed in 1926: "For Doug Junior with sincerest good wishes from his friend and contemporary Jack." It was the first time he had used the Christian name in their relationship, and Douglas was thrilled. Up till then it had always been Mr. Barrymore, and in his uncritical hero worship he consciously adopted the great man's Byronic attitudes and flowing hair style. Barrymore was something of a Jekyll and Hyde personality in real life, liable to be found drunk and disorderly in all sorts of company, but he only allowed Douglas to see the best side of his character, and he made it a point of honor to be at his most urbane and charming to his young admirer. He was a fascinating talker, always ready to expatiate on literature, the origin of alcohol, or how Leonardo da Vinci mixed his paints.

He gave Douglas much fellow sympathy and kindness, when there was no one else to turn to, and used to intervene with Senior on his behalf, saying: "You don't know what a good young fellow you have."

Douglas was plagued by people who insisted that he would never rival his father in reputation or ability. He was understandably sensitive to the untrue suggestion that life must be very easy for someone with such a wealthy and influential parent. As he had been living for some time exclusively on his own earnings, supporting several members of his mother's family, this naturally excited the rebellious strain in his nature. His chief reaction was to cultivate precisely those qualities which might distinguish him from his father. He developed a taste for "arty-crafty" interests and intellectual pursuits.

His assumption of John Barrymore's appearance and mannerisms was more than superficial. He harked back to Byronic romanticism in his behavior, and sought expression in drawing, writing short stories, and composing poems. With memories of his delicate childhood, he developed a romantic illusion at the age of seventeen that he would die at the age of twenty-five in a blaze of creative talent. A friend of the family, Margaret Case, daughter of the owner of the Algonquin, who had become the associate editor of the magazine *Vanity Fair,* saw a couple of his poems and devoted a full-page spread to them.

They were, it is to be feared, highly derivative, and anyone with the slightest acquaintance of Milton's "Hence, loathed Melancholy" can hardly have been in ignorance of the source of inspiration of the following opus, but published it was:

Dive, O most unnatural mind
And drown thyself within the bowels of my perturbéd spirit
So that in such a way thou might'st dissolve
The one, the other and so cleanse my deform'd soul
Of such impious meditations.
O rude morbidity, thou bastard son of our mortality
That can on will transfer a happy mood
To thoughts of depravéd suicide. . . .

Barrymore's courtship of Dolores Costello provided Douglas with another field for emulation. After a brief boy-and-girl infatuation for Betty Bronson, who had created the movie part of Peter Pan in America and then disappointed Douglas by her lack of interest in the cultural sessions with old Thomas Patten, Douglas fell violently in love with Dolores Costello's sister, Helene. When she decided to marry a real estate man his grief was awe-inspiring. Nothing is so tragic as the thwarted and frustrated infatuation of a boy of seventeen.

He was suicidal, drowning himself in Shelley, Byron, and Keats, sitting up drinking sherry, and playing all the records of Grieg to develop his somber outlook. His drawings became copies of Doré, and he started illustrating the works of Edgar Allan Poe, while his poems became more morbid than ever.

He turned for consolation to John Barrymore, who for all his Bohemian cynicism was extremely fond of the young man and gave him excellent advice in his own brand of pure-blooded Anglo-Saxon. It cannot have been without effect, as the wife of his old mentor, Henriette Patten, can remember him saying in the depths of his woe: "This is a tragedy, but it will probably help my career."

His career was not, in fact, making very great strides. Somehow the promise of *Stella Dallas* had not been fulfilled, or at any rate not exploited by the film companies. Nineteen twenty-seven was a difficult year. He was given quite good parts in minor pictures at several studios, including *Man Bait,* with Marie Prevost, and *Women Love Diamonds,* with Lionel Barrymore and Pauline Stark, under Edmund Goulding's direction. In another picture, *Dead Man's Curve,* for a company called Film Booking Offices, which was later absorbed by the present RKO organization, a young man named Joel McCrea played his first part. He was another alumnus of the girls' school to which Douglas had been sent when he first arrived in Hollywood.

To raise much-needed cash Douglas approached Lotta Woods, one of his father's close associates, who allowed him to write some of the titles for Senior's film *The Gaucho,* giving him fifty dollars for his pains, and later he wrote all the titles for some of the Ronald Colman–Vilma Banky pictures.

Thwarted on the screen, Douglas lobbied around to find an opening on the stage. After all, that was where his father had started.

One of the major milestones in his life came in the autumn of 1927. On October 17 he appeared at the Majestic Theater in Los Angeles in the John van Druten play *Young Woodley.* His name guaranteed the attendance of the elite of Hollywood, and there is no doubt that he was a success in the part:

"The debut of young Fairbanks is, both from the standpoint of the play and of personal considerations, a distinct success," said one critique. "Ideally cast as the student, he also conveyed the deeper emotions inherent in the story with an air of sincerity that was more marked because he has not yet acquired the stock tricks of the established actor."

"With the fall of the final curtain, Who's Who in Hollywood was on its feet," wrote a local columnist. "Doug, Mary, Gloria Swanson, Louis Wolheim, Lowell Sherman, and scores of others were stomping and cheering and calling for a speech. The leading woman had had a big scene, and young Doug thought they were cheering her. Three stagehands finally pushed him out front, and when he realized what it was all about he stumbled to the footlights and with tears in his eyes and on his cheeks said, 'I thank you.' "

The last sentence Douglas denies. "I was under perfect control and very pleased. In fact, I recall I was quite unemotional about it all. Rather smug, as if to say, 'Well, it's about time you all treated me as something less than a shadow!' "

His mother was ecstatic: "Douglas had that natural thing that an actor needs. You either have it or not, you never can learn it. It's timing."

It was indeed a big moment. Charles Chaplin came round to his dressing room and talked until two in the morning. Douglas Senior underwent something of a change of heart. "Have you seen my boy's play?" he went around saying. "I guess I was wrong. He shouldn't be doing it at seventeen, he should be in college, but pay no attention to me; he's an independent cuss, and by God he's got away with it." To Douglas' delight he gave him a copy of the limited edition of *The Drama* by Henry Irving with the dedication: "To Junior: 'Let your own discretion be your tutor,' Dad 1927. The occasion being your first appearance on the dramatic stage."

Among the audience there had been a strikingly beautiful young woman who had been captivated by his performance. She was herself just making a reputation as a newcomer in the film business. Her name was Joan Crawford.

5

JOAN CRAWFORD is perhaps the last woman screen star in the grand tradition of Hollywood. Nearly fifteen years after such great rivals as Greta Garbo and Norma Shearer have slipped quietly into the limbo of retirement, she can still put the clock back to her beginnings and display as comely a figure in tights as many a touted newcomer, plus a considerable measure of acquired dramatic ability. Hers is a classic example of the film world's favorite "night-club chorus girl to great star" theme. Her whole career has exhibited a single-minded ambition and dedicated exploitation of herself, which makes her perhaps the most completely typical product of the demanding and fickle profession which she has made her life.

She has practically no being outside Hollywood. One of the phrase-makers in which the film colony abounds has suggested that if she were ever transplanted out of the media with which she has so identified herself, she would suddenly become and look a hundred and fifty years old, like Maria in James Hilton's *Lost Horizon.*

With the years she has acquired dignity, intellectual attainments, a long record of philanthropic acts, and an unassailable position. Childless, she has adopted four children, lavishing on them maternal care at set hours in the back-breaking timetable of work to which she still adheres. At an age which may be reasonably assessed at not far short of fifty, she is still a strikingly handsome, vital woman carried along irresistibly by the momentum which she has given to her life.

Three unsuccessful marriages, the recurring threat of professional oblivion resulting from totally unpredictable changes in box-office appeal, and the consciousness of a limited talent have resulted at each crisis in her career in an almost embittered counterattack to maintain her position as one of filmdom's queens. She talks, thinks, eats, lives, and behaves in Hollywood terms, with herself as the center of any activity in which she engages.

Her early life, in all conscience, was hard enough. Much of the frantic drive of her nature must stem from the memories of poverty and the desperate scramble for almost any source of income. Born Lucille Le Sueur Cassin in San Antonio, Texas, "on the wrong side of the tracks," she moved as a child, with her mother, whose two marriages had been dissolved, to Kansas City, washed dishes for pocket money and started to work her way through Stephens College by waiting at table. Her only academic distinction during the short time she stayed there seems to have been good marks in the dancing class. This talent won her a prize at the local Jack O'Lantern café and an introduction to show business in a night-club chorus in New York.

Spotted there by a film talent scout, she moved to Hollywood at the beginning of 1925, adorning the cheese-cake publicity stills which engulf so many aspiring starlets and progressing through a series of minor parts to a modest degree of recognition. There was something in her unquenchable vitality and vivid looks, the enormous eyes and lithe figure, which could not be denied even in that grave of so many hopes. She became widely known in the film colony, even if not necessarily for her acting abilities.

She can still remember that first night at the Majestic Theater back in 1927. "Douglas in *Young Woodley* was the most exciting thing I had ever seen—sensitive, colorful, a great talent," she recalls. He was appearing before a very distinguished audience and the acclaim he received must have given added weight to the title of "Crown Prince of Hollywood" accorded him by those ignorant of his struggle for recognition and the strained relations with his father. He was clearly a young man of some consequence, and Joan wrote him a very warm and pleasant letter of congratulation on his performance.

After the six weeks' Los Angeles run, the company then presented the play in San Francisco, and on his return Douglas met this new admirer. When he left a few days later for a short vacation at Del Monte, the young man was already in a condition of telephoning Joan every day and writing her passionate poems.

"He was charming, with a divine sense of humor," Joan remembers. "He liked me, too, and understood my serious attitude toward my work and life." They were, in fact, a well-matched pair; Douglas, old beyond his years—just turned eighteen—in manner and cultural attainments, but still to some extent constrained by the overpowering devotion of a doting mother—and the vital, self-reliant, ambitious girl a few years his senior. He was groping in the gargantuan shadow cast by his father and weighed down by responsibilities at an age when he should have been entering college. Joan talked him out of his lack of confidence in himself, providing the spur and the arguments for him to concentrate on his career and develop his acting abilities. Douglas, with his different social background, was able to open up a new world of behavior and interest for her.

They became inseparable companions, barely daunted by the implacable hostility of his father and mother to any suggestion of marriage. The very idea of it put Beth into a panic. She found Joan a strange, moody girl, overflamboyant in her dress and alternating between gushing enthusiasm and gauche aloofness. "The first time I met her they took me over to see a picture, and she sat in the car, read a book the whole way, and never spoke to me. She was scared," Douglas' mother remembers, but she soon found that Joan had her compassionate side too, often paying hospital bills for the poorer employees on the set, and Beth's opposition softened. "It'll do him good," Mrs. Patten, the wife of his tutor, told her. "He needs a steam roller."

Douglas Senior was violently opposed to the idea. As the romance took a more serious turn, he even got in touch with Beth and said she must do something to stop it, and tried to enlist mutual friends like Irving Asher, the producer, in the same cause. Jesse Lasky recalls how Joan and Douglas often used to come and sit on his private beach at 400 Ocean Front, although they seldom ventured the couple of hundred yards down to his father's beach house. Outwardly a front of civility was maintained in order to avoid wagging tongues, but relations between father and son dropped well below freezing point. Those close to them suggested that Senior and Mary Pickford were horrified at the possibility of becoming grandparents, but the antipathies were largely personal and never fully smoothed over.

The net result was to spark young Douglas into rebellion, and although his best friends told him he was too young, he determined to escape once and for all from parental influence and marry.

He had been supporting eight or ten people since he was thirteen, and this had engendered a premature maturity. He was still living with his mother, and although everything was made as pleasant as possible at home, he kept straining at the leash. He felt he ought to be in control of his own life.

Egged on by Joan, Douglas' career took a turn for the better. He was given a good part in *The Power of the Press,* the very first film made by Frank Capra, but the real break came with the advent of the talking film. The Warner Brothers' Company, in low financial water at the time, decided to stake everything on the new invention, which swept a hurricane swathe through established stars, who might rival Venus and Adonis in looks but had hideous corn-crake voices, whining Kansas twangs, and thick foreign accents. In the frenzied search for anyone who could face up to a camera and produce a reasonable speaking voice, Douglas had a head start. By this time he had appeared in several further "little theatre" successes, including Maxwell Anderson's *Saturday's Children.* The title came from the nursery ditty "Saturday's child works hard for its living." This Douglas had always done, but from now on he was to see some return for it.

He was put into *The Barker,* one of the earliest talkies, with Dorothy MacKail, Betty Compson, and Milton Sills, a film version of a stage success on a serious social theme. On Broadway the star was Claudette Colbert, in her first big hit. But she was not considered sufficient of a name and not photogenic enough for Hollywood. Static as the film was, due to the primitive conditions under which it was made, with all the cameras housed immovably in soundproof booths, it caused a sensation, and Douglas was given special mention in the critiques for his "tender love scenes with Dorothy MacKail."

With the overnight swing in popularity so typical of Hollywood, his services were suddenly much in demand, although his next film was again a silent one and the only time he has ever appeared with Greta Garbo. It was in *A Woman of Affairs,* the movie version of Michael Arlen's *The Green Hat.* Garbo and her co-star John Gilbert were in the middle of their much publicized romance, which was punctuated by stupendous quarrels. Douglas found himself acting as a sort of Cupid's messenger, going up to Garbo and saying, "Jack told me to tell you so-and-so," and returning with the answer, "Miss G. [as she was always referred to] says so-and-so."

Douglas had known Garbo from the time she first came to America with Mauritz Stiller, the director, later to be joined by Emil Jannings, the famous German actor. They formed part of a very intense group from Mittel-europa. At that period Douglas was anxious to act in and produce Rostand's *L'Aiglon,* the play about Napoleon's son which had been one of Sarah Bernhardt's most famous roles. His head was full of advanced ideas on the use of this pictorial art. The only positive sympathy he could get was from this particular coterie.

He did, in fact, make two films in French, *L'Athlète Malgré Lui* and *L'Aviateur.* His films had been going over quite well in France, so Warners asked if he would be willing, although it was not in his contract, to make two additional films entirely in French, with an imported French cast. The producer, Irving Asher, one of his lifelong friends, remembers: "When the pictures came out in Paris nobody would believe he was speaking such absolutely perfect French."

Joan and Douglas announced their engagement on December 20, 1928, and at the same time his career took another step forward. Warner Brothers put him into a series of puppy-love films, with a ravishingly beautiful young girl they were just grooming named Loretta Young. She was fifteen, claimed to be eighteen, and had the wide-eyed, exquisite, china-doll face she retains to this day. "Gretch," as she is known to her friends, is another Hollywood phenomenon. At a cheerfully acknowledged age of forty-one, she is still as slim as a girl, and can confound all her contemporaries by slipping quite comfortably into a child's nursery chair. "Douglas was absolutely charming to me," she says; "very much the gentleman. I hardly saw him outside the studio, as we had a different group of friends. He used to tease me about my age, but would always stand up for me when I got in trouble with the director."

In fact, however, as they now candidly admit to each other, they did not get on very well.

One of these productions was called *The Forward Pass,* a football story. Douglas' great heroes at the time were the University of Southern California team. They took part in the film, which helped release some of the pent-up frustrations of his lost youth and lack of schooling. To the exasperation of the director, Eddie Klein, who was afraid he might injure a leg and interrupt the shooting of the film, Douglas often succeeded in persuading the players to cut short their lunch and organize practice games for him. In another of their films called *I Like Your Nerve* a minor part was played by an English newcomer named Pratt, chiefly remarkable for his enthusiasm for cricket. This taste he retained, but he changed his name to Boris Karloff.

With this upswing in his career, Douglas and Joan married. To avoid any possible exhibition of family dissension, the wedding was held in New York. "He obtained his marriage license in the same place where his birth was registered, City Hall," his mother recalls. "He was nineteen, but supposed to be twenty-one, so he asked me to confirm the later age. They only needed to go up a floor to find out the truth, but fortunately they didn't ask him." The ceremony took place quietly in a chapel at St. Malachy's Catholic Church on June 3, 1929. His father sent a cable with his last-minute blessings, and superficially all was well. A week later the two younger Fairbanks were back in Hollywood on their respective film sets.

Not long after, his mother left for New York to marry Jack Whiting, the musical comedy star. Although he is some years her junior, they have been the happiest of couples ever since.

Beth Whiting now passes very largely out of her son's story but has never ceased to be an influence on him. She is, and always has been, a *grande dame,* her intense and sensitive nature complicated by vicissitudes for which the ease and grace of her early upbringing prepared her ill. During the years which brought Douglas to maturity, she provided in her personal attitudes and tastes a leavening contrast to the brash, even somewhat uncouth, atmosphere of the film colony. During periods of financial stringency she always contrived to maintain the air of a salon in their home. The conversation was good, manners decorous, and interest in the arts and music lively and constant. For years she fought and scrimped, disposed of family heirlooms, and devoted the fervor of her affections to furthering the career and growth of her handsome only son.

In the midst of his full life Douglas has never failed to write to her faithfully every week. Much of the gentleness in his character derives from her, and for a man who at first glance looks so like his father it is curious to note how very much more he resembles his mother. His interest in public affairs grew out of the wider background his mother made possible in his youth, but during the period after his own marriage, both he and his wife had to concentrate first on the consolidation of their film careers.

Joan by this time had become a star in her own right in *Our Dancing Daughters,* portraying a gin-swigging flapper with a wind-blown bob. Her studio, M-G-M, in an attempt to exploit the publicity value of her marriage, borrowed Douglas to make a sequel called *Our Modern Maidens.* It was the only film they ever made together.

Even Pickfair could scarcely withhold recognition. A few weeks after their return from New York, the young couple received their first invitation as man and wife to dine with the senior Fairbanks. It must, if the long-cherished recollection of a fellow guest is any criterion, have been an electric occasion. Joan had been fully conscious and resentful of her father- and stepmother-in-law's objection to her marriage. On the way up Summit Drive in the car she was seen to bend down as if she had dropped something under the lap rug. The carriage entrance to Pickfair is under a long overhanging terrace and guests must climb one story to the main hall. The drawing room is off to the right down three steps, and Joan paused at the top as Senior came over with his athletic lope to greet them. Just as they shook hands Joan said, "Oh dear, my shoe has come undone"; and there, before his guests, Douglas Senior bent down at her feet to do it up. It was indeed a superbly calculated and symbolic moment.

The party can hardly have been a success. The hosts had long adopted the curious habit of placing Mary at the head of the table, with Douglas Senior on her left. This put the guest of honor on her right and his wife on Senior's left, forming two unchanging pairs, to the exclusion of intercourse with anyone else at the table. Junior and Joan, farther down, had developed an exasperating doggerel language of their own, in which they used to communicate at all times with shrieks of laughter, leaving everyone else to suppose that they were the subject of the conversation. The groundwork was hardly laid for any easy exchange of hospitality.

Among Douglas' friends of the time was Robert Montgomery, his present television rival. They used to see a good deal of each other, fish, swim and box together, and on one occasion borrowed Cecil B. de Mille's ocean-going yacht *Seaward* for a fortnight's cruise. Laurence Olivier was another close friend and the victim of some fearsome practical jokes. On a visit to Mexico, Douglas arranged with the local police to have Olivier thrown into jail on a charge of being an Englishman. Olivier took it seriously and was nearly frantic by the time he was released.

Douglas was spreading his talents far and wide. He appeared in two more stage plays (his mother remembers him buying up empty blocks of seats so that the statement at the end of the week would look encouraging), continued to dabble in painting and sculpture, and wrote a number of short stories, some of which appeared in the *Redbook, Cosmopolitan,* and other periodicals. *Vanity Fair* commissioned him to write a series of profiles about Hollywood personalities, which he illustrated with his own caricatures. Two or three of these were striking and original, but his drawing of Charlie Chaplain was clearly based on an earlier pencil sketch by the Mexican artist Covarrubias.

The production that really established young Fairbanks as an actor of unusual charm and quality was *Dawn Patrol,* a classic film of the wartime exploits of the Royal Flying Corps, so well written and authentic in atmosphere that it has been remade twice since. It was a sort of *Journey's End* of the air, with an all-male cast.

When Howard Hawks, the director, and Richard Barthelmess, the star, were trying to cast the film, Douglas was due to appear in the John Barrymore version of *Moby Dick*. "Howard had his heart set on young Fairbanks playing one of the three principal roles," Barthelmess recalls. "I'd known Doug since he was a boy, so I went to him and asked which part he thought would be better for him. He leaped at the chance in *Dawn Patrol*. I told him to call Jack, tell him the problem, and see if he would release him. Which he did.

"I remember one amusing thing that happened. Young Doug in those days was a fancier of Barrymore. He affected the same rather Byronic collars and he wore his hair rather long. This was a military picture, so Howard told him to go and get his hair cut. He did, and when he came back Howard took one look at him and said: 'Now go and get your hair cut.' So he had two haircuts, but this time he had it almost clipped off."

Hawks was a hard taskmaster and a perfectionist. Douglas remembers him as "gentle and intelligent, but at the same time cold as ice and hard as nails." The company worked extremely hard, including one stretch of thirty-six hours' shooting sustained only by a few sandwiches, but the result was worth it.

The shorn locks were another milestone in Douglas' life. When the film appeared, his interpretation of the role of the happy-go-lucky Douglas Scott received the best notices.

The immediate result of his performance was that on June 25, 1930, he signed his first long-term contract with Warner Brothers. On the crest of a wave, he was quickly put into *Outward Bound* with Leslie Howard. Two lighter parts then led to his appearance in perhaps the greatest of all gangster films, *Little Caesar,* in which he played the young gigolo Joe Massara, with Edward G. Robinson. Douglas surprised everyone with the perfection of his dems, deese, and dose accent in this character role, but he had not lived in New York for years for nothing.

Highly delighted, Warner Brothers rewrote his contract, giving him authority in all his forthcoming films to supervise details of script, direction, production, and costume design. His father's mantle seemed about to fall on him. He was just twenty-one-and-a-half years old.

He was now required to make only four films a year, but over the next two years their quality was uneven. He played in *Parachute Jumper,* with Bette Davis, one of her early films; two or three indifferent dramas; scored a hit in *Union Depot,* with Joan Blondell, and was lent to RKO to make *Morning Glory,* with Katharine Hepburn. This was, as Douglas says, the nearest he ever came to an Academy Award. It was his co-star who won it.

The only drawback to this professional recognition was the deterioration in his marriage. Within a year it had become clear to them both that it was not going to last, but they struggled on, determined to try to maintain an understanding, if only to prevent those who had tried to stop it from saying that they were right all the time. Hollywood makes almost impossible demands on a couple if they are both stars. Half the time they barely see each other, and even if one partner is free while the other is working, it only means that one of them is too tired to make any normal married life possible.

Even professional rivalry plays its part. In 1931, according to their tax return, Douglas' income from First National was $72,791.67 and Joan's from Metro-Goldwyn-Mayer $145,750.00, but in 1932 he had caught her up.

The tremendous drumbeat of publicity had chronicled every minute aspect of their lives, and the strain of maintaining the necessary front had been too great. Their interests simply did not coincide. Joan concentrated almost entirely and exclusively on her job as an actress. Douglas had much wider interests. He could already talk lucidly about literature, the arts, and politics. He liked books and reading, but Joan was only interested in film scripts. Douglas, with the mirror of his father always before him, was eager to branch out into direction and production, whereas Joan's chief concern was the perfection of her acting technique. Even their guest lists clashed.

In the middle of 1932 they decided to make a two-month trip to Europe together in an attempt to compose their differences. At first all seemed to go well. They traveled over on the *Bremen,* and Noel Coward, who had known Douglas and his father for years, was there at the dockside to meet them. He arranged for them to see *Cavalcade* from the royal box at Drury Lane, introduced Douglas and Joan to the gay social whirl of London life, and held a party for them at which Douglas met again Prince George, later the Duke of Kent, for the first time since his visit many years before, as a midshipman, to the United Artists studio and Pickfair.

"My brother tells me an awful lot about your father and what a good golfer he is. . . ." the Prince greeted Douglas. (Senior had long been a friend and golf partner of the Prince of Wales.) Then they started discussing certain mutual friends, things they had in common, and before the party broke up the Prince had invited Douglas and Joan for a drink at St. James's Palace the next day. The foundation had been laid for a warm friendship, which lasted until the Duke's tragic death in the war, and led to Douglas' entrée into the circle of personal friends of the royal family.

Douglas was delighted by his reception, happy to be back in London renewing old acquaintances and making new friends. He felt completely at home. Joan, it seemed, was rather out of her depth. When Margot Asquith arranged for them both to be invited to a garden party at Buckingham Palace, Joan got cold feet and at the last moment refused to go. By the time they had spent a fortnight in Paris and made their way back to Hollywood, it was clear that there was nothing left to be patched up.

The last film Douglas made for Warner Brothers was called *The Narrow Corner,* adapted from the novel by Somerset Maugham, but so freely that Douglas received a signed copy with the dedication: "From almost one of your authors." The director was Al Green, a Hollywood perennial with many successes to his credit, both before and since. He had already directed Douglas in *Union Depot* and *Parachute Jumper* and, most recently, in *It's Tough to be Famous,* a story based on the national adulation of Lindbergh after his Atlantic flight. This had to be withdrawn from circulation because its release coincided with the kidnaping of the Lindbergh child. Green had known Douglas since the old Lasky days, and did not spare his criticism. One day on the *It's Tough to be Famous* set Douglas was having difficulty in the interpretation of one scene and Green delivered a dictum which was quoted and requoted around Hollywood: "You don't seem to know whether you're John Barrymore or Ronald Colman," Green said. "Why not try the scene as Doug Junior?"

"When he made up his mind to be himself he was very good," says Green, who found him an easy man to have on the set. They hardly ever needed to run through a scene more than a couple of times, and when not actually engaged in the action Douglas would sit next to Green and pick up tips on direction. A deceptively quiet man with thick-lensed glasses, Green had a taste for preposterous practical jokes. He especially delighted in shocking Douglas out of his normal mood of quiet dignity. Once when Douglas was conducting a minor scion of Eastern royalty around the set, Green joined them for tea and deliberately sat sucking it out of the saucer, to his star's embarrassed horror. Years later, when Douglas was appearing everywhere with Marlene Dietrich, Green practically broke up their tête-à-tête in a restaurant by walking over to their table and engaging Douglas in conversation while noisily operating a toothpick.

Part of *The Narrow Corner* was shot at night in the open air, on a superstructure representing the deck of a sailing ship. Not only was it surprisingly cold for California, but there were a couple of mild earthquake shocks during the evening. To quiet his nerves and keep out the cold, Douglas had taken a few shots of whisky. "I suppose you might say he was a trifle 'woozy,'" Green chuckles. "It was a storm scene, which involved emptying about forty tons of water on the deck. I did not like the first take, so Doug grabbed a few more tots, and we shot the scene again with another forty tons of water. And so it went on. It must have been one of the worst nights he's ever spent."

More than that, it was symbolic of a crisis in Douglas' career. The ground was indeed shaking under his feet, and both his private life and professional ambitions were about to suffer a series of cold douches.

When *The Narrow Corner* was finished, Warner Brothers did not renew his contract. The situation had been building up for some time owing to a number of factors. Some of his recent films had not been box-office successes, and the Brothers Warner had never been entirely happy about the veto powers given to such a young star. They were also a little out of humor at discovering that in lending Douglas to RKO to make *Morning Glory,* they had allowed him to keep his entire fee.

Douglas for his part was consumed with ambition to blossom as an actor-producer, like his father. There is more than a hint that he had become a little bumptious and demanding. His friend Gene Markey recalls with astonishment how Douglas used to lunch in the Warner Brothers directors' room and take part in the planning of the year's productions. There were plenty of people who found him a little too pushing and too sure of himself.

Hollywood was suffering at the time from the delayed effects of the great depression. As a panic measure, many of the stars had accepted a fifty per cent cut in their salaries. Douglas, William Powell, and James Cagney were three of the actors affected, and they had agreed to the cuts only on the personal undertaking of Darryl Zanuck, at that time Warner Brothers chief of production, that they would be restored to the original level as soon as business improved. Such is the way of Hollywood that the upswing was not slow in coming, but their incomes remained obstinately stationary. Zanuck, who had pledged his word and comes very well out of the affair, resigned in protest. Shortly afterward he joined Joseph Schenck in the formation of 20th Century-Fox. Douglas himself became involved in the sort of infighting typical of a Hollywood situation of this kind. While he went around saying that he would sign no new contract except at the restored figure, *The Narrow Corner* was released without any mention of his name in the credit titles. Threats flew, lawyers were consulted on both sides, and the inevitable resulted. His option was not taken up and he was out of a job.

This internecine shin-hacking behind the scenes coincided with the final breakup of his marriage to Joan Crawford. The trip to England had brought about no renewal of warmth in their relations. Although they continued to live under the same roof, they maintained what were to all intents and purposes separate establishments. The Hollywood gossip columnists, who dote on divorce almost as much as they love a marriage, had already printed a few hints, but these both Douglas and Joan had as promptly denied. Privately they had agreed that a separation had become inevitable.

It was not the fault of either. They had married too young and neither temperament, profession nor the torrent of studio publicity which had trumpeted the most intimate details of their existence were conducive to a long and happy marriage. As it was, each had done the other far more good than harm. Joan had injected her husband with some part of her own driving ambition, giving him confidence in himself, and helped to crystallize his personality; while Douglas had opened up new worlds of appreciation and interest for her.

Douglas had become involved in an alienation of affections suit brought by one Jorgen Dietz, which was filed on March 16, 1933. Joan Crawford immediately told a reporter: "There's nothing for me to say except I have known all about this from the start. We've discussed these flagrant charges together. It is an outrageous injustice and there is no truth in them whatever." In the end the plaintiffs thought better of their intention to bring the case before the court.

However, the atmosphere in the Fairbanks' home at 426 North Bristol Avenue was by no means as calm as this announcement might suggest. Events quickly assumed a hilarious degree of melodrama. Joan was in something of a dilemma. Not long before she had given an interview to a fan-magazine writer, when she had grown confidential and told of her troubles, and the girl had written a big story for the April number. These revelations were not going to coincide with the sympathy stories of Joan's devotion to her young husband and their beautiful romance, with which the local Los Angeles newspapers were likely to greet the announcement of the Dietz suit and her reaction to it. She would be picking buckshot out of her neck for years if she did not quickly square things with the influential Hearst columnist, Louella Parsons. So this redoubtable lady was invited over and informed of Joan's intention to apply for a separation.

The next unfortunate to be dragged into the melee was Mike Levee, business manager of both Joan and Douglas. She rang him up from the Metro-Goldwyn-Mayer studios and asked him to come out at once. When he arrived he was told that she wanted all Douglas' clothes removed from the house before she returned home that evening.

He was in a fine quandary. Joan was obviously in no mood to vouchsafe explanations, and he felt that if he were to go straight over to the Warner Brothers studio to ask Douglas what the trouble was, he would put him off work for the day. So, sending his chauffeur and the chauffeur's wife to collect Douglas' clothes and belongings from North Bristol Avenue, he drove to the Warner Brothers studio later in the day to meet Douglas as he came off the set. In his dressing room Mike Levee suggested that it might not be a bad idea for them both to have a scotch and soda. By the time he had plied him with three, he told him what had happened. Douglas' reaction was to roar with laughter. He had been rung up hours before by Louella Parsons and asked for a statement. Mike Levee's nervous delicacy had provided some needed comic relief.

6

BY APRIL 29, 1933, when Joan Crawford filed suit for divorce on the grounds of incompatibility in the Los Angeles Superior Court, Douglas was in England. He heard the news while sitting on the beach at Bournemouth. The break had brought an unexpected compensation. Young Fairbanks' marital difficulties coincided with the protracted and painful termination of his father's marriage to Mary Pickford. The two men, almost strangers to each other, had found unwonted communion and pleasure in each other's company. Douglas Senior had already sought escape from his mental confusion in the purposeless peregrinations which had resulted in one of his last and very poor films, *Around the World in Eighty Minutes,* which had been followed by an even more pathetic venture, *Mr. Robinson Crusoe,* the last film he ever produced in America.

The wonderful partnership with Mary Pickford, which had covered the dazzling years of his success, was beginning to disintegrate. Together they had been the acknowledged and outstanding heads of the film world. The aftermath of resounding success he could not hope to repeat had formed a vacuum in Senior's mind that only restlessness could temporarily satisfy. There were faults on both sides. Mary, with her practical common sense, perhaps did not share his dogmatic idealism and fanatic insistence on total abstinence as an essential component of physical well-being.

His trips to Europe had involved him in the company of people more hedonistic and sophisticated than his usual sphere of acquaintance, and some echoes may have reached her ears. It is probably true to say that the possibility of reconciliation always existed, but circumstances were to prevent it. Perhaps with a twinge of conscience, he turned briefly to the companionship of his son.

Junior had also developed a case of wanderlust: "Hollywood was getting to be a grind," he told a newspaper reporter at the time. "They had me doing five and six pictures a year. Some of them looked all right on paper, but they had a habit of slipping down into the program class. Only once in three years would I get a part I cared anything about. I kept going up and down the ladder and not getting any place, there was nothing stable about my career. . . . I decided to dip my finger in the production pie. To become a producer in Hollywood I would have had to start way far back and work years to get anywhere. The producing business was practically a closed corporation, it was in the hands of a few who didn't want to let in any outsiders. In England I stood a much better chance. It was just beginning to go in for movie making in a large way and drawing frankly on Hollywood talent."

Mike Levee, his manager, and a man of parts, who helped to form the Academy of Motion Picture Arts and Sciences, goes even further:

"He was young, aggressive, ambitious, with a good brain, and at times I wasn't quite sure that he should even be an actor. He had a little more I.Q., you might say, than the average actor or actress that one comes in contact with. He didn't like this chi-chi business that goes on. It is a part of our business, but he tried to dignify his association with it."

In the spring of 1933 the two Fairbanks sailed to Europe with Tom Geraghty, the irrepressible Irish pixie who had long been Senior's court jester. This trip introduced young Douglas into the financial stratosphere of the film world. Senior was seeking to expand the international ramifications of United Artists, and he and Junior were so enthusiastic over an uncut version of *The Private Lives of Henry VIII* that Alexander Korda, who had previously failed to make his mark in Hollywood, was invited to become one of the contributing owner-members. Douglas Junior, full of his ambition to graduate from mere acting, received his first insight into the production and financial aspects of his profession. It was also agreed that he should star in the first picture Korda made expressly for United Artists.

A tour of Switzerland was followed by a visit to Italy, which still further widened Douglas' horizons and gave him his earliest contacts with the affairs of foreign nations. It was probably the inception of this abiding interest in his life. Senior knew many of the leaders of Italian life and introduced his son to Mussolini and Ciano. Young Douglas also had a number of conversations with Count Sforza and Count Volpi, the Minister of Communications, who had introduced himself to them on a train. These experienced statesmen found Douglas a very intelligent young man, and his father was amused and a little flattered at the attention they paid him. "Well, look at old longhair over there," he would say to other friends when Junior stayed ensconced in a corner for hours settling the fate of the world. "Can't make up his mind whether to be a poet or a diplomat." They also met several members of the Italian royal family, including the dukes of Aosta and Spoleto. This meeting had a curious sequel many years later, during the war, when the Duke of Spoleto, who had succeeded his elder brother in the Aosta title, entered into communication with Douglas at the time of the Italian capitulation and surrendered to him the flotilla of Italian MTBs under his command.

It was one of the happier periods in the checkered relationship of Fairbanks *père et fils*. Junior always insisted on paying his share of the expenses, and when his money ran out, left the party. But they were discovering each other as friends. Senior used to introduce his son as his brother or nephew or his "Uncle Ethelbert." "He's the best friend I have, I don't have any children, you see," he used to say.

Unhappily it was not long before warmth lapsed into estrangement again. Senior's name at that time was being connected with that of Lady Ashley, whom he subsequently married as his third wife. When he was working at Elstree with Alexander Korda on his last film, *The Private Life of Don Juan,* in 1934, he rented the nearby estate of North Mimms Park, a vast mansion filled every week end with dozens of house guests, where Douglas Junior was never invited. On December 9 of that year Mary Pickford sued for divorce.

Even so, the ties that bound Senior and Mary were so strong that spasmodic attempts were made to effect a reconciliation. Yet, paradoxically, much of the revived coolness between father and son was due to the fact that Senior felt that Douglas was taking Mary's side.

In the meantime young Douglas had been asked to return to Hollywood to appear in the Lubitsch film version of Noel Coward's *Design for Living,* with Fredric March. But on his arrival in New York he was stricken with pneumonia and the part was given to Gary Cooper. Three lobes of his lungs were affected and, before the days of antibiotics and serums, only good luck and nursing care pulled him through. Dr. Samuel Brown, who had brought him into the world, was out of town, as was his assistant, and Mrs. Whiting called in a young physician who had just joined the practice, named Dr. Mason Hicks. He has since become one of his patient's closest friends and recalls this first contact well: "In those days your temperature came down by crisis. One morning they called me to say that his temperature had dropped to normal but his pulse rate was forty-five. I thought, oh! my God, here he is getting a heart lock—jumped into a taxi, rushed to the hospital, and ordered an electro-cardiogram." Douglas finally asked what all the excitement was about. "No excitement," the doctor forced himself to say, "your pulse is just a little bit slow." "But my pulse is always slow," Douglas replied. "He was quite right," says Dr. Hicks, "a lot of athletes are the same."

When the scare was over and Douglas saw the newspapers for the first time, with their headlines: "Joan ready to fly to Doug's bedside," Dr. Hicks still remembers his patient's rueful comment: "Well, for heaven's sakes, I get sick and nearly die and she gets first billing."

He was left with a spot on one lung and told that if he did not convalesce slowly in some high, dry climate, no one would answer for the consequences. Obstinate and self-willed as ever, he determined to return to London to fulfill his contract with Korda. The film in question was *Catherine the Great,* with Elisabeth Bergner. Under the sensitive direction of his co-star's husband, Paul Czinner, Douglas scored one of the major successes of his career in an extremely complex part —that of the unbalanced Peter III of Russia.

Douglas had a small flat at 6 St. James's Street at the time, above Lock's the Hatters, a building that intrigued him because it is one of the few dating from the time of the Great Fire of 1666, full of switch-back floors and low-slung beams. He had struck up a friendship with one of his great theatrical idols of the time, Sir Gerald du Maurier, who used to come round for breakfast and bring little toys he had bought from street hawkers, which fascinated him. Sir Gerald was already so ill that he used to stain his face with iodine so that people would say how well he looked. He had a small part in *Catherine the Great* as the King's valet, and Douglas was terribly embarrassed that this great figure of the theater should have such a relatively small part when he was the star. Such was his admiration for the veteran that the first day he got to the studio he replaced his name on the star dressing room door with that of Sir Gerald, who went through four weeks on the picture, and never, to the day he died, knew what had been done. Douglas then inherited his dresser-valet, a man named Buckley, who would always lapse in his service into, "Yes, Sir Gerald. I mean Mr. Fairbanks, I'm sorry."

The film had triumphant gala premières, first in Paris, and then in London, on February 9, 1934. The audience included a number of the society friends Douglas' gay personality had already made, among them, the Prince of Wales, Queen Victoria of Spain, and King George of Greece. Douglas himself escorted the mother of the enchanting stage personality whose frequent public appearances with him were exciting the constant attention of the gossip columnists, Gertrude Lawrence.

Douglas had been one of her admirers for years. He saw her for the first time just after the Great War in a Noel Coward revue in London. Then she came to dazzle the United States with Jack Buchanan and Beatrice Lillie in *Charlot's Revue,* which he saw during its New York run and later in Los Angeles. At the age of sixteen he used to haunt the stage door, and then met her at Pickfair. In their turn the three stars took a great liking to the eager adolescent. Douglas still remembers thinking of Jack Buchanan: "There is the best-dressed man in the world. How can I get my clothes to look like that?"

When he arrived in London with his father, Gertrude Lawrence gave a large party at the Café de Paris in his honor, and for the best part of two years they became, as the contemporary phrase has it, great and good friends. She was a very great theatrical personality, and a mature woman of wit and character, who not only provided a new dimension in Douglas' professional career but helped his development from a still somewhat uncertain twenty-four-year-old to the assured man of the world he quickly became.

She had the effortless quality of appearing at ease in any company. Gilbert Miller, who put her in many of his best productions on both sides of the Atlantic, still speaks nostalgically of her charm. He watched her career from the first time he saw her as an understudy to Beatrice Lillie at the Vaudeville Theatre in the Strand in 1916 to her last appearance in *The King and I* in New York in 1952. "She was a most darling woman," he says. "Gertie was a very serious girl in many ways, but she had a definite streak of the clown in her. I never knew anybody who had greater audience perception. She was not a woman of great culture or learning, but she was always abreast of any situation. If she was talking with a little chorus girl, she could still remember when she was one herself. If she was in aristocratic company at a big party, she was just as much at ease. She was the complete sophisticate. It was a great joy to see her act with Noel Coward, I'll never forget when they did *Private Lives,* just like two parts of a wonderfully intricate machine."

Douglas appeared in two plays with her in England, the first an indifferent success by Philip Leaver, called *The Winding Journey,* and the second Clemence Dane's *Moonlight Is Silver,* which had the gallery in ecstasy but left the critics relatively unmoved. Gertrude Lawrence received the notices but Douglas cornered the stage-door fans. Once when he was besieged by autograph hunters, she grabbed away one of the books and deliberately signed her name. The little girl looked at the signature and then turned to her friend and said: "Well, anyway, the handwriting ain't so bad."

At the beginning of 1935 they made a film together, an adaptation of the *La Bohème* theme, called *Mimi,* but by this time they were providing the newspaper diarists with far less copy and their lives reverted to separate paths, to cross again one awful evening many years later when Douglas took the wife of his second happy marriage backstage after the first night of *The King and I* to congratulate the star. They found Joan Crawford already in her dressing room. Gertrude Lawrence was at her naughtiest, producing an inscribed cigarette case Douglas had given her and commenting with cheerful malice on their past friendship. It is probably one of the few occasions in his life when Douglas has been really embarrassed, especially as Mary Lee Fairbanks still delights in recounting the story. "Mary Lee and I behaved beautifully, I thought. My respect for her jumped two hundred per cent," Joan Crawford comments.

Douglas' excursion into the London theater had not improved his finances. There had been a slump in his earnings. He had purchased a motor yacht called the *Grateful* in which he and Gertrude Lawrence used to visit friends along the Thames, where he became quite a figure. He knew every pub, every lock-keeper, became darts champion of Clifton Hampden, and was on Christian-name terms with all the old farmers. But he was subjected to the continuing drain of supporting impecunious relatives, his old nurse and other dependants, and by the beginning of 1935, when he moved to a diminutive flat in Conduit Mews, Paddington, he was in debt to the tune of several thousand pounds. The friend in need turned out to be his Hollywood companion, Irving Asher, who had moved to London in charge of the whole of Warner Brothers European operations. In a gesture which Douglas still remembers with gratitude, Asher lent him enough to put him on an even keel again, and then suggested that he should pay it back by appearing in one of the quota films Asher was producing with his own wife, Laura La Plante, called *The Man of the Moment.* It was filmed largely on location in Monte Carlo.

But quota films were not what Douglas had left California to make. Mike Levee from Hollywood made suggestions from time to time that he should return, and warned him against the many difficulties of independent film making in England, but Douglas was still fired with the ambition to emulate his father as an actor-producer. In a series of talks with Murray Silverstone, European head of United Artists, he came to an agreement for the distribution of any films he should make. This made it possible to obtain American financial backing, and Douglas set about the formation of his own company, Criterion Films. Sir Adrian Baillie, M.P., was one of his first partners, and Silverstone persuaded him to co-opt Marcel Hellman, a refugee from Hitler's Germany, with long experience in Continental films, to help on the production side. They were later joined by Captain A. Cunningham-Reid, M.P., then the husband of Lady Louis Mountbatten's sister.

Douglas was full of enthusiasm at his new status, and for a time all went well. Their first production was *The Amateur Gentleman,* starring Douglas and Elissa Landi, from the story by Jeffery Farnol, and this was followed by *Accused* with Dolores del Rio, *Jump for Glory* with Valerie Hobson, and *Storm over London.* In spite of Douglas' high standards, only the first could be described as a success. Its cast included a young actress playing her first film part, Margaret Lockwood. Nor was hers the only name later to become well known. Googie Withers was in the stock company, playing comedy parts and pleading unsuccessfully that she was a serious actress. Douglas played the lead in *Accused,* stepping in at the last moment when the leading man they wanted was not available. A young barrister who was recommended to them as technical adviser for a court-room scene told Douglas on the set that he was interested in the theater and had always wanted to play a film part. He was given a few lines to say in the role of a junior counsel. His name was Leo Genn.

Ambitious plans were made for a Highland costume film with a story by one of the many friends Douglas had made, John Buchan. Duff Cooper, at that time Minister of War and a member of Douglas' growing circle of acquaintances in the political world, was so keen on the project that he offered a regiment of troops to act as extras, but nothing came of the idea.

Unfortunately, Douglas, Cunningham-Reid, and Hellman soon failed to see eye to eye on company policy, and reached the regrettable point of communicating with each other through their solicitors. Toward the end of 1936 Douglas was writing to Hellman: "I find my position and our activities as well as our business relationship in its present form incompatible with my ideas of the company when we first launched it. . . . Our pictures, for what they are, have been disastrously expensive. . . . My own career has been devaluated beyond recognition."

7

THIS RETURN to the professional doldrums had its brighter side, with Douglas' growing acceptance in London society and the inception of his passionate interest in the more serious affairs of the world. One of his lifelong friends, John McClain, now drama critic of the New York *Journal-American,* remembers visiting London during this period and seeing Douglas for the first time in a couple of years: "He had become a tremendously suave man of the world since I had last seen him," says McClain. "He was completely at home in London, knew several members of the royal family, and his whole personality seemed to have taken an enormous step forward. I was tremendously impressed; it was quite a transition. He was the gay young man round the West End, had a penthouse in Grosvenor Square, was entertaining all the important American visitors and big people in Mayfair—he was really living."

During the thirties Douglas was already on a first-name basis with the younger members of the royal family, a confidence he never abused and a relationship he always had the good taste to keep to himself. He was gay, amusing, an excellent companion, with inborn good manners and an ever present sense of the necessary protocol. Members of the royal family have a personal circle of good friends like any other people, and Douglas was accepted into it on his personal qualities. Nor should it be supposed that celebrities in other walks of life are not attractive to royalty, and acceptable Hollywood stars were more of a rarity twenty years ago than they are now.

His principal sponsors were the Mountbattens, who had spent part

of their honeymoon at Pickfair in 1922 and were delighted to recipro-
cate to the son the hospitality they had received from the father.
Douglas was a frequent visitor at their London home, Brook House,
and their country estate at Adsdean. Over the years their friendship
has remained close and constant, strengthened by Douglas' wartime
naval service under Lord Mountbatten's command and their mutual
interest in international understanding.

Douglas was free to ring up the Duke of Kent whenever he arrived
in London, and as he had the good sense never to exploit their friendship, he was always a welcome guest at the homes of the royal family's
entourage and other friends. He was one of the intimate spectators
of the Abdication crisis in 1936, has remained a friend of the Duke
of Windsor, and first met Queen Elizabeth and Princess Margaret
when they were little girls.

Acquaintance with society at this level provided a natural introduction to the growth of his interest in the affairs of nations. It is not the
sort of process that can easily be traced to its origins. As an inveterate
traveler he had been given unusual opportunities of seeing at first
hand the countries and of studying the conditions and politics he had
discussed as an earnest young man with old Thomas Patten. In retrospect he recalls that the first example of voluntary application to more
serious matters was given him by a young man he met at this time,
Viscount Carlow, son of Lord and Lady Portarlington. Carlow, who
could speak half a dozen languages and rendered some service to
British Intelligence before he was killed in the war, provided Douglas
with a fascinating model. He would ask his parents if he could have
a few friends in to dinner, and when the Portarlingtons returned from
their own evening party it was to find that their son's companions were
H. G. Wells, Lawrence of Arabia, and similar outstanding figures.
Lawrence, in fact, made Carlow one of the executors of his will.

The idea that someone not much older than himself was already, as
Douglas puts it, getting his feet wet in world affairs, and managing
to live at several different levels was a revelation. He started consciously to seek out the sort of personality who seemed in a position
to influence events, and offered himself in any capacity, courier, con-

fidant, or catalyst, or merely as host to people who might find it useful to meet on his neutral ground and discuss problems of moment.

Douglas was constantly commuting across the Atlantic, and one of his chief mentors in the great world of politics and international affairs was Herbert Bayard Swope, who for many years conducted one of the few political salons in the United States. A former editor of the New York *World*, he is a man of tremendous vitality, an indefatigable talker, a great conversationalist and wit, with a wealth of reminiscence and acquaintance and friends in every walk of life, from the racing world to high politics. He and his wife maintained two shifts of servants, and they expected their guests to arrive at eleven o'clock at night after dinner or the theater.

The guest list was always an extraordinarily interesting cross section; representatives of the world of music, arts, or the theater, together with Wall Street bankers, Middle West industrialists, a radical or two, Washington politicians, and foreign diplomats. Someone would always come up with a controversial topic, and the conversational ball would be thrown from one to the other until dawn broke. At three o'clock automatically there were ham and eggs for everybody.

These endless contacts and ceaseless flow of information gave Swope the status of a highly valued independent adviser in American government circles. He made something of a protégé of Douglas, who would always receive an invitation from him whenever he passed through New York. He clearly detected that there was more to this young actor than met the eye. Swope would pass on Douglas' impressions of European countries and figures, and call attention to him in Washington and also to other people in his varied and influential group, which included such figures as Bernard Baruch and Harry Hopkins, both intimates of President Roosevelt. It was not long before Douglas was introduced to the Secretary of State, Cordell Hull, and the Under-Secretary, Sumner Welles.

Douglas first met Winston Churchill at the Savoy Grill one night in 1936, as bearer of a note of good wishes and a short message from Swope. Churchill was in the middle of his political wilderness period at the time, and Douglas was fascinated at the prospect of making his acquaintance. He sent a note over to Mr. Churchill's table, and was highly flattered when he was asked to join it. Anxious not to abuse the invitation, he started excusing himself after about five minutes, but Mr. Churchill insisted that he stay and have a drink, and then sounded off on every subject under the sky for about two hours.

Anthony Eden was another leading figure Douglas had met in the course of his active social life in London during the thirties, and the two men have remained close and firm friends ever since. Shortly after Eden had resigned from the Chamberlain government over the Abyssinian affair, he and Douglas found themselves in the same ship traveling to New York together. Eden was on his way to make a speech to the American Manufacturers' Association, accompanied by Lord Hinchingbrooke and Ronald Tree, another Member of Parliament who had been his parliamentary private secretary. It was some time since a former minister of Eden's importance had visited the United States, and the trip received much advance publicity in view of American interest to know which way British policies were really leading. Douglas spent most of his time on the ship with this group, and was made privy to their intentions and opinions. He was invited to make comments on Eden's speech, which was being drafted on board, a number of which were incorporated in the text, a highly gratifying procedure.

Even Douglas himself cannot pin down when he first became engaged in his quasi-diplomatic activities. He remembers that back in 1936 the American Ambassador in Budapest said to him: "If you're going to be in Paris on the such-and-such, would you mind seeing so-and-so and telling him this." Another link in the process came during a visit he paid to Austria in the days before the *Anschluss*. One evening he had dinner with the theatrical impresario, Max Reinhardt, at his *Schloss* just outside Salzburg. The Austrian Chancellor, Schuschnigg, was a fellow guest, and as a result of his conversation with him Douglas sent a long report back to the American State Department in which he warned against any expectation of Austrian resistance to German demands. Another contact during the Popular Front troubles in Paris at the same period was Paul-Boncour. Such people would start talking to Douglas because he had the freak celebrity of a film star, and then were sufficiently surprised to find that they were talking to someone with a very good mind, able to converse intelligently on political topics, that they were more free with their comments and inside information than they would have been to a professional diplomat.

He continued to see Ciano not infrequently, and had several talks with Count Grandi, the Italian Ambassador in London. He met Ribbentrop on a number of occasions, disliked him, and liked even less the evidence of military resurgence he saw in Nazi Germany. Douglas' automatic acceptance in the salons of London, Paris, and Rome made him privy to a constant flow of pertinent gossip and information. Alarmed at much of the evidence, he became passionately anti-Axis and sent long reports back to friends in America. Often he would get a note back saying, "So-and-so showed your letter to Cord[ell Hull] or the President. He was very interested."

Douglas had an observant eye, an actor's sense of atmosphere, and a solid background of travel and interest to reinforce his developing judgment. He held a privileged position as an independent celebrity, could not be suspected of ulterior motive, and often found himself the authorized transmitter of a point of view which could not conveniently be entrusted to paper. It is the sort of service few people can render.

Cordell Hull, sitting sick and old in his suite in Washington's Wardman Park Hotel, long after the war, still talks with warm appreciation of the high-level inside information and the clarity of the reports his young protégé used to bring him from the countries of Europe. "He always had my views before going on one of his trips," Mr. Hull says.

The development of these wider interests covered quite a span of time in Douglas' life. In London he still continued to supply the gossip columnists with material. For some time they had been noting his frequent public appearances with Marlene Dietrich. She had taken a flat two floors below his Grosvenor Square penthouse, and they were made welcome at the country houses of friends. Among them were Constantine and Lady Morvyth Benson, two of his most constant British admirers, he a well-known merchant banker and his wife the sister of the Earl of Dudley. They had a lovely house at Shawford in Hampshire at the time. Lady Morvyth's chief memory of Marlene is of the glamorous star disappearing constantly into the kitchen, where she used to delight in taking over the cooking for the weekend.

At a time when he needed a steadying influence in his career, Douglas could not have found a better friend. Behind her *femme fatale* exterior Marlene Dietrich is a woman of great good humor and common sense, and it was she, more than anyone else, who persuaded him to take the next step in his profession.

The situation at Criterion had become untenable. At two o'clock one morning, early in 1937, Douglas received a transatlantic telephone call from Los Angeles. It was David Selznick on the line offering him the role of Rupert of Hentzau in *The Prisoner of Zenda*. It was not one of the starring parts; these were reserved for Ronald Colman and Madeleine Carroll. It would be a wrench to leave London and in a way Douglas felt it would be an admission of defeat, but it was a splendid role. Many years earlier, in the first version of the Anthony Hope story, it had rocketed Ramon Navarro, then a rank amateur, to stardom.

In his dilemma Douglas cabled his father for advice. Senior had not lost his touch. Back whipped the answer: "Of course you must do this; it's one of the best things ever written. You'd be a fool to turn it down." That, Marlene's promptings, the handsome fee offered, the attractions of an all-star cast, and the blandishments of one of the most brilliant producers in Hollywood turned the scale. Douglas accepted and sailed for America in the *Aquitania* in February, after selling out his interests in the Criterion company. It was Marlene who suggested that he looked perhaps a little modern for the part and should curl his hair. Unfortunately, the story his friends tell that she performed the operation with her own fair hands is pure romantic embellishment. The job was done by the studio barber.

Another shrewd stroke was his choice of costume. Lavishly produced, the all-star cast was dressed regardless of expense, the women in exquisite period gowns, and Colman, C. Aubrey Smith and Raymond Massey in exotic uniforms. Douglas remembered an old maxim of his father's—never wear anything fussy around the neck, whether a spotted tie or a fancy uniform collar—it detracts from the expression of the face. To the baffled amusement of his fellow actors, Douglas rejected the costume offered him and designed his own—plain black, almost devoid of ornament. Only the rushes showed how the contrast enabled him to dominate each scene in which he played.

The film was a tremendous success and earned Douglas enthusiastic notices. "The best performance of his career as the flashy and scheming Rupert." It was a fine, swashbuckling, entertaining production, and perhaps not the least reason for Douglas' success was the fact that he was playing the sort of costume part with which the Fairbanks' name was indelibly associated. There followed his three most successful years as a film actor, and he was voted the outstanding romantic character star of the year 1938 by the Class on the Motion Picture of New York University for his work in *The Prisoner of Zenda, Having Wonderful Time* with Ginger Rogers, *The Young in Heart* with Janet Gaynor and Paulette Goddard, *The Joy of Living* with Irene Dunne, *The Rage of Paris* with Danielle Darrieux, and the Kipling epic *Gunga Din* with Cary Grant and Victor McLaglen. The plaque they gave him lies covered in dust in the stationery cupboard of the office at his Westridge home. But although he earned $194,270 that year, his came only twenty-first in the list of stars' incomes.

Janet Gaynor had known him since the days when she appeared with Charles Farrell in *Seventh Heaven*. They gave the youthful Douglas a lift home one evening. At every traffic light along Sunset Boulevard he stood up in the open car and announced the identity of his companions to the waiting pedestrians, causing a near riot. Now she found him much changed, dashing off to the telephone at every lull in the shooting to engage in some long conversation about his public activities. Irene Dunne remembers chiefly a long argument Douglas had with their director, Tay Garnett, over the pronunciation of the word "futile." Douglas, freshly back from England, wanted "fewtile," but Garnett insisted on "fewtle"—probably not the least factor in the rumor that he had returned from London completely anglicized and with a British accent.

Somewhat less of a success was the test he made for Sam Goldwyn in the role of Heathcliff in *Wuthering Heights*. He overacted so badly that the reel has become a collector's piece, shown at private parties in Hollywood and never failing to reduce the privileged to helpless laughter. The part went to Laurence Olivier.

Douglas soon assimilated himself into the Hollywood background he had deserted for four years. His father had in the meantime married Lady Ashley, and they were living in his old beach house on Ocean Front in Santa Monica. To his pleased surprise, Junior was invited to stay with them. He found his father happy and seemingly relaxed in the company of a wife twenty years younger, who was clearly doing everything in her power to create a pleasant atmosphere in the twilight of her husband's career. The great business enterprise of which he had once been the head was reduced to one man, Art Fenn, the accountant, who had a bedroom and office in one wing. Senior still had grandiose plans, continued to live extravagantly, kept up his frantic round of physical exercise, and then tried to match the gregarious night-club habits of his wife.

But the old, latent mood of black despair and jealousy was nearer the surface. One day, to Junior's hurt and dismay, Senior sent his one remaining intimate, Kenneth Davenport, to suggest that his father would be happier if he moved out. No explanation was ever vouchsafed. Perhaps the old pathological objection to having a younger man around had reasserted itself. Junior left within the hour, mortified and miserable. It was to be months before he and his father came together again.

Douglas' own career was making great strides. By the end of the thirties he was commanding the handsome fee of one hundred thousand dollars a picture. Yet it is a curious fact that during his whole life as a Hollywood star, both then and until today, only two of his seventy films have ever made the list of the ten best pictures of each year as recorded in *The Year Book of Motion Pictures*. One of these was *Stella Dallas,* made in 1925, and the other *Morning Glory,* which won the 1932–33 Academy Award for Katharine Hepburn. In both he only played supporting roles.

How is it then that such giants of the film industry as Mary Pickford, Charles Chaplin, and Samuel Goldwyn can state so categorically that he is a very much better actor than his father ever was, when Senior's best films swept the world?

Mary Pickford has this to say: "We all knew that he was making a desperate effort to create his own type of role, which I think he actually did. Yet, some of his best parts have been those in the tradition of his father. It is amazing how few people can wear costumes; most of them look like stuffed sofas. That's where the English, the French, and the Italians have it away over us. They don't look upholstered, they look as though the costumes actually belonged to them, that they lived in them and were quite comfortable. It takes a certain amount of strutting and wide gesture, poise and pose to be a successful costume actor, and I think Douglas has that, I won't say to the full extent that his father had it. But when it comes to reading lines and playing a dramatic role, I think Douglas Junior is really more capable than his father was."

That is still not the final answer. Senior made better use of more limited talents. He was totally integrated with the films he made and sought expression only in the medium of the motion picture. His personality had more sheer impact than his son's, and although Douglas Junior is a very fair hand at the rapier-wielding, knight-errant role his father made famous, he simply does not possess, nor has any actor before or since, the bewitching athletic grace that his father brought to his roles. Senior in his heyday had the superb physical co-ordination of a panther, and some of his best action sequences were a species of gymnastic ballet. Junior is very attractive in the same sort of part, has a gift for sophisticated light comedy his father never possessed, and can display a surprising range of emotion in romantic modern parts. Sam Goldwyn says in exasperation: "He is one of the best leading men in films. He could go on earning his living here for years. Why doesn't he drop all this stuff about politics and come back where he belongs?" But that is the operative phrase—"one of the best." His father was an elemental force and had sufficient intelligence to know it. These days there is no scope for anyone like him.

Viewed in the cold light of retrospect, Douglas Fairbanks, Sr., was neither an artist nor an actor in the accepted sense. As Paul Rotha, in his monumental critique of the early cinema, has said, "Fairbanks Senior was an acrobat, unable to put drama into his gestures or emotion into his expression. His fame rested on the fact that he was a pure, and to this day unique, product of the medium of the cinema in which he sought fulfilment."

In his great costume films he had the insight to employ advisers of real artistic merit: Leloir, the great French illustrator; Carl Oscar Berg, the Swedish artist; Dwight Franklin, the authority on buccaneer life; Robert Nichols, the poet; and William Cameron Menzies, a designer who made his name with *The Thief of Bagdad*.

Nowadays the making of a film is a vast and complicated business, run like a complex military operation, but in Senior's time it was a much more simple process. His story, situations, and stunts would emerge more or less day by day. He would take a pencil, put it on a desk, and say: "That's me, now where am I and what happens to me?" Then he would get one simple idea, perhaps that he was locked in a castle. With his close collaborators, Lotta Woods and Kenneth Davenport, he would expand the situation ad lib., have someone take down rough notes in longhand, and they would have a story sequence which would then be formalized in terms of the set.

One trait at least which he has passed on to his son was the extraordinarily happy atmosphere which always reigned in his studio, more like a private house party. Senior kept the same staff and camera crews for years and could never bring himself to fire a man. The same is true of the more limited operations of the son. Once asked about "following in his father's footsteps," Douglas answered: "His footsteps were so light they left no trace for anyone to follow. My respect for his work is so considerable that I don't believe *anyone* could successfully emulate him."

The plain fact is that Douglas Junior's heart is not in his profession. Friends who are big names in Hollywood put it another way: "He is just too intelligent to be an actor," although they will not suffer themselves to be quoted, as they do not mean it in a sense derogatory to others. He has, over the years, acquired this multiplicity of interests, and his film work is a means to an end. It provides him with the only sort of income, in the only way he knows how to make it, which can support him in the manner he deems necessary for his other activities.

Douglas himself says: "I think the idea of creating has always been paramount in my affections in terms of work, something more tangible than the mere interpretation of a role. I began to be embarrassed that the interpretation was really someone else's creation. I fully realize now that that is not the case if you get an artist of the stature of, say, Larry Olivier—but still in my own mind, realizing my own limitations, I became aware that I could never be a creative actor. I would only be an interpretative one or an imitator. I would think back on something I'd seen, put together a hodgepodge of four or five things, and apply them to whatever I had to do, and as such became fairly expert—like anybody who makes ten thousand shoes, he ought to be pretty good by that time or give up the job—you just develop a sort of professionalism about it."

Nevertheless it has been a remarkable career and there is hardly a major woman star with whom he has not appeared. His favorite? Prosaically enough, he confirms the prejudices of many older filmgoers. It is Greta Garbo. "She is a great personality, no great intellect, but what she has is star quality. There are some people, I suppose, who could act rings around her, but don't have that star dust, as they call it, that one little subtle thing where you don't have to do anything except look from left to right and everybody swoons. It's not beauty particularly. She is beautiful in a way, but there are other people more beautiful. It's just that indefinable something that makes a star or doesn't, and different grades of stars, and she has it. You can meet her in life, she'll have mascara running down, her hair will be matted, she'll have on an old sackcloth for a dress and you'll just sit and drool over her, just fascinated, and you'll hang on every word, and the words when they come out are sometimes banal, and still they seem like pearls of wisdom at the moment. It's just incredible personality."

He has warm words for Irene Dunne: "One of the more civilized women. She's a dream, an absolute dream, thoroughly professional, one of the most professional women I've ever known. Nothing is instinctive, everything she does is very carefully thought out; she knows her camera and lighting as well as any cameraman, she knows every movement, every intonation, every nuance. Her hours are like office hours, she's never late, she never slips, but instead of being dull and perfect, she's absolutely enchanting and perfect."

And of Katharine Hepburn: "We've been very good friends ever since *Morning Glory*. She's very amusing, with a very masculine mentality and attitude, nothing dainty or feminine, but extremely intelligent and very well informed about things. She is no respecter of conventions and will say the most insulting things to anybody if she feels like it. Exactly what she appears to be she is. She's not an actress in the sense that she can simulate characterization or anything else, she just is herself and as such is a very striking personality. But it is fascinating to watch her in this, because she does have a very good instinctive sense of timing."

Douglas was much in the public eye and, as an eligible bachelor, had his name associated with many glamorous figures. But he had reached a point in his life where he was seriously exercised by the necessity for settling down, in more ways than one.

The end of the thirties provided the watershed in Douglas Fairbanks, Jr.'s, life. If he had remained quietly integrated in the career which had been forced on him and in which he had now achieved a very considerable measure of success, he would have remained just another movie actor. Instead he was about to embark on a progressive departure from the norm which involved him in the multifarious public activities associated with his name today. In the years which led up to the war, Fairbanks started quite deliberately to exploit his celebrity value for the purpose of advocating measures he considered essential to the welfare of his country and the survival of the Western democracies against outside threat.

Men acquire a sense of mission from many different motives. Some have political ambitions and others social resentments. Scientists seek to uncover the workings of nature and missionaries to spread the conception of truth. Fairbanks is none of these. He is a twentieth-century romantic, one of those rare people in this sour materialistic world who has a genuine affection for his fellow human beings, who by dint of seeing in all his acquaintances a possible knight errant has become one himself. It is an attitude which his contemporaries find easy to mock and one which in an actor may lead to the impression that he is hamming a part in public. But with Fairbanks it is perfectly genuine.

From now on his work as an actor is always overshadowed by his earnest striving to play some part, however small, in the great events of his time. But first he was to experience within one short year great personal happiness and numbing personal tragedy.

8

MOST NEWSPAPER ASTROLOGERS enjoy the advantage of knowing that their predictions usually help to light the next day's fire. Their readers have no opportunity of making a subsequent check. This prompt oblivion may absolve many errors, but it would have been a pity in the case of the practitioner in the Los Angeles *Times,* who on February 19, 1939, wrote, with remarkable pertinence: "Douglas Fairbanks, Jr., will undertake a journey on a matter of sentiment, an elder will cause him some anxiety and loss, his fortunes will be mixed ones this year. This is a fortunate year for marriage for Fairbanks and he will probably marry this year."

The forecast was, indeed, astonishingly accurate, the year was to bring Douglas both joy and sorrow. He had met, and in the spring married, Mary Lee Hartford, a happy union which has been the cornerstone of his subsequent career, and served to bring about a final *rapprochement* with his father. But Fairbanks Senior's happy adoption of his new daughter-in-law and the enthusiastic plans he evolved for business partnership with his son were brought to a tragic end by his sudden death at the onset of winter.

Douglas first met his future wife when Mary Lee paid a short visit to Hollywood as the guest of Merle Oberon in the latter part of 1938.

At that time she was married to George Huntington Hartford, heir to the Great Atlantic and Pacific Tea Company fortune.

The newspaper astrologer could not know that his subject had already made the sentimental journey to which he referred. Even Douglas did not know its import and outcome at the time. He traveled East to spend Christmas and the New Year in New York with his mother in her apartment at 325 East 57th Street. The New York World's Fair was about to open, and a clubhouse with a glassed-in terrace was already available for distinguished visitors. The party decided to see in the New Year there. Douglas' companion was Genie Chester. As he drove her across the town in his car she remembers him saying: "You know, I really ought to settle down and get married; don't you know anyone suitable?" It became one of the conversational themes of the evening and the other members of the party subjected Douglas to a lot of good-natured chipping. He had even more sober considerations preying on his mind at the time. During the evening there was a monster firework display, and Genie remembers Douglas turning to her and saying: "I don't like it; in a year or so they will be watching this sort of thing in Europe, and it won't be a firework display, it will be war."

On the way home Douglas asked what she was doing the next day: "I've been invited out to the Herbert Bayard Swopes' and I don't know whether I'll go or not," he said. "If I don't go I'll call you up; we might go to a movie."

"Why don't you go?" replied Genie. "It'll do you good to get out into the country."

The next morning he rang to say that he had decided to go to the Swopes' after all. In the muted atmosphere of a New Year's morning his hostess had deputed one of her house guests to receive him. Unbeknown to him, it was Mary Lee. An hour before he arrived she had received a telephone call from her husband saying that he wanted to end their marriage.

Their relationship had largely been a matter of keeping up appearances for some years, but the conversation had not been the best start for the New Year. Mary Lee had more or less made up her mind to spend the rest of the day in bed, and it was only with reluctance that she dragged herself down to do the honors of the house. Recognizing each other from their previous meeting, they were soon deep in conversation. They remember, rather sheepishly, that when they retired to the library after lunch to compare their woes and aspirations, the door stuck and to the huge hilarity of the house party they had to summon assistance from outside to get it open again.

Mary Lee comes from an old Virginia family. Her father's name was Epling and her mother was a White, claiming descent from the first white child to be born in New England, Peregrine White. Giles Epling was descended from a branch of the family of John Evelyn, the diarist, and the name became corrupted when his ancestors went to live in Germany and then migrated to the United States. The Eplings, Mary Lee's father, grandfather, uncles, and brother, were all doctors and had built up a considerable reputation in the mining area of West Virginia for their devotion to their profession and sponsorship of free clinics.

It was a family of substantial, professional folk, and Mary Lee was sent to the best girls' schools in Philadelphia. Then she took a postgraduate extension course at Harvard in child psychology, and there met her first husband, a fellow student at the university. Two months later they were married in secret, Mary Lee, then eighteen, giving her age as twenty, and George Huntington Hartford, still a minor of twenty, giving his age as twenty-one. Their families, without engaging in dramatic opposition, had considered that they were both too young to marry. It turned out that they were quite right.

Within a couple of years it was clear that the whole thing had been a mistake, although appearances were kept up for another five. George Huntington Hartford was a very wealthy young man with immense expectations, and he and his wife were ornaments of the Virginia–New York–Palm Beach–Newport, Rhode Island social round, but Mary Lee was a fundamentally serious person, with a mind more attuned to the severe practicalities of life. When the final break came, it only formalized a hopeless situation.

Mary Lee filed a suit for divorce in out-of-the-way Okeechobee in

Florida, where such matters are handled expeditiously and with minimum publicity, on the grounds of incompatibility and mental cruelty. She received a generous settlement, which included their estate at Boxwood Farm, near Hot Springs in Virginia.

Beth Whiting found her enchanting. One night Douglas called up and said: "Mother, have you gone to bed yet? Don't go, I want to bring a friend of mine up"; and he brought in Mary Lee. "I can see her to this day," Beth recalls, "that beautiful head that's always held high and that lovely voice, the dress she had on, black silk, high-necked, short sleeves with a little lace and turquoise-blue velvet on it. She was just a dream. I thought this is too good to be true. Jack and I just lost our hearts to her, and her mother was just as crazy about Douglas."

The shrewd suspicion that his son had found a new interest in life wrought a wondrous change in his father's attitude to him. Early in 1939 both Fairbankses were invited to a party given in New York by Mr. and Mrs. Harold Brooks, to welcome Senior back from a trip to Europe. Douglas asked Mary Lee to accompany him. No sooner did Senior see them enter the room than he said to the hostess: "That is the girl Jayar is going to marry." This was jumping the gun by several months, but Senior's intuition was not at fault. He took an immediate liking to Mary Lee, and he was beside himself with joy when his son asked if he would act as his best man. "It was one of the few times I had ever seen him acting really like a boy," Douglas remembers. All the years of misunderstanding and bitterness and estrangement were suddenly wiped out. Douglas Senior and Beth met again for the first time in twenty years, and it was a very happy family indeed that collected for the wedding.

Douglas had made up his mind that this was not going to be one of those typical Hollywood ceremonies. In fact, the only time he has ever employed a personal publicity agent in his life was during the four months after he met Mary Lee, solely for the purpose of keeping their names out of the papers as much as possible.

The ceremony took place in Los Angeles, very quietly, on April 22, 1939, at Westwood Community Episcopal Methodist Church on the corner of Wilshire Boulevard and Warner Avenue, and there were only fifty guests, mainly members of the family and close friends, many of them middle-aged. At the reception the bridal bouquet was thrown gently and carefully to Genie Chester, sitting radiant in her wheel chair at the bottom of the stairs.

He was back in the film capital working in *Rulers of the Sea,* and Frank Lloyd, director of the film, played a last-minute practical joke on him by chalking up a shooting schedule on the board which would have kept him busy the whole day. When the star exploded in indignation, Lloyd pointed to the small type at the bottom which made it clear that the notice referred to the following Saturday. Even so, Douglas and Mary Lee had to spend the first week of their honeymoon on Santa Catalina Island, completing the film.

Returning to his apartment in the Waldorf Astoria Towers in New York, Douglas Senior looked back over the barren thirty years of his fatherhood and waxed nostalgic: "You may be sure that my son and his bride will find time to slip away to visit Watch Hill and the scenes the boy and I used to know together," he told a reporter from the Providence, Rhode Island, *Evening Bulletin,* who came to interview him. "I'd like to be with him when he stands before Kenneth Ridge again. It will bring back memories, and I know they will be happy memories. Watch Hill in summer when you're a carefree boy gives you something that Paris, London, and Hollywood can't disturb. My son will look up some of the old gang that used to make up the boys' club when William Freeman conducted it. The boys didn't have a clubhouse, but they did have the Atlantic Ocean, that was enough for my son. He learned to swim at Watch Hill, and he learned right, he's still a whale of a swimmer. He'll probably take one look at the surf and then go swimming just as in the old days. And then he'll probably drag his bride round to Fenelon's garage. That used to be a favorite hangout of his during several of the summers he enjoyed at Watch Hill. Maybe he'll even try to show the mechanics how to adjust a carburetor or reline a brake. I know he used to try to show them how to do things, and if he gets in their way like he used to do they'll probably ease him out of the garage, just like they used to do."

And when he talked of his son's career the tone was much softer than in the days of his opposition and indifference. "It was something of a problem for a while. There's no doubt my son was a little annoyed at the thought professionally of merely being my son. He wanted to be somebody on his own, and to that end he carefully avoided doing the kind of pictures I had done. Now he's all right, he's arrived, he's an actor in his own right. I like his work. I was just thinking how funny it would be if one day I got to be known as Douglas Fairbanks, Jr.'s, father—or no, maybe that wouldn't be funny."

There were long discussions between the two about forming a company for the production of films all over the world, in which, for the first time, Douglas Junior was to be admitted as an equal partner. Even so, the barriers of confidence were not completely down. When Douglas knew that Mary Lee was going to have a child, it took him weeks to pluck up sufficient courage to tell his father. Knowing Senior's hatred of growing old or being thought of in any way as belonging to an older generation, he was afraid that the news would disturb him and turn his father against Mary Lee and the marriage. Both his mother and his uncle Robert insisted that he would be pleased, but Douglas still lacked the nerve.

Eventually he managed to break the news, and his father was more pleased than at any previous time that he could remember. Senior began to take Mary Lee as a personal responsibility and frequently asked her out to luncheon by herself. They would drive together to hamburger stands and discuss the future. The two generations saw each other constantly, at Senior's beach house on Ocean Front or with other members of the family. At dinner one evening Senior was very touched when his son stood up and, after a gentle review of their relations, gave him a toast. Senior was becoming sentimentally pleased with the new relationship and seemed to be trying to make up for past errors of omission and commission.

Thus it was that when Cousin Flobelle gave a party for Douglas on his birthday on December 9, it went off extremely well. However, the next day when Douglas called his father, he learned that he was not feeling too well. He had a touch of indigestion and was going to stay in the house with a good dose of bicarbonate of soda. Later in the afternoon a doctor was sent for, a sufficiently alarming occurrence, as normally Senior would allow no member of the medical profession anywhere near him.

After a few tests the inevitable verdict was pronounced. Senior had strained his heart. The doctor told him that he would have to stay in bed, that he must not turn on the radio or listen to the war news, or read anything exciting, but just rest. Senior had always prided himself on playing thirty-six holes of golf a day, in addition to swimming, exercising, and going to board meetings. But then he would stay up late at night and get overtired. He boasted that he had men many years his junior puffing and blowing and knocking themselves out. Now he was faced with six months at least of semi-invalidism, and that he could not stand, he had no will to resist it. When Junior visited him during the afternoon of the next day, he found his father terribly depressed. He read to him from a book of poems, which he seemed to enjoy, and found him very gentle, but impatient with his illness and despondent.

Douglas was on the set making *Safari* for Paramount at the time, and his co-stars, Madeleine Carroll and Tullio Carminati, sensed that there was something on his mind. Normally word perfect in his part, he fluffed his lines several times and kept going away to the telephone. At two o'clock in the morning he was rung at home by Sylvia Fairbanks' sister, Vera Bleck. Her sobs told him what had happened. He and Mary Lee rushed down to the beach house in a matter of minutes to find that his father had passed quietly away. His last request to the male nurse who was in attendance was to have the windows opened a little wider so that he could hear the sound of the sea.

Nearly three thousand miles away, in New York, Beth Whiting did not sleep a wink that night, obsessed by some vague dread. In the morning Mary Lee called her; Douglas was too upset to talk to her himself. For thirty years he had striven to do honor to the name he bore, to prove himself worthy of his father's affection and esteem. The whole drive of his career had been a subconscious essay in emulation. Now, at last, when they were happy and relaxed together, tragedy had intervened.

Some surprise was caused when the details of the estate were published. Long assumed to be one of the richest men in Hollywood, Senior's fortune amounted at his death to just over $2,300,000. During his heyday in the twenties he was probably worth more in the nature of twelve or fourteen million dollars, but the value of his holdings had depreciated disastrously in the great depression, and in the years of his decline he had continued to live an expansive and extravagant life.

Under the terms of the will half his fortune, not to exceed one million dollars in value, was left to his third wife. Douglas Junior was to receive twelve-fortieths, not to exceed six hundred thousand dollars, his brother Robert two-fortieths, not to exceed a hundred thousand dollars, and Norris Wilcox, his half brother, one-fortieth, not to exceed fifty thousand dollars. His four nieces—John's and Robert's daughters—were each left the same amount in trust, and another fortieth was left to his son for distribution to various friends and charities in accordance with instructions given him by his father. The appearance of the name of Norris Wilcox was the first indication to many people of his very existence. He was the son and only child of Ella Fairbanks' second marriage, and had been brought up by a distant aunt, after being more or less deserted by his mother in circumstances which were never fully explained in the family.

The estate was very complicated and it took a long time to settle. The value of many of the holdings had diminished so much that in some cases the original intentions of the will were nullified. There was also a distinct coolness between Sylvia and some of the other beneficiaries. This arose partly out of the right granted to a widow under California law to draw out of the estate, pending settlement, a sum which will enable her to maintain the standard of living she enjoyed before her husband's death. This was assessed by the courts at a sum of three thousand dollars a month, little enough compared with the Niagara of expenditure of his halcyon years, but a considerable drain on an estate which it took the best part of three years to settle. By the spring of 1942 this allowance had been halved, but even this involved a court hearing and more lawyers' fees.

In a community avid for gossip, garbled accounts of these difficulties got into the press, and Hollywood factions took sides according to the mood of the moment. One well-known actor rang up Douglas one day to protest at the way the family were treating "poor Sylvia"; but he was out, so the caller protested to Mary Lee. She lost her temper with him, told him to go and look up the Los Angeles court records and then ring back and apologize, which he did. Douglas, in fact, was at pains to keep neutral in the squabble. He realized that Sylvia had made his father happy, and always did his best to keep their relationship a pleasant one for that reason.

For all the checkered nature of their relationship, Senior bequeathed Douglas more than just part of his estate. His name alone had opened more doors than it had closed. In his art, until his touch began to fail, he was a perfectionist, and Douglas measures his own efforts by the same exacting standards. They share the same energy, the same charm, although with Senior it was more calculating and less all-embracing than with Douglas, many of the same mannerisms, and the same carriage.

Their physical resemblance is almost too obvious to comment on. Photographed full face it borders on the uncanny, yet there are important differences. Senior had a round head and Douglas has a narrow one. Junior is fair and his father was dark. He is taller, slimmer, and finer drawn than his father. Good athlete that he is, he has never matched the sleek puma-like co-ordination and grace of Senior.

Their laugh is the same, but their voices are not. Senior's was higher in pitch and not basically suitable for the talking films which arrived as his career ended. Douglas, all the gibes of those countrymen who object to the anglicization of his accent to the contrary, has always spoken in the mild mid-Atlantic tones he uses today.

Above all, both brought romanticism to a materialistic modern world. But where the father found complete expression in the films that sealed his fame and then was left rootless and bewildered as the superb athletic grace which made them possible thickened into middle age, his son has sought ultimate expression outside the world of the cinema. For Douglas Fairbanks, Jr., the romance of pageantry and the affairs of nations, the historical associations of great names and places, the castles in the air and the unrequited aspirations of his fellow human beings, provide the greater and more lasting appeal.

Douglas and Mary Lee soon found a dream house. Standing in seven and a half acres of eucalyptus wood at 1515 Amalfi Drive, where the hills of Pacific Palisades tumble into the ocean, it overlooks the virgin slopes of the Will Rogers State Park. It had belonged to Elissa Landi, and they bought it for the bargain price of twenty-five thousand dollars.

Both then and since the war it has been the western end of their axis of hospitality. It has become the legitimate successor of Pickfair as the mecca of distinguished visitors; the Mountbattens, Lord Halifax, Anthony Eden, Prince Bernhard have all stayed there. In the jealous hierarchy of Hollywood, actors tend to be regarded as the hired help, but Douglas has never had a refusal to an invitation to such leaders of the industry as Louis B. Mayer, Sam Goldwyn, David Selznick, Joseph Schenck, and Darryl Zanuck. He will never match his father as their equal in films, but his personal prestige stands even higher.

The house itself is built in California Spanish style, two stories high with blinding white walls and a low cambered roof of semi-cylindrical tiles. The front entrance drive encloses a grove of lemon and orange trees, with the blossoms wafting their scent into every room. It is U-shaped in form, with a wall joining the ends of the two wings, enclosing an oblong patio, with a covered colonnade on three sides and tangerine, lemon, and magnolia trees, camellia bushes, and a large goldfish pond.

For all the exquisite taste of its decoration and English period furniture, the foibles of the owner are most apparent in two side rooms in the wings. In the office which leads off the library, Douglas keeps his remarkable collection of five thousand toy soldiers, arranged in four shelves round the room, and above them, a set of Speed maps of the English counties. On the right of the patio is the imitation English pub called the "Rose and Crown," which Fairbanks uses as his trophy room.

Every inch of the wall is hung with signed photographs of people with whom he has worked or acted, under whom he has served, or met in his social life. There must be two hundred of them, all with famous names. It has a dart board and a large, brick, open fireplace for a log fire. Above is an old carved motto which says in the Scots: "Ye canna baith be grand and comfortable."

Some of his friends find the vast collection of photographs a little overdone. As a joke, David Niven posed for a fake picture of himself in naval uniform receiving a decoration, with his face set in a horrible leer, and had it nailed on the wall when the host was out. Douglas knows his faults and gives it a place of honor.

With its sea breezes, open-air swimming pool and tennis court, Westridge provides a perfect background for relaxation. It is one of the most attractive of the many lovely houses of Hollywood. Douglas and Mary Lee lived there for a year and a half, and then never set eyes on it for nearly five years of war.

9

THE STAGE was set for Douglas Fairbanks' emergence as a character in the round. We are all products of our environment. In his case, the dominating interests in his life result from attempts to escape from it. Established again as a Hollywood star, he was identified with a group of mass entertainers, whose members are not expected to step outside the fantasy world to which they belong in the eyes of the public, and who have no real influence outside their profession. Now he met a new series of challenges in the larger universe outside its confines. His long intimacy with personal conflicts had forged in him an obsession to heal quarrels wherever he found them.

Fairbanks' firm personal conviction was that if the two English-speaking countries did not draw closer together, they would not be able to confront the growing menace. However small one man's influence might be, he saw it as a contribution to the desired end. In its inception the emphasis of his activities was on Anglo-American relations. Over the course of time he has sought to render any service of which a private citizen is capable in fostering relationships between the United States and the other countries of the Western world.

One of the first examples of something tangible emerging from Fairbanks' growing sense of mission and his frequent conversations and discussions with people of mark was the visit paid to the United States, in May and June 1939, by King George VI and Queen Elizabeth. No project could have appealed more directly to the romantic streak in Fairbanks' nature or combined more successfully the currents of his ideas. It became a matter of high policy between sovereign states involving the whole machine of government, obliterating the part played by any individual, but this does not detract from the fact that Fairbanks started using his persuasive arts on the Duke of Kent to advocate such a visit as far back as 1937. The Duke thought well of the idea, discussed it with his brother, the King, but for some time could report no progress. The project lay fallow, although several members of the household and other public figures to whom Douglas had suggested the plan continued to regard it as a highly desirable possibility.

During the period succeeding the Munich crisis Douglas redoubled his efforts, communicating again with the Duke, broaching his suggestion to President Roosevelt, during a long discussion they had on Anglo-American relations, and enlisting the aid of John Buchan, who had become Lord Tweedsmuir and Governor-General of Canada. He and Douglas had worked on film scripts together at various times, particularly on stories dealing with the life of Bonnie Prince Charlie and a Scottish border tale, the abortive Criterion venture which had attracted Duff Cooper's interest.

Buchan, better known to the British and American public as the author of *Greenmantle* and *The Thirty-nine Steps,* was much more closely identified with the central figures of these books than has ever been generally realized. For a period between the two wars he was nothing less than the head of Britain's secret service, an appointment which over the centuries has always been shrouded in a decent veil of anonymity. Nothing is more typical of the sort of friendship that Douglas Fairbanks has made a habit of contracting during his life than the warm appreciation and confidence he succeeded in winning from this dour, demanding, and undemonstrative Scot. This must not be interpreted as a suggestion that Fairbanks was in any way connected with Buchan's intelligence work. Rather did the older man take pleasure in widening the horizons of the younger.

Buchan was a man with the affairs of the world at his fingertips, fully alive to the nuances of a political gesture. He espoused the idea of the royal visit wholeheartedly, recommended it on his own authority to the British Government, and became one of those chiefly responsible for the organization of the tour. When the project was well under way, Douglas effaced himself. The formal arrangements were outside his province, although for months he lobbied his growing circle of friends in the American Government, particularly Cordell Hull, to support the invitation. After the resounding success of the visit, Buchan sent an appreciative letter to Douglas in California: "You must have been pleased at the way your plan worked out so well."

Tweedsmuir died in office in 1940. By that time Douglas had acquired considerable notoriety as one of the public figures most clamorous in demanding all-out American aid to the Western Allies and the entry into the war at their side of the United States. One of the last letters Tweedsmuir wrote to his son was devoted largely to praise of Fairbanks' efforts. Such an expression of warmhearted approval of anyone was so unusual, coming from his father, that the second Lord Tweedsmuir kept it as a curiosity. More than a dozen years later he quoted from the letter when introducing Fairbanks as the guest of honor at a dinner of the City Livery Club in London and afterward presented it to its subject.

Fairbanks found his own medium of the film a useful outlet for the message he so tirelessly propagated. At what was probably the peak period of his acting career he demanded, and obtained, a veto power on his scripts, and deliberately set out to make films with a pro-British or "internationalist" theme. They were not straight propaganda, although each had the same sort of message written into the situations or dialogue. Fairbanks had by that time become sufficiently conversant with mass psychology to know that preaching was not a particularly constructive form of getting a message over. It had to be done with subtlety, stating the ideas in such a way that people would both be persuaded and interested. He tried to inject more than a mere jingoistic appreciation of an individual country as such, but a positive belief in the system by which America and all it stood for operated. If that coincided with Franco-Anglo-American interests, he felt it was all grist to the same mill. He tried to pose a situation, a certain set of reactions, which sometimes had nothing to do with politics but which subconsciously reflected on general human behavior and human rights and decencies on a mass or individual scale.

It was far from an easy undertaking. Prosperity in the film industry was bound up very largely with the necessity for pleasing as many people as possible most of the time. Controversial subjects were bad enough, but the idea of taking sides in the international political struggle of the times, which a very large number of Americans considered to be a squabble that was no concern of theirs, was enough to give the panjandrums of the box office an acute attack of the ague.

Fairbanks insisted, and in between the light comedies which were needed to maintain the demand for his services, he took a leading part in four films whose entertainment value was heavily larded with a moral. The first of these was *Gunga Din,* a highly successful epic concocted from the Kipling poem of the same name, grafted on to his *Soldiers Three* and the exploits of Privates Mulvaney, Ortheris, and Learoyd. It was made on location during months of grueling heat in the sweltering California valleys and deserts. Douglas had as his co-stars Victor McLaglen and Cary Grant.

Every evening he would sit down with the director, George Stevens, and work over the shooting script for the next day, often rewriting it completely. It reached the cinema screens about the time of Munich, and although this unashamed piece of tub-thumping earned some anti-British boos in a few Middle-Western towns, it proved immensely popular and effective.

By a curious coincidence the film had its première in London on the same day as the remake of *Dawn Patrol,* with Errol Flynn and Basil

Rathbone in the principal parts, and David Niven in the role Douglas had originally created ten years earlier.

Next came a melodrama called *The Sun Never Sets,* in which a pair of stiff-upper-lipped Colonial civil servants, played by Basil Rathbone and Fairbanks, outwitted a villainous "Fascist" planning world overthrow from some eyrie in Africa. The story was trite to a degree, but the cast of the picture was sufficiently popular for it to sell very well. Some critics objected to the excessive pro-British slant, and the *New Yorker* sighed: "The spirit of Empire can weight down a picture."

Then followed *Rulers of the Sea,* an account of the history of the first ship to sail by steam across the Atlantic. This brought a protest from the American National Maritime Commission, which announced in June 1939 that its highest officials had entered an appeal with the Motion Picture Producers and Distributors of America and with the directors of the Paramount Corporation to abandon its production. It was added hastily that the agency had no quarrel with the Cunard White Star Line, but only asked that the equally glorious tradition of the American merchant marine receive equal recognition.

Safari, the film Douglas was making when his father died, was less blatant and direct, although Douglas had the script altered to again make the villain a "Fascist."

One immediate result was that Mussolini banned all his films from being shown in Italy. Nearer home, this outspoken partisanship created quite a body of criticism in Hollywood against Fairbanks. Some of the more extreme isolationist organizations threatened to boycott his films, there were demonstrations in front of several cinemas, one or two exhibiting circuits intimated that they would be happier not to book his films, and some of the higher Hollywood executives made it clear that he would have to be less controversial or they would be unable to engage him for further productions.

The prevailing mood of the movie colony was to stick their heads into the warm California sand. They knew that a war would deprive them of a certain number of stars, would affect the markets abroad which would be involved in the war, and the general attitude was to say: "Hands off, let's wait and see how it comes out." Fairbanks was the first actor of importance to take sides publicly and say that this was America's war. There was a definite attitude on the part of the older heads of studios: "Well, young Fairbanks is doing his best to get us in this goddamn thing. He's an actor, why doesn't he stick to acting!" It required considerable courage to fight this trend. It was not the policy of powerful columnists like Louella Parsons or Hedda Hopper, or of the Hearst newspaper group, or the studios, but Fairbanks stuck to his guns.

He refused to be deterred. As a result, during the twenty-two months between January 1940 and American entry into the war, he made only two films, the bare minimum necessary to keep his financial head above water. Into one of these, *Angels Over Broadway*, with Rita Hayworth in an early Hollywood part, intrinsically one of the best films he ever made, he put more propaganda—together with an investment from his own limited financial resources. In the other, *The Corsican Brothers*, he was more or less compelled to return to more innocuous entertainment. In fact, he was too busy with other work to do more. The story of how he exploited his celebrity value during that period to help range the might of American intervention on the Allied side in the conflict is the story of his emergence as a public figure of consequence.

September 3, 1939, was Labor Day weekend in America. With Laurence Olivier, Vivien Leigh, David Niven, and Nigel Bruce, Douglas and Mary Lee had chartered a boat to fish off Catalina Island, twenty-four miles out to sea from Los Angeles. There was very little fishing. They were too busy crowding round the radio for the latest news flashes. Then came the climax, Chamberlain's announcement that hostilities had begun. Ronald Colman, who had come alongside in his own boat, listened in too and joined the circle of grim faces.

David Niven, a former regular officer with the Highland Light Infantry, returned to join his regiment in Britain. He was given a rousing send-off, with a bagpipe serenade and all the Hollywood flourishes. Olivier left for Britain as soon as he finished the picture he was making and presented himself to the Royal Navy's Fleet Air Arm as a fully qualified pilot. Unbeknown to any of his friends, he had been getting up at five-thirty every morning to take flying lessons before reporting to the studio. He was frightened of planes at first and hated every minute in them, but stuck it out so that he could be of the greatest service possible.

Within a week of the outbreak of war Douglas had written to two of his oldest friends. Appealing to Genie Chester to enlist the help of her influential multimillionaire father, he said: "Aren't these horrible days? Did you hear the King and Chamberlain? I trust you are swinging *all* your weight—in your family and out—to writing your senators and congressmen—to lift the arms embargo. We *must*. We cannot face a world wherein we are the sole surviving democracy—nor where Britain no longer is a great power. It's unthinkable that we can pay lip service to freedom and justice and yet remain aloof in this death struggle. Are you doing your bit?"

To his British friends the Bensons, he sent this note of reassurance: "I have gotten hundreds of petitions signed to be sent to our congressmen, asking for a lifting of the arms embargo and repeal of the Neutrality Law as it exists. . . ."

The Battle of America, in which Douglas had just fired a few lone sniper's bullets, lasted until Pearl Harbor day. It became a complex, bitter political struggle, and his part in it will be told. But first there was a personal service he could render and to this he turned his driving enthusiasm. The letter to the Bensons also answered an appeal from Lady Morvyth to help in the financing of an urgent welfare project she had undertaken. "As to your wire about raising funds, there's some problem about subscribing money for the benefit of a belligerent, although the law says nothing about charities. I've unofficially approached several people including my father, and somehow or other, sooner or later, you will, I promise, have your $10,000, even if I have to do it all myself."

Shortly after Munich, Lady Morvyth Benson had started to organize convalescent homes of a dozen to fifteen beds for the R.A.F. territorial squadrons manning barrage balloon sites in the South of England, some of which were miles from their headquarters. When the war broke out Lady Morvyth equipped her station wagon as an ambulance, took over a small cottage in Southampton, co-opted her cook and personal maid and put their services at the disposal of the squadron doctor. With the onset of the winter and its influenza epidemic, the men went down like ninepins. The nearest nursing facilities were about twenty miles away and completely overwhelmed, so the little cottage was turned into a fourteen-bed hospital. After the appeal to Douglas, they were able to move into a larger house, and Lady Morvyth opened up two more homes, at Portsmouth and the Court House Hotel, Newton Ferrers, providing total accommodation for over a hundred cases.

Fairbanks maintained them entirely out of his own resources for nearly three years, and they were called the Douglas Hospitals in his honor. After the first year he was compelled to write: "I am trying to get the British War Relief Association here as well as in California to earmark a certain percentage of their takings to the Douglas Hospitals. I am not sure as yet whether they will agree to this or not. I am hoping so. For me to do it on my own would be a little difficult just now, as I have been so active with war work I have done only four weeks' regular work this year and am rapidly becoming as poor as the proverbial church mouse. There is no reason for you not to be optimistic, because somehow or other we will get it to you, but when, how, or in what form, I do not at the moment know. If my father's estate were settled I could take some from that, but unfortunately it is in a frightful mess and I do not think it will be straightened out for many, many months to come."

He had to carry the burden until the end of 1942, although, as the money had to be transferred through Red Cross channels, even the Bensons did not realize that each donation was coming out of his own pocket. In the end, Fairbanks managed to arrange for their support on a more official basis through the American Red Cross, and the three hospitals were kept open until the end of the war. With their future assured, he got this note of thanks from Lady Morvyth: "Darling Doug, you are doing so much for us that I am really speechless with admiration. All I can say is that I never expected you to do otherwise because of that close affinity which you have always had, more than the majority of your countrymen, with England, born out of the fact perhaps that you have never outgrown enjoying seeing the Changing of the Guard."

Another of his major interests was the Franco-British War Relief Fund, which he took a leading part in founding in California. He worked in conjunction with Francis Evans, the British Consul, later Sir Francis; Ronald Colman and Charles Boyer helped to back it, and prodigious sums were raised in the film colony. An all-star series of productions of the nine *Tonight at 8:30* plays by Noel Coward, lasting three weeks, raised sixty thousand dollars. Fairbanks himself played in *We Were Dancing* with Constance Bennett. He helped Noel Coward in sponsoring the journeys to the States and the upkeep of sixty children from the Actors' Orphanage in London.

Headquarters of the Franco-British War Relief Fund were later moved to New York and, when France fell and it became the British War Relief Society, Winthrop Aldrich became its head. The day France fell, Charles Boyer, heartbroken, gave Douglas a bottle of 1825 brandy, telling him to keep it for them to celebrate the day of ultimate victory. They have met again since but not at the site of the bottle, which Fairbanks still has.

Ranging the country on fund-raising drives, plotting with fellow internationalists how American aid might best be swung behind the Allies, making speeches and firing off letters to newspapers, Douglas met Professor James T. Shotwell, dean of the Columbia University law school. In long discussions together they produced a remarkable plan to implement an idea that had been revolving in Douglas' mind for some time, for a form of mutual honorary citizenship between Britain and the United States of America. It was the sort of symbolic gesture that appealed to Fairbanks' romantic nature.

He had received private assurances from the President and the State Department that the project would receive serious consideration. It stamped him as quite an original thinker, and attracted the attention of a number of people who had hitherto dismissed him as just another movie star. Professor Shotwell produced the legal arguments and justifications and related the whole to international law.

The draft took the form of a proposed Act of Congress, and the imposing preamble read: "The freedom of the United States of America is hereby extended to all subjects of the Crown of Great Britain, Ireland and the British Dominions beyond the Seas, who are citizens of Great Britain and Northern Ireland, of the Dominion of Canada, of the Commonwealth of Australia, of the Union of South Africa, of the Dominion of New Zealand, or of Newfoundland, and to all citizens of the Irish Free State; that is to say, all such citizens, and their children being minors, shall be entitled to enter the continental United States, to reside therein, and to depart therefrom, in every way as if they were citizens of the United States of America. . . ."

The intention was to make mutual honorary citizenship no more than a symbol, like the freedom of a city, without in any way undermining the sovereignty of either country. The sponsors went back into common law for centuries, quoted several historical examples, and examined the procedure in other nations and ancient Greek city-states when individuals had been made honorary citizens.

Although the plan was designed to operate on a reciprocal basis, presentation of the British cause was still so muted in the States during the early months of the war, for fear of engendering more antagonism than support, that it was considered desirable to make the first move in Congress. If the initiative had come from London, it was felt that American suspicions might be aroused.

Douglas discussed the plan with Lord Lothian, the British Ambassador, and forwarded copies to Anthony Eden and Lord Halifax, who sent encouraging messages but queried the political timing. Sumner Welles, the Under-Secretary of State, liked the whole idea and was in process of giving it practical support when Germany invaded France. The project had to be shelved under pressure of events, although its essential theme appeared in another context in the Churchill offer to the French a few weeks later and found expression after the war in his Fulton speech. It is a perfectly feasible proposition and every now and again Douglas receives inquiries for the text from his political friends.

In the midst of all this activity, Douglas began to inquire through

Lord Tweedsmuir whether he could join the Canadian Navy. As a young man of military age, he felt that he should back his constant advocacy of support for Britain by some more tangible action on his part. Friends in the American State Department heard of his intention and sent unofficial messages that it was considered, in view of the strong isolationist attitude in the country, that he could render a greater service by continuing to make public his pro-Allied views. He was the only major film personality who had shown himself willing to exploit his celebrity value in support of this cause, without regard to the effect on his career.

On one of Douglas' visits to Washington, Secretary Hull suggested that, although he was free to do as he wished, it was felt that he would be more useful proclaiming his beliefs in the country at large, because he could approach a kind of public and a wider public than a politician, who might appear to have some ax to grind. Fairbanks did as he was requested and plunged into the fray.

10

UNITED STATES leadership of the Western world and the decisive nature of America's contribution to the war are factors now so readily acknowledged that the long and bitter political struggle between President Roosevelt and the isolationists during the period which ended on Pearl Harbor day seems like ancient history. Yet without American aid—the repeal of the arms embargo, the destroyers-for-bases deal, Lend-Lease, the neutrality patrol, and the convoy system—Britain might well have succumbed. But every step in that vital program of assistance was taken in the face of violent and vocal opposition and was only made possible by the successful mobilization of a sufficient body of public opinion, by tireless volunteers and the agencies they created, to support and sometimes to inspire the President's measures. The most powerful and influential organization in this struggle was the Committee to Defend America by Aiding the Allies, whose first chairman was William Allen White, whose national director and administrative co-ordinator was Clark M. Eichelberger, and in which Douglas Fairbanks, Jr., was probably the most active of its three original vice-chairmen.

The war in Europe had broken out at the beginning of the year of strenuous political campaigning that always precedes an American presidential election. The early part of 1940 was additionally confused by the five months of the "phony war." During the life-and-death struggle into which Britain was plunged during the second half of the year, President Roosevelt had to contend with political opponents who might have ousted him from office if he had given them grounds for convincing the public that he was about to involve the country in active participation in the conflict.

Not only were most of the President's opponents against U.S. involvement in the war, but most of his supporters as well. American opinion had been overwhelmingly isolationist ever since the Republican election victory and America's refusal to join the League of Nations in 1920. The mood was so strong that even in 1935, three years after the Democrat comeback and the first election of President Roosevelt, Congress passed a law designed to keep America neutral in the event of another war, prohibiting the export of arms, ammunition, or implements of war to any belligerent nation and making it illegal for an American vessel to carry arms for or to any belligerent. The President was left no latitude to discriminate between aggressors and victims, and this prevented the United States from playing any decisive part in the events which led up to the outbreak of World War II.

Three weeks after Germany invaded Poland, the President sent a message to Congress urging the repeal of this arms embargo.

The American political system tends to involve public opinion far more actively and passionately in the actual voting on controversial issues than is the case across the Atlantic. In European parliaments, party lines are more clearly defined, the authority of the whips more rigid, and the mandate of the representatives, once elected, less liable to the fluctuating influence of their constituents. Both the major American parties cover a much broader arc of the political spectrum and are controlled by faction rather than doctrine. Senators, it should never be forgotten, are the representatives of the sovereign member states of the Union, and both they and the representatives form part of a mesh of patronage and influence no longer characteristic of the body politic in such countries as Britain.

The vast expanse of the United States and the decentralization of its institutions make the political pressure group a much more important factor than in the smaller and centralized countries of Europe. Professional lobbyists are an accepted and recognized part of the Washington political scene. Controversial issues, both major and minor, call into being volunteer organizations bent on bombarding the nation's representatives with propaganda and messages from influential constituents for the purpose of influencing their vote. It is hardly surprising that the question of aid to the Western allies and eventual participation in the war aroused the most violent controversy.

Fairbanks, as we have seen, early added his mite to this mass movement of expression. During the confused winter of 1939–40 his propaganda films, his fund-raising activities, and the death of his father compelled him to spend a large part of his time in California. Likeminded friends in the East, with whom he maintained active contact, including Professor Shotwell, the Swope group, and such figures as Fiorello La Guardia, Mayor of New York, Herbert Lehman, Governor of New York State, Clarence Streit, the advocate of "Union Now," Robert Sherwood, the playwright, Herbert Agar, the editor and historian, and John G. Winant, later Ambassador to Britain, were combining under the initiative of Clark Eichelberger, at that time director of the League of Nations Association, to form an organization which would rally public opinion behind the repeal of the arms embargo. In their search for a respected non-partisan figure to act as chairman, they approached William Allen White, an outstanding liberal Republican who, as editor of the Emporia *Gazette* in Kansas, had become something of a folk hero to millions of Middle-Western Americans. Twenty years earlier he had fought, unsuccessfully, with such figures as Elihu Root, Charles Evans Hughes, and Henry L. Stimson, for American membership in the League of Nations, and had spent his whole life campaigning against injustice in the social and economic system.

This first William Allen White committee developed the tactics which were later to make it perhaps the outstanding example in American political history of the nation-wide, voluntarily organized political pressure group. Its operations came to involve intimate personal liaison with the President, the principal contacts being William Allen White himself, Robert Sherwood, and Douglas Fairbanks.

In a preview of the methods perfected in their later mass campaigns, the White committee stirred up public opinion to support the repeal of the arms embargo. Instructions were sent out to members to persuade their friends and neighbors to bring the matter up before their clubs and societies, to wire or write to their congressmen and senators, organize meetings to discuss the issue, and write letters to local newspapers. Each member received a copy of a Senate poll showing where various senators stood on the bill, and were urged to influence their votes in its favor.

With the support of this barrage, the arms embargo was lifted on November 3, and both the President and Cordell Hull, the Secretary of State, sent messages to the committee in which they made it quite clear that they considered its contribution had been decisive.

Then, while people waited for the "phony war" to end, the campaign lacked a focal point and the original committee more or less went into suspension. However, such zealous partisans as Douglas Fairbanks never slackened their efforts to promote assistance for the Western Allies. "I haven't worked for five months and probably won't for several weeks to come," he wrote to his friends the Bensons in England on April 23, 1940, announcing the birth of his first daughter, Daphne. "Unfortunately I may be obliged to do something inferior just because economically I can't hold out much longer."

Three weeks later, after the German Army had launched its blow in the West, he wrote them again: "The President, as usual, is doing his best to rouse the country from its lethargy. We have indeed suffered from it right up until the invasion of the Low Countries—rather like Britain before Munich. The American people seem frightened to do or

say anything too decisive. Being over 3,000 miles away makes it understandably hard for many people to see how their own welfare is
affected by the outcome. They have been as critical as usual of 'other
people's fights' and were either disappointed or bitter at British actions
in Norway. They started out to applaud and ended up jeering. Recent
Nazi propaganda has been most effective here. It is not that the Germans seek to make friends for themselves, but they have managed to
put a question in people's minds as to whether there is anything to
choose between the two belligerents. Any argument against the Allies
has been welcome to people here as a sop to their consciences. Along
with others of like mind, I continue doing all I can. I write letters and
articles under various *noms de plume* and send copies to isolationist
groups or indecisive people. In addition, there are interviews, broadcasts and recordings, all of which draw on my head a great deal of
widespread and highly unpleasant critical attacks."

This outspoken and unpopular stand attracted quite a lot of attention, most of it derisive. Among those who took a more approving view
of his attitude was the United States President himself who, in the
critical years that followed, extended to Fairbanks his hospitality and
his confidence.

Fairbanks' first contact with the Roosevelt family came at the age
of six or seven, when he occasionally played with the future President's
younger sons in New York's Central Park. Douglas Senior had a passing acquaintance with the then Assistant Secretary of the Navy, and
this had mollified Dedie Dowd, the Fairbanks' nurse, who always liked
to cross-check on the social standing of the playmates of her charge.

As he started to acquire friends in the political world on both sides
of the Atlantic, young Douglas' name had occasionally been mentioned
approvingly to the President by Herbert Bayard Swope and Cordell
Hull. His first meeting with Franklin D. Roosevelt took place shortly
after the Munich crisis in 1938, when Fairbanks was asked to expand
on his European reports and observations and make any suggestions
for improving Anglo-American relations. It was during the course of
this conversation that Douglas was able to present his plan for a visit

by King George VI and Queen Elizabeth. The President made a great point of encouraging earnest, eager, and intelligent members of the younger generation to support his policies or take up an administrative career. Douglas was a celebrity, the son of a celebrity, clearly had the knack of making himself acceptable in influential company, and had unequivocal ideas about where he stood in the mounting international conflict of the time. Soon after their marriage Douglas and Mary Lee were invited to spend a weekend at the White House, and Roosevelt took a warm liking to the handsome young pair.

Nevertheless, as Fairbanks himself is at pains to make clear: "The degree of my intimacy with F.D.R. was never that great. I was not a boon friend of the family or anything else. I had a very warm entrée, but no account of his life, however intimate, would ever include me, and no history of the United States at that time would mention my association in any positive degree." Even so, the access he enjoyed was sufficiently frequent, and indeed unusual in someone from the entertainment world, to excite disproportionate attention and comment. There was more than a little jealousy in the attitude of some of these critics, and they have reacted in the same fashion to evidence of similar acceptance by important personages since.

"The President was very kind to us," Fairbanks recalls, "and often when we came to Washington we would be invited to stay at the White House. The President always seemed completely relaxed, whatever the day's pressures had been, and I was immensely complimented by his apparent interest in our discussions. He somehow found time to give attention to what must often have been just *trivia*. We were usually part of a small house party, although sometimes we were the only guests. At other times one of the boys would be there—young Franklin was the one I knew best. Occasionally some extra 'visiting firemen' or a politician would be in at cocktail time for an informal chat.

"It was like staying in the country, instead of within a stone's throw of the heart of the city. It was an informal life. Mrs. Roosevelt was always extremely warm and cordial, and when it was time to go to bed she would come with us to our room and sit down on the bed while we had a sort of good-night chat."

The Fairbankses would also go to Hyde Park for occasional week-ends, where there would be long discussions into the night on international affairs and politics. Franklin Roosevelt, Jr., a good and enthusiastic friend, championed Fairbanks with his father in a private capacity, and Cordell Hull and Sumner Welles on the more official side. The President responded most affectionately and almost as an older family friend. "But," says Fairbanks, "he would frequently put me in my place with my ideas."

His relationship with the President gradually became firmer. They would discuss details of the aid-the-Allies campaign, and the President would congratulate Douglas on a particular article or speech, or write a note saying how useful it had been. Sometimes when Douglas was in Washington the President would ask him round in the evening after dinner. Douglas would tell him what he and the committee had been doing, and the President would comment on the possible repercussions of their campaign, indicate what trial balloons he would like to have launched, and ask questions about their proposed activities. At that time Douglas was bristling with every sort of project, and he would frequently put forward his own suggestions of how best to counter the influence of the isolationists.

Part of Fairbanks' appeal was that he was one of the few people granted access to the President who did not seek personal advantage from the acquaintance. On the only occasion when he tried to discuss an issue which directly affected him, he was snubbed for his pains. Returning to California after one visit, Douglas told his colleagues in the motion-picture industry that he had attempted to secure from the President sympathetic consideration of their heavy tax problems, by proposing that so ephemeral a thing as talent, dependent for its livelihood on the whims of an unpredictable public, should be granted the same concessions as owners of oil wells. He suggested that their tax liability should be spread over a number of years and not levied in the ordinary way. Actors would have one good season and possibly two bad ones, and it was difficult to spread the load and save something for the lean years. The President received these proposals with a loud "horselaugh," adding that they had better find some satisfactory method of saving when they could. "You're not as necessary to the national welfare as oil wells," he said, and dismissed the whole matter from that point on.

Douglas was on close terms with several members of the White House entourage, and Robert Sherwood often saw him there. "I know the President was very grateful for all that Doug had done to help his foreign policy," he was to say in after years. With Harry Hopkins, Douglas was less certain of himself. "Harry was around a great deal," he wrote in one of his long letters to Genie Chester. "I can't remember a time when he was not. I am always a little apprehensive about him and don't think that he likes me very much. He does tend to be a little sour and sarcastic sometimes, which puts me off and embarrasses me. I realize I am a much younger man and my background is one to make him a little suspicious as to what I am doing in this kind of world." However, he learned later from Franklin Junior that when he was not there, Hopkins spoke of him very cordially and at times enthusiastically. But Douglas never knew this at the time, and when Hopkins was present he was always on the alert.

Fairbanks' visits gave him an intimate view of Roosevelt's thoughts and foibles, and sometimes he saw him off his guard. The President had a very real and understandable concern for polio research and treatment. But he was extremely sensitive about his own incapacities. Once, when Douglas and Mary Lee drove up from New York to Hyde Park, they arrived just as their host came in from the farm himself. Douglas was carrying a little ciné-camera, with no intention at that moment of doing anything with it. One of the secret-service men in the driveway, fearing they belonged to the category of picture-collecting guests, came up to Douglas and politely asked him to put his camera back in the car until the President had been taken into the house. "The Chief doesn't like to be photographed when he is being moved, so I've got my orders," he explained. Out of his wheel chair, the President would be carried like a baby in some big burly policeman's arms, and both guests and friends were expected to absent themselves when that happened.

Not only did the President not want to be photographed, he did not want to be looked at. Even in the house, when it was time for dinner, he usually had himself wheeled in first, and the guests looked the other way while he was lifted out of his chair and into the dining chair at the head of the table. Members of the family and close friends, like Sherwood, who would live there for months on end, and Hopkins, were excepted from the rule, but for others the custom was tactfully to disappear into the next room or get involved in a conversation with backs turned. The President was very sensitive and very touchy about it.

His mother, Mrs. James Roosevelt, a wonderful and dynamic old matriarch, was always at Hyde Park. In many ways she was the head of the family and always had been. She often talked to her son, as most mothers will, as if he were still a little boy, and the President was usually careful not to let her see him should he decide on a second cocktail. Once, when he and Douglas were sitting in the library after dinner and having a serious discussion on psychological warfare and propaganda, his mother came in and tipped back, rather playfully, the office-type swivel chair in which the President was sitting. He went into an instant panic and yelled out at his mother to stop. He was immediately sorry for his outburst, but was obviously unnerved. "He resented dependency in any form, because he was physically a very muscular man," Douglas recalls. "From the waist up he had colossal shoulders and very strong forearms. His hands were strong but soft, and when you shook hands with him the flesh was sensuous and meaty. Yet his very illness, aided by his wife's inspiration and character, gave him a strength of mind and will which before had only been latent."

Fairbanks has since recorded a few of his more intimate glimpses of Roosevelt's political outlook and personal attitudes:

"The President had that particular brand of calm and easy assurance often found in men accustomed to high office and authority. His bitterest enemies melted before his personal charm, only regaining their objectivity when they had left him. He had a way of taking off his coat, rolling up his sleeves, and leaning back in his chair, head cocked one way, the cigarette holder pointing the other, which made one feel that everything was very agreeably under control and that *you* were the one person he had been wanting to see. Your own common sense reminded you this was not so, but the warmth thus generated gave common sense a temporarily rosy glow.

"There was something so authoritative about his easiness, however, that very few people took liberties with him. He was, as a man experienced in American public life and truly gregarious, a keen 'first-name-caller,' even to those he met for the first time. I can remember no one outside the family who dared to return the compliment and only a very limited number who managed to match his ease with their own.

"It was almost impossible to draw the dividing line between the Man and the Office. F.D.R. himself was fully aware of the possibilities of his destiny and of his place in history. He had an overwhelming respect for the office of the presidency and expected everyone else to share it. Most did. Even his own mother, warm, possessive, devoted, and as intimate an influence as any mother could be, made a point of standing, in deference to 'the President of the United States,' whenever he entered a room.

"Most men who achieve positions of great power suffer from some form of megalomania. Roosevelt was no exception. His enemies, of which there were many, were convinced that this megalomania took a vicious form. I do not believe it did. I had a great fondness for him and a great respect. That he was a shrewd and adept politician, and a very human being with many frailties, was self-evident. But I believed him to be a man devoted to his country and to the policies of which he believed. If his method of operation was occasionally high-handed or brusque, the times and circumstances called for it. A less tough, less determined—or less ambitious—man might have permitted the New World to forgo its destiny by default.

"The President was very much alive to the eminence of his position and appreciative of the natural powers of persuasion which time and again inspired the popular support which put and kept him there. Being a professional politician, but also a man of ideals who had arrived at just the right time in history, he was fully aware of the fact that he would be a major paragraph in the chronicles of his times.

"One day, I was at Hyde Park and he asked me if I would care to drive up with him to a lodge he had on top of a hill. It was a little stone house, to which he would repair from time to time to sit and contemplate the Hudson River valley and his estate. It was done up with books and chairs and couches, a retreat where he could go off and confer with somebody or be quite alone. He drove up himself in a specially constructed small car, with hand controls so he would not have to use his legs. It was a lovely warm day and we were sitting outside. He was feeling relaxed and intimate about matters in general, and we talked about my particular job at the time, whatever it was, about politics, world affairs, and family problems.

"While we were chatting we could see ships passing way off down the Hudson River through the trees. He interrupted his conversation to comment that it was interesting to meditate on the fact that there would very possibly come a time in history when ships passing that spot would recall the times in which we were living then and dip their flags as they passed. I had no recourse but to agree with him—he was almost talking to himself—but it was one of the few times I heard him speak out loud of his awareness of his place in history. He would occasionally let things of that nature drop. If you were fond of him they were not offensive, they were rather endearing; of course if you were his political enemy they became something to hate.

"Not that he did not give indications of this consciousness in other ways. He would half jokingly invite attention to the fact that whenever the Big Three met he was the only real Head of State, the others being legally only the political leaders.

"He was immensely tolerant in many things, but very stubborn in others. For example, both he and Secretary Hull, whom he profoundly admired, shared an intemperate attitude toward General de Gaulle. Toward the British they shared a strong admiration, but also a strong suspicion. The President, in spite of a general affection for Winston Churchill, could not quite believe the British to be as altruistic as they proclaimed themselves. But neither, as many of his critics will say, was he. Roosevelt frankly opposed the old idea of 'Empire' and, although welcoming the evolution of the Commonwealth, he sometimes expressed distrust of reports and assurances of progress in that direction.

"He firmly believed that the British were a fine influence in the world and that a strong association of British nations was vital to peace, but he encouraged, in so far as he was able, British relinquishment of Imperial India and increased American interests in the Middle East. He was persuaded that the U.S. enjoyed more widespread moral support than Britain and was therefore destined to be the inheritor of her mantle of world influence. While loyal to our closest ally, he was intent on America filling, by influence, commerce or example, any vacuum occasioned by British withdrawal.

"Of all his contemporaries, Winston Churchill commanded his greatest admiration; yet he evinced a certain envy. Twice at different periods he asked me, as he asked several other people, whether it was really true that Churchill wrote his own speeches, as he himself had a highly literate team to assist him. It seemed incredible to him that anybody who was the chief executive of a major power could possibly find the time—he just could not believe that it was possible and thought there must be some catch to it. That was another facet of his curious conceits. I do not mean to sound disloyal when I recount this, because I say it in great fondness, but it is in recognition that human beings are human beings and all have their frailties."

11

ON MAY 15, 1940, the beleaguered British Prime Minister in London sent a letter to the President, asking if some way could not be found to release forty or fifty overage American destroyers to make good severe losses at sea which would not be covered by new construction for at least a year. Over the next four months, the means of meeting that request was to provide the crucial issue between America's internationalists and isolationists and the touchstone of the country's attitude to the war.

Within a week the William Allen White committee was reactivated. White, Eichelberger, Henry Stimson, Senator Ernest W. Gibson, Robert

Sherwood, and about thirty others met in the Bankers' Club in New York and launched it on a truly national scale. Local chapters were formed more or less spontaneously, and inside a month there were three hundred of them, representing every state in the Union, except North Dakota. Douglas Fairbanks became head of the Southern California branch and a national vice-president, enlisting the popular appeal of some of his fellow film stars, and raising a constant flow of funds and public support from airplane, oil, and shipping magnates and industrialists, labor leaders, intellectuals, and scientists.

Fairbanks, by reason of his close friendship with the British Ambassador, Lord Lothian, was one of the first Americans to hear through him and through Lord Tweedsmuir in Canada that destroyers were the crying need of the hour. He also received letters on the subject from Anthony Eden and Duff Cooper. Although he was only one of the many channels through whom such information reached the committee his exceptional contacts on both sides of the Atlantic and the confidence he enjoyed made him into one of its most active and useful members.

Although he was to come under violent criticism as a British "stooge," his friendships in United States administrative circles, particularly with such professional officers as Admiral Standley, formerly Chief of Naval Operations, had confirmed his conviction that aid to Britain was a prerequisite of the defense of America and the survival of his own country in the face of Axis aggression.

The invitation to become a vice-president of the committee was largely due to the realization that he had a curious and unorthodox type of entrée into Washington, the White House, and the Department of State. He had also begun to cultivate Felix Frankfurter, the influential Supreme Court justice, who was always extremely cordial, and advised Douglas on the content of many of his speeches.

The central office of the committee set up its national headquarters at 8 West 40th Street in New York. The staff issued for its more influential members regular summaries of current voting opinion in the Washington Capitol, named the legislators it was essential to concentrate on, arranged for statements to be made by prominent public figures, which were printed and distributed on a vast scale, refuted the allegations of isolationist opinion and provided the necessary counter-arguments. Organization at the ward level was minute. The women's division enrolled enough volunteer workers for each of them to take one page from the telephone directory in the major towns, call the names in order, and explain why aid for Britain was essential to national defense.

Co-ordinating each phase of their campaign with the White House, the committee was able to provide a firm body of support for the President in each of his successive moves. The campaign became one of the greatest demonstrations of the mobilization of public opinion in the history of the United States.

The committee was successful in two ways: first, because it created a general atmosphere of support for the Allies and then for Britain when she stood with her back to the wall; and secondly, because it was always able to concentrate public opinion on a specific thing, whether it was bombers, bases, destroyers, Lend-Lease or the neutrality patrol. It was one of the few examples of a popular movement advocating a great ideal which could always express itself in terms of specific requirements. Thousands of people all over the country wired the President and Congress to send this material or take that measure, which gave the President the evidence of public support he needed to drown the counterblast of the outraged isolationists.

It was essential to know the President's mind and the exact requirements of the British. Here Fairbanks' contacts with Tweedsmuir and Lothian, and later with the latter's successor Lord Halifax, whom Douglas had known back in the early thirties when he was Lord Irwin, were invaluable. Robert Sherwood describes the liaison work he and Fairbanks and others maintained with the President thus: "We could find out what they were urging the President to do and from the President how much he wanted them to do. He was a master of the technique of getting everybody else far out ahead of him and then doing something not quite as far ahead, so that it would seem sweetly reasonable to the public at large. He used members of the committee and his cabinet officers in that respect to fly kites and balloons in speeches that were just breathing fire. A great deal of criticism would descend on the individual who had made the speech, but a new trail had been blazed and the President could advance along it."

William Allen White had exceptional access to the President himself, although the conservative and cautious line he took in the committee's councils was to lead to his resignation before six months were out. Fairbanks, less inhibited, was frequently able to report the President's views to the committee. Sometimes they felt Roosevelt ought to act more quickly and decisively, and in certain cases took the lead themselves.

They had a formidable body of isolationist opinion to combat. While France was falling, the Chicago *Tribune* commented: "Inflamed by commercial radio commentators the East has fallen into a complete state of hysteria, the mental confusion could hardly be worse if the enemy were in Long Island again." Senator Nye, a Republican leader in the Senate, said: "A campaign of fear is pushing the country into Europe's war, a war which is nothing more than a continuation of the old European conflict of power politics, a fight to save an empire." Colonel Lindbergh added the opinion: "In the future we may have to deal with a Europe dominated by Germany. An agreement between us could maintain peace and civilization throughout the world as far into the future as we can see."

The President was at first very dubious about the possibility of making the destroyers available. He had been nominated by the Democratic Party as a candidate for his third term and was not prepared to take undue risks affecting his political position. William Allen White was somewhat disturbed at Roosevelt's relative inaction in the matter. "Since he's won his third-term nomination," White is recorded as remarking, "he seems to have lost his cud." The committee set to work during the next few weeks to demonstrate to the President that the public would support such a move.

With disaster leading to Dunkirk in France, the committee launched a campaign of cables to the White House urging that aircraft be sent to the Allies. Time was bought on the radio for Mrs. Dwight Morrow, the mother-in-law of Colonel Lindbergh, to refute his isolationist standpoint. The next day there were fifteen thousand telegrams on the President's desk advocating release of the planes. Two days later two hundred and fifty of them were on their way. Another whirlwind barrage of cables and letters deluged the White House and Congress, advocating shipment by the American Government of enough rifles, 75-mm. guns, and other material to re-equip the British Expeditionary Force. Petitions with more than two million signatures demanded all-out aid to Britain.

With their campaign gathering momentum, the committee scored a telling blow when they persuaded the venerable and respected figure of the only General of the Army of the first world war, John J. Pershing, to make a nation-wide broadcast supporting the release of destroyers. This contribution was largely the work of Herbert Agar, one of the members of a ginger group of the committee, calling itself the Fight for Freedom Committee. Its members, who included Fairbanks, were in favor of immediate American participation in the war. William Allen White was never prepared to take up a position very far in advance of the public opinion he was trying to organize, and toward the end of the year this caused him to resign his responsible position as leader of the parent organization, continuing in a merely honorary capacity.

Nevertheless, the active protagonists of the destroyer deal had to contend with a stalemate in Washington. The President was unwilling to submit the matter to Congress for legislation, and a considerable proportion of the senators and representatives desired the President to take direct administrative action. No one wanted to accept the political responsibility.

By the beginning of August, Eichelberger was able to advise Fairbanks and his immediate associates that a way had been found out of the impasse. They had approached one of the most brilliant legal minds in the Roosevelt administration, Benjamin V. Cohen, at that time in the Department of the Interior and later consultant to the State Department. For years Roosevelt had leaned heavily on Cohen to rationalize the legal tangles involved in much of his New Deal legislation. He had an astonishing capacity for work and employed a day stenographic staff, which he kept in a state of hectic activity until the inevitable Washington cocktail time, and then, after a leisurely dinner, would return to his office about nine o'clock at night and give his night staff enough further work to keep them busy until eight o'clock the next morning.

Eichelberger, on behalf of his colleagues, asked him to determine if any legal method could be devised of transferring the destroyers without additional congressional authority. In the course of a single night's work he produced legal proof that such an action fell within the terms of the President's constitutional powers. His brief was passed to some of the lawyers on the committee, six of whom, including Dean Acheson, later Secretary of State in the Truman administration, signed a letter to the New York *Times* on August 23, 1940, in which they outlined the legal basis for the transfer. A copy of the letter was sent to every newspaper in the United States, and many of them printed it. This expression of opinion from eminent constitutional experts broke the back of the opposition. The destroyers were released as part of an exchange agreement for the granting of facilities for the United States Navy in British possessions in the Western Hemisphere, and the President was able to sign the necessary order on September 3.

In a letter he wrote a week later to a former Hollywood colleague, John Farrow, by that time a lieutenant in the Canadian Navy, Fairbanks was able to say: ". . . It was indeed an exciting event, this transfer of the destroyers, and we on the White committee have been proud as peacocks of the part we played in it. Both the President and Lord Lothian have admitted off the record that had it not been for our activities in preparing public sentiment for such a deal, it could never have gone through. I am doing my best to get a job somewhat like yours in our Navy. . . ."

More sensitive than ever to his position as a young man of military age so vigorously sponsoring the active intervention of the United States in the conflict, Fairbanks had in August made formal application through the 11th Naval District in San Diego for a commission in the United States Naval Reserve and was waiting to hear the outcome.

During the campaign to release the destroyers, Fairbanks had helped to organize a nation-wide series of mass meetings, to culminate in a much-heralded attack on the main isolationist stronghold of Chicago. His name had proved one of the most effective "draws" in the campaign, and he was deliberately chosen by the committee as the key speaker.

By the time the rally in the Chicago Coliseum finally took place on September 18, the immediate battle was over, but his address to a capacity crowd of sixteen thousand served to underline the triumph, and brought home to a radio public across the nation the fact that he was an orator of uncommon ability. On their arrival, Douglas and Mary Lee received scores of abusive letters, many of them threatening violence, had their hotel picketed, and had to be placed under a strong police guard. The local organization of the meeting was in the hands of the Chicago chapter of the committee, which was headed by a highly successful lawyer and internationalist named Adlai Stevenson. Douglas had been in constant contact with him during the preceding weeks, and their friendship has lasted during the succeeding years.

Many of the things Douglas said on that occasion he still propounds today: "Now, I am frankly pro-British. But only because I am radically pro-American. . . . The question posed by some of our diehards as to what we have in common with Britain is the easiest of all to answer. The first and very important reason is that we have in common the language of Chaucer, Shakespeare, Milton, and the King James version of the Scriptures, of Keats, of Byron, and of Shelley. We have in common a tradition of representative government dating from the time of the Druids—more than two thousand years ago. We share the history of an idea which men wrote of, thought of, shouted and fought for. An idea which will allow us to say what we please, think what we please, write what we please, and do what we please—within the limits of the laws which our representatives legislate on our behalf. An idea that gave us the Magna Carta, the Bill of Rights, and the Common Law. That idea, in the face of seemingly insurmountable obstacles, has never died."

Then he added an interesting footnote dating from a conversation with Ribbentrop, Ciano, and Count Grandi in London: "Prominent

Nazi officials, as long as two years ago, said, in my presence, that a military invasion of the Western Hemisphere 'may not be necessary' to bring us to within the Nazi-Fascist orbit. They had other methods equally effective. Their organization has already been so thorough that Central and South America are wincing under their pressure. Dr. Goebbels, the notorious director of 'Filth' Columns, said, no longer than thirteen months ago, to a personal friend of mine, 'I'll see you in America within eighteen months.'" The remark had been made to his father in Venice just before Senior left Europe for the last time.

This meeting was designed to stimulate support throughout the Middle West, far beyond Chicago, increase membership, and raise more funds. It was a turning point in American support for the internationalist program and positive aid for the Allies. There had always been a degree of passive support, but when the Middle West came into line more actively, in spite of the opposition of the Hearst and McCormick press, it was of enormous assistance to the national campaign.

This successful incursion into their very heart roused the isolationists to fury. Their most vocal organization was the America First Committee. One of its leading members, General Hugh S. Johnson, within a week, picked on Fairbanks' speech and personality as a means of discrediting the White committee campaign and wrote in his United Features syndicated column: "We have been harangued by several eminent breast-beating war criers. . . . We were advised on this serious strategical question by a movie he-vamp from Hollywood, young Douglas Fairbanks. He, as everybody knows, has a long, heroic and varied celluloid military and diplomatic experience—in all parts of the world that can profitably be imitated on photographic film in Hollywood."

It was typical of the sort of attack to which Fairbanks was being subjected at the time. When he ventured to protest to General Johnson, he received this reply: "Dear Douglas: When you are as old as I am and my friend your father was you won't take yourself so damned seriously. You may know a lot beside acting—although I am not so sure you know that very well—but I don't think you know very much about strategy, defense, politics—and especially fighting Britain's wars. I know the latter even if not the former.

"You are being a propagandist's little agent—and the direction of that propaganda is disaster. When you call me an isolationist, you are calling names. It isn't isolation to prepare to defend—and get ready to defend—half a world. I don't know what you would call protagonists for our involvement from Singapore to Aden and dear Old Baghdad— except silly suckerism.

"Forget it, kid—I neither meant nor did you any harm, but you can't get down into the arena without getting sawdust or tanbark on your shoes."

Douglas and Mary Lee went to spend the weekend after the Chicago speech at Hyde Park, where the President congratulated him warmly. Douglas was working at this time on a revised version of his honorary citizenship plan. In view of the difficulties of initiating the necessary legislation in Congress, one suggestion was that the British should take the initiative by the formation of an international order of chivalry, with the King as its symbolic head, conferring honorary citizenship of the British Commonwealth on all those assisting in the fight for freedom. It was described in another paper Douglas prepared at the time as "A revival of the Knights Templars, combining the spirit of the orders of the Middle Ages for those who fought against the infidel with the theory of guest citizenship extended by certain Greek states in antiquity to aliens who had served them."

The President was sympathetic and interested in the broader aspects of the plan, but Harry Hopkins was outraged. He turned to Franklin D. Roosevelt, Jr., who was a fellow weekend guest, and said: "What is this stuff you're getting this young friend of yours to push? It's time he learned a few political facts of life. How the hell does he expect the President to fall in with any scheme which puts the King of England at its head?" Hopkins at that time had by no means developed the friendly feelings for Britain which resulted from his subsequent visits on behalf of the American Government.

Douglas also decided to enlist the support of Winston Churchill, and sent him a long letter on the subject a few days later, to which he received a friendly acknowledgment. In it he said: "There has been much talk of creating common citizenship between this country and Britain . . . would it not be a magnificent gesture if the British Commonwealth proclaimed that every man actively supporting the fight of Britain will be regarded . . . as honorary citizens? . . . In effect, the proposal would state to the world, 'Democracy is a living religion. The world is now faced with the most terrifying and complete challenge with which this faith has ever had to cope. Most of our friends have fallen; others of our friends are not yet inclined or able to join us actively, although they are lending us every possible support. We alone are able to continue the fight. We denounce as a sacrilege the accusation that we are fighting solely for our own safety. Rather do we say that we are fighting for an idea and an ideal which transcends national boundaries. Therefore, in gratitude to those who feel as intensely as we and are joining with us in this struggle, we, through the symbol which represents us and our ideas, offer to them the same rights and privileges which we enjoy as free men in a free commonwealth. The idea of democracy is above religious, racial, and party-political affiliations.' "

Fairbanks' letters to the President over the next fortnight, during which he saw Roosevelt again in Washington, reveal that they had discussed other matters as well: "It was so very kind of you to be so gracious and not feel we were interlopers on such an intimate family party. [It has been the eighty-sixth birthday of the President's mother.] I am grateful for the length of time you gave me personally. . . . I have been terribly excited about the possibility of being of service along the lines you tentatively suggested. . . . Saw young Franklin yesterday and outlined the article which I am writing for the Hearst papers on your behalf. From my vantage point the election appears to be in the bag."

The "possibility of service" was to mature the following year as a confidential mission to South America. Support for the President's third term in the election had become another item in Fairbanks' furious round of activity.

He was still in top demand as a convention speaker on behalf of the aid-the-Allies committee. He made another speech which caused a considerable stir, and was reprinted and rebroadcast several times, at the New York World's Fair on October 19, the anniversary of the British surrender at Yorktown.

During the same period he received a cable from Duff Cooper, by that time Minister of Information, asking him to make a series of transatlantic broadcasts for the B.B.C., and his encouraging voice became one of the features of the dark winter of 1940–41.

Political support for Roosevelt was something new for Fairbanks, who to this day remains registered as an independent voter. Only two years previously he had replied to his fellow actor Melvyn Douglas, who had written asking for help in the mid-term elections of 1938 on behalf of the Studio Committee for Democratic Political Action: "I don't think much of the New Deal as a liberal, and had better be left out of it."

But, as he later admitted, "Roosevelt was such a dynamic personality and in a great many ways he answered the questions which were in the majority of minds both in domestic and foreign affairs. Certainly he did as far as I was concerned. I didn't always go along with him on domestic affairs, but that was not my particular cup of tea, I was not up on farm problems or internal banking problems or states' rights, except from an historical sense. I didn't have any clear-cut views and wasn't terribly interested. My private interests had always been in the world of foreign affairs and in that I was for him."

Fairbanks' position was complicated by the fact that he had conceived a strong personal liking for the Republican candidate, Wendell Willkie, and had played his part, in a series of talks in the New York Waldorf Towers, in persuading him not to make the destroyer deal a political issue. Moreover, his character being what it is, he could not bring himself to take the accepted political stand that to justify yourself you attack the opposite side. It is one of the main reasons why he has never been able to bring himself to enter elective politics. He had several meetings and an exchange of correspondence with

Willkie, and never did anything but praise him as a man in the many speeches he was called upon to make.

Fairbanks felt that Roosevelt carried a greater international confidence, and that if he lost the election the world would misinterpret the defeat as a renunciation of his foreign policy. "I don't suppose that I influenced more than about five voters anyway," he says, "but quite a lot of people listened to my broadcasts." Robert Wagner, the Washington columnist, thought otherwise: "So far as the participation of the motion-picture people in the recent campaign is concerned, the bright hero in administration circles is young Douglas Fairbanks," he wrote. "His speech from Hollywood on the big broadcast the night before the election is regarded as one of the finest of the entire campaign."

The President himself also sent due acknowledgment: "Dear Douglas, I want to felicitate you on your fine performance over the radio on election eve. I am sure Secretary Hull will keep your offer of service in mind and I hope he will find some place in which you can render real service. With all good wishes and again my sincere thanks, very sincerely yours, Franklin D. Roosevelt."

Other unsolicited messages were less favorable. "Never again do I expect to see a picture of yours. Some of us movie 'fans' are gonna try to keep your pictures from ever being shown at our theaters and the theaters of the surrounding towns. Consider yourself socked in the puss with rotten eggs. Boo Douglas Fairbanks, Jr.," said one letter from Milton, Oregon. A cable from San Francisco stated succinctly: "You fool."

The President invited Mary Lee and Douglas to stay at the White House again for a few days during his inauguration. At a very quiet dinner after the ceremony, the President complained how tired he was from having taken the salute and of the pain in his legs. But then he relaxed and began to enjoy himself, inquiring about the inaugural balls that night. Two or three of these had been arranged, at the largest of which Robert Sherwood was to act as master of ceremonies, make the dedication speech, and introduce the distinguished participants. In the middle of dinner—scrambled eggs, deerfoot sausages, and bacon

—word came that Sherwood had been taken seriously ill and would be unable to carry on. He had actually arrived at Constitution Hall before being obliged to return home.

The President looked down the table and called, "Hey, Doug!" He showed Douglas the note about Sherwood and said: "Will you do me another favor?"—"Why, certainly, sir. What?" Douglas replied. "Will you not have any more dinner, run over to the big auditorium and take Bob Sherwood's place?" Fairbanks said he would be delighted but that he was completely unprepared. "I know you'll do it all right," said the President, "they'll brief you on the way over in the car. Here's my aide, who'll tell you more."

With three minutes of preparation, Fairbanks did a first-class job.

The New Year found Fairbanks busier than ever. December 8 had seen a second major appeal from Winston Churchill to the President, raising as a matter of urgency the problem of Britain's ability to pay for further essential supplies with her dwindling dollar resources. Roosevelt, re-elected by an overwhelming majority, was in a position to take much bolder steps on his own initiative. In a press conference on December 16 he enunciated the fundamental principle of what was to become the Lend-Lease program. A bill containing the necessary legislation was prepared for submission to Congress, but in order to be quite sure of the outcome the President called on the aid-the-Allies committee to make a further lunge in his support. Fairbanks was again to the forefront as a key speaker at a major rally at the Bay Front Park in Miami on February 2, 1941, before twenty-five thousand people, and a coast-to-coast radio audience.

In a letter to the Bensons in England on February 21 he gave some indication of what the almost reckless exploitation of his reputation had meant in personal terms: "You would be surprised at some of the violently insulting letters and write-ups I have received. I have been threatened and cajoled, patronized and offended. I will have to admit that my activities have probably had a deteriorating effect upon my so-called career. After eleven months of this work I've not done any professional work. However, I don't really care except for the fact that bills have to be paid and I am obliged to do something soon, although with each day it is getting more difficult, as people in our profession are not supposed to be active in controversial affairs. There are not more than half a dozen of us who have done anything about it, in fact the only ones I can think of are the Lunts, Bob Sherwood, Bob Montgomery, Connie Bennett, and Melvyn Douglas."

The United States Senate passed the Lend-Lease Act on March 8 by sixty votes to thirty-one and the House of Representatives, three days later, by a majority of two hundred and forty-six. The long battle the committee had waged was almost won. The further stages of American intervention during 1941, the neutrality patrol and the convoy system, became largely a matter of administrative action on the part of the President, although the members of the committee continued by their now tried and proven methods of organizing mass support to provide him with the public backing he needed.

On November 7, a month before Pearl Harbor day, Congress approved, largely as a matter of formality, the repeal of those sections of the Neutrality Act which prevented the arming of merchant ships and forbade American vessels from entering belligerent ports and sailing through combat zones.

The immediate successor of William Allen White as chairman of the Committee was Senator Gibson. When he joined the Army during 1941, he was succeeded by Clark Eichelberger, who had been the committee's spark plug and organizing head during the whole of this momentous period, and after the war continued his unselfish activity in a similar capacity as head of the American Association for the United Nations. It is Eichelberger who pays this unreserved tribute to Fairbanks as a colleague: "He was a glamorous figure and we needed glamour in the movement, we needed people who could get public attention, people we could put on the radio easily, who could make headlines, people whose identification with a cause of this kind would influence masses of people. We soon realized that he had a very good mind, he had a mind that Hull respected, Welles respected and Roosevelt respected—a person who could talk about world citizenship, a person who could write his own speeches, so that he became an intellectual power in the movement. He became one of the people that we leaned on very heavily. I value his friendship almost more than anyone else I know."

12

THE ACTIVITIES on their behalf of this unusual young movie actor had made a good impression on the President, Cordell Hull, and Sumner Welles. His unselfish willingness to place his celebrity value at their disposal, the clear evidence that he was a public figure of considerable appeal, and his enthusiasm made him an unusually effective advocate of the administration's foreign policies. Fairbanks, for his part, blossomed visibly in their confidence, pressed on them further offers of service in any capacity, and steeled himself to the carpings of his own industry and the derisive comments in the press.

However, his public identification with Roosevelt caused one setback. His sponsors were asked to withdraw his nomination for membership of the exclusive New York Racquet Club. Some of his friends in the States, who cluck indulgently over what they describe as his Thespian weakness for sartorial display, insist that he had been foolish enough to be seen wearing the club tie and boater before he came up for election, but this he has always indignantly denied. "If people accuse me of being pro-British, they should at least be consistent," he complains. "Anyone who has had contact with the old-school-tie tradition has at least enough sense of the protocol of such things not to try such a silly trick."

It was Sumner Welles who finally suggested the next outlet for Fairbanks' energies. With the French collapse, the American administration had become increasingly perturbed at the possible effects of the vigorous Nazi and Fascist infiltration in the South American countries. The German and Italian governments were maintaining swollen embassy staffs, subsidizing subversive organizations, pouring out a flood of propaganda, and acquiring a dangerous degree of control of newspapers and such strategic enterprises as airlines. Of all the dangers

Above: H. Charles Ulman and Daniel J. Sully, Douglas Fairbanks, Jr.'s grandfathers. *Below:* Douglas, Jr., and his mother, Beth Sully Fairbanks.

Douglas, Sr., introduces his son to his first Indian

This photograph of the Fairbankses, Sr. and Jr., was taken
at the Sully mansion near Watch Hill, Rhode Island

A scene from Fairbanks, Jr.'s first motion picture, *Stephen Steps Out*

With Richard Barthelmess in *Dawn Patrol*

The Fairbankses, Sr. and Jr., in Switzerland, 1933

Left to right: Cecil Parker, Barry Jones, Martita Hunt, Gertrude Lawrence, Richard Addinsell, Douglas Fairbanks, Jr., Clemence Dane, and Helen Hayes

Studio portrait by Hurrell, presumably in 1934

The Fairbankses in 1938

The stars of *The Prisoner of Zenda*—Fairbanks, Madeleine Carroll, Ronald Colman, David Niven, C. Aubrey Smith—appearing on a charity show with Ray Noble (seated)

Above: Fairbanks' first visit to the Douglas Hospital in Southampton. *Below:* Fairbanks shortly after being commissioned a lieutenant j.g. in the U. S. Navy

Fairbanks with his staff communications officer during the
landing in the South of France

Fairbanks receiving the Distinguished Service Cross from Lord Halifax

Fairbanks and his stepmother, Mary Pickford

Above: Fairbanks with Cesar Romero, Ernst Lubitsch, and the Duke and Duchess of Montoro. *Below:* Fairbanks, as president of the Share through C.A.R.E. Committee, handing a package to a woman in the Roman slum district of Trastevere

Above: Douglas and Mary Lee Fairbanks with the Duchess of Kent, Cecil Beaton, and others. *Below:* Fairbanks with President Auriol of France

Fairbanks making a television film in the British National Studios, Boreham Wood

Douglas and Mary Lee Fairbanks with their daughters Daphne, Melissa, and Victoria

inherent in Hitler's triumph on the continent of Europe, the United States Government regarded as the most direct threat to its security the very real possibility of developments in the Latin-American republics, calculated to disrupt the unity of the hemisphere.

There were more than a million and a half Germans or people of German descent in the South American countries, and as many more Italians. In southeastern Brazil and southern Chile large areas were almost completely German. Through blandishments and pressure, agents had forced their co-nationals into Nazi organizations, some of which were para-military in nature. In one or two of the smaller countries, such as Uruguay, a *coup d'état* was a distinct possibility.

Deprived of vital European markets, alarmed by the suddenness of the Nazi victories, relatively defenseless, and threatened with subversion from within, many of the South American governments were finding it difficult to resist German pressure. Nazi diplomats and businessmen were endeavoring to convince them that the defeat of Britain was imminent, were even guaranteeing delivery dates for goods on the resumption of trade that would follow, and warning those who demurred that it would be the worse for them if they failed to co-operate.

Latin-American affairs had long been Welles' particular province. He decided to see if a somewhat unorthodox diplomatic *démarche* would help to influence events. On January 24, 1941, he sent this memorandum to the President: "Douglas Fairbanks, Jr., came in to see me this afternoon and spoke again of his efforts to find some opportunity of being of service to the government. . . . It has occurred to me that if we sent him some time in April on an official mission to some of the larger South American countries, ostensibly to give us information with regard to the effects, beneficial or otherwise, of American motion pictures in those countries, he could probably do some very helpful work. . . . As you know, there has been a somewhat marked pro-Fascist tendency on the part of the younger generation of the well-to-do groups in Brazil and in Argentina and in one or two of the other larger republics of South America, and I think that Fairbanks could probably do a pretty effective job in combating this trend.

Both his moving-picture celebrity as well as his personality will appeal to the elements I have mentioned. Will you let me know what you think of this suggestion?" Roosevelt made the marginal comment: "S.W., very good, F.D.R."

Welles lost no time in inviting Fairbanks to undertake the mission. Douglas was staying with his mother in New York at the time and on the last day of January received this letter:

My dear Mr. Fairbanks,

With reference to our talk when I last had the pleasure of seeing you a few days ago, the President has authorized me to ask if you will be willing to undertake an official mission for us at the end of April. The mission would ostensibly be a mission to investigate in a broad way the effects on public opinion in the other American republics of American motion pictures. In reality your mission would be directed principally toward getting in touch with certain national groups in some of the larger countries to the south which are now believed to be veering toward Nazi ideology. Your mission would entail the making of addresses in the countries you visit.

I hope very much that you will find it possible to accept this invitation since I believe you could render a very highly useful service to our government.

Will you let me know what your reaction may be?

    With my kind regards, believe me,

           Yours very sincerely,

              Sumner Welles

Douglas was delighted. It seemed as if the diplomatic career for which he yearned was opening before him. Both the President and Cordell Hull had inquired on a number of occasions what his plans for the future were, and Hull had also suggested that if he ever took the decision, it might be possible to start grooming him for election as a member of the House of Representatives. But Douglas, while he hoped that bigger things would come in due course, was also acutely conscious of the type of press criticism to which he was being subjected, which taunted him for his willingness to involve the young men of his generation in actual war without giving any signs of getting into uniform himself. That this was manifestly unfair in view of Fairbanks' attempts over a year earlier to join the Canadian Navy, and his application for a commission in the United States Naval Reserve, did not prevent the criticism from hitting its mark.

Douglas returned to California, amidst his usual turmoil of activity, and while the details of his forthcoming trip were being settled, pressed for a decision on his application to the Navy Department. A difficulty had arisen, as the authorities demanded that any applicant for a direct commission should hold a university degree or prove an equivalent education. Douglas, whose schooling had been haphazard and unorthodox, had to obtain affidavits from his former tutor, Carlton Hoekstra, and the widowed Mrs. Patten, together with half a dozen recommendations from prominent friends before the Navy would even consider his case. Then they relented and his commission as a lieutenant, junior grade, was signed by Frank Knox, the Secretary of the Navy, on April 10, 1941, eight months before Pearl Harbor.

By the time it arrived, Fairbanks was already back in Washington for his final briefings from Sumner Welles and State Department officials before embarking on his South American trip.

It had been decided that his mission should be undertaken under the harmless and general pretext of studying cultural relations. His formal letter of authority was dated April 11, and read: "Sir, In compliance with instructions received from the President you are hereby assigned as a special representative of the Department of State to the other American republics. In order that you may carry out the directions of the President which have been given to you orally, you are requested to proceed to South America for the purpose of visiting certain cities in Brazil, Uruguay, Argentina, Chile, Peru, Panama, and any cities of the other republics which you may deem advisable for fulfillment of your mission."

The sum of five thousand dollars was allotted from the "Emergency Fund for the President" for the purpose, and Edward Hutchinson Robbins, a member of the staff of the Office of the Co-ordinator of Commercial and Cultural Relations between the American Republics, was deputed with his wife to accompany Douglas and Mary Lee.

In an oblique tribute to Douglas' work over the previous eighteen months, Welles sent this confidential instruction to all the American ambassadors on his route: "It is highly desirable to ensure adequate police protection for Mr. Fairbanks, the objective of course would be to save him from molestation not only from his admirers but also by persons with views opposed to the strongly pro-British position which he has consistently taken and on behalf of which he has spoken in the United States and plans to speak in the other American republics. Please emphasize as strongly as possible to the appropriate authorities of the government to which you are accredited the necessity of taking a maximum of precautions in this respect."

Just before leaving, Douglas paid a courtesy call on the President at Hyde Park and could not resist wearing his new uniform. Roosevelt was visibly surprised: "Well, what are you all dressed up for?" he asked. "Mr. President, you've just handed me a commission," said Douglas with pardonable pride. It is a tribute to the fabulous efficiency of the expansion of the United States Navy during the war to note that at this time there were considerably less than three thousand Naval Reserve officers on active duty. By the end of hostilities their number had swollen to a quarter of a million.

With the State Department's approval, Douglas had discussed with Lord Halifax, the British Ambassador, the possibility of preparing an unofficial and impartial report on the conditions he might find as they affected British interests. Unorthodox, even illegal, as the procedure was, it gave an indication of the extent to which the United States' administration was willing to go in furthering the British cause. Fairbanks was permitted to do whatever he thought was best under the circumstances for British interests, while maintaining his identity as an American and keeping the Secretary of State advised. Douglas was already under the authority of the United States Office of Naval Intelligence, which, with the State Department, maintained a veto on the divulging of any matters affecting American security.

The tour started on April 21 and lasted nine weeks. Behind the façade of his acceptance as a popular movie star, Fairbanks had been given instructions to sound out the heads of government in the countries he was visiting on a number of subjects which could not be raised as formal matters through regular diplomatic channels. He was to make it clear both in direct conversations and in all his speeches that the United States stood firmly by the side of Britain and looked to South American countries to support her attitude.

Douglas was to introduce such topics as the granting of naval and military bases for the use of United States forces as an extension of the destroyers-for-bases agreement recently concluded with Britain. He was to suggest that steps be taken to counteract the flood of Axis propaganda and the number of Nazi-controlled newspapers and was to impress Fascist-minded people, especially the vociferous younger element of his own age, of the growing military might of the democracies and the certainty of their eventual victory. Welles felt that if offense was taken at any departure on Fairbanks' part from the overt purpose of his mission, it would be perfectly simple to disown him and no harm would have been done. In fact, this was at no time the case, and the flow of information he and Robbins were able to send back to Washington proved invaluable.

Before leaving, Fairbanks spent several weeks in concentrated sessions with Spanish and Portuguese tutors, and during the tour amassed the respectable total of twenty-five speeches in Spanish, seven in Portuguese, and twenty-five in English.

The films of both Senior and Junior Fairbanks had long been extremely popular in South America. Very few movie stars had appeared there in the flesh, and Douglas' visit attracted banner headlines in the press for days in each of the cities he visited. No other representative, however eminent, could possibly have had the same mass appeal. When, instead of the capers normally organized by Hollywood publicity departments for their big names, it was discovered that he was a modest young man of sense and sensibility, who talked with tact and spoke with a genuine conviction and gift of phrase, the impact of his mission was considerable.

In Brazil he was soon on excellent terms with President Vargas and the Foreign Minister, Oswaldo Aranha, both of whom were pro-American. Many of the other ministers, however, were not and Fairbanks, in due course, was able to comment on this fact in a manner quite impossible for the accredited Ambassador. There were scores of pro-German and German-language newspapers, and only one in English. Fairbanks had been instructed to disapprove strongly of this discrepancy. Behind the scenes he was also able to discuss in general terms the possibility of acquiring bases, or at least supply and refitting facilities, for the American Navy.

In due course, the pro-German newspapers were shut down. Less tangible and equally effective were the results of his conversations with those who sympathized with Germany or regarded a Nazi victory as inevitable. To them he gave stirring accounts of the mass of armaments being manufactured in the United States to back Britain and quoted all the economic and political factors which made the defeat of Germany certain. His carefully prepared speeches, which underlined American determination to see Britain through, were extensively published.

In return, government leaders felt free to expound in conversational terms the difficulties and requirements of their economic and political situation, which could never have been revealed in formal diplomatic talks. This information, together with the observations he and Robbins were able to make of the degree of Nazi infiltration, included much pertinent matter, and the pattern was repeated in each of the countries he visited.

"Much of the German strength in Brazil is due to a growing defeatism on the part of responsible officials and society leaders," he wrote to Sumner Welles. "To counter this I invented out of thin air more terrifying statistics of our rearmament program and of growing British strength than the legendary Munchausen could have conceived. I seriously feel that it did have some effect, as before I left I had repeated to me rumors of a great mysterious power which I myself had started on the way. In short, it had gone the rounds and had come back. Even the pro-Nazis admitted that perhaps Brazil's place was in line with the States, although it was really 'too bad.'"

The labor was not without its reward. First in the formidable array of honors Fairbanks has since collected was the award to him by President Vargas of the Republican Order of the Southern Cross, in recognition of his contribution to relations between the two countries.

The connection forged at this time also resulted some years later in his appointment as Grand Officer of the *Orden al Mérito* of Chile.

The only jarring note was a contretemps with the famous Brazilian painter, Portinari. As part of the general junketing, Mary Lee was asked to sit for him, only to discover when the portrait was delivered that there was a very large price tag attached. She sent it back, saying that her husband had been busy with his voluntary work so long that he could not afford it. However, they did buy it two years later, when it was being shown in a Washington exhibition.

Douglas also gained an insight into the improbable world of Phillips Oppenheim, although he did not expect the final twist. During his stay at Rio de Janeiro he became somewhat suspicious of the zealous attentions of one of the people deputed to attend to his requirements. Douglas was fascinated by his ability always to come in at the most awkward moment, to be in the room when he wanted most for him to be out, and to be around during several confidential talks. The man stuck to him like glue. Douglas could not shake him off, and decided he was there to collect as much information as he could on behalf of one of the pro-Nazi ministers.

When Douglas arrived in Buenos Aires a member of the British Embassy began to tell him very intimate details of his visit to Brazil. Douglas laughingly asked: "How do you know about these things?" —"Oh well, we have means and methods of getting information," the official said. "Do you ever remember seeing——?" and began to describe the object of Douglas' suspicions. "Why yes, of course."—"Well, he's one of our chaps."

In the Argentine he had to endure some of the drawbacks of a film star doubling as a diplomat. One of the pro-German papers called him a "spy extraordinary" and promised to return his visit with a radio crooner named Antonio Caggiano, "among the worst we have in our country." When a firecracker exploded near Fairbanks as he was entering a radio station, *El Pampero* reported the incident under the headline: "Hero of a Hundred Films almost Dies of Fright." The same paper published a front-page picture showing him stretched out on a sofa, without his trousers, a woman's hat on his head, his torso covered with a mink coat and a sign tucked in the cushions reading: "Keep off the Grass." The caption read: "America's unofficial Ambassador to Argentina," and commented caustically on the character of the men sent by the United States to South America. Fairbanks had posed for the picture in 1938 as part of a scene from the film he made with Irene Dunne, *The Joy of Living*.

While in Buenos Aires he was able to act as channel for a request from the British Embassy that the United States Government should bring pressure to bear on American oil companies to restrict the provision of bunkering oil for Japanese ships, calling at Atlantic and Pacific ports in the Americas, in order to stop one of the leaks in the blockade of the Axis powers.

A week after he left, the American Ambassador, Norman Armour, wrote to Cordell Hull: "I shall be lacking in frankness in attempting an objective report on Mr. Fairbanks' visit were I not to say that the first reaction to the news that he had been delegated as President Roosevelt's personal representative on a cultural mission was greeted with considerable surprise and skepticism. Certain elements, particularly among the intelligentsia and *estanciero* classes, and even in official circles, did not hesitate to suggest that in deference to Argentine culture it would have been expected that a distinguished man of letters from the United States would have been chosen for such a mission. It is all the more satisfactory therefore to be able to report that despite such an initial reaction Mr. Fairbanks' visit proved an unqualified success. That it did so was due in a very great measure to his personality. His evident sincerity, his modesty, quick intelligence and, above all, his truly remarkable talent as a public speaker won over the great majority of his critics and in the end those who had come to scoff remained to cheer."

Diplomatic representatives are not always so ready to acknowledge the incursion of visiting firemen in their domain. Fairbanks could never have built up and maintained his present position on the basis of his movie celebrity alone, and these formal comments from his own compatriots convey something of the quality of his personal appeal. The same day, the Ambassador in Santiago, Chile, Claude G. Bowers, was writing in similar terms to the President: ". . . He is much liked by all who meet him. They expected a flamboyant Hollywood person and are surprised and delighted to find him a modest and gracious young fellow." To which Roosevelt replied: "Dear Claude: The report . . . regarding Douglas Fairbanks' visit is a happy confirmation of the success of his trip. I am really appreciative of the help which you gave him."

Indeed, the rest of his tour went off extremely well. In Montevideo, across the River Plate, they dubbed him *El Embajador de la Sonrisa*— the Ambassador of the Smile—and he addressed an open air meeting of thirty thousand organized by the grandiosely titled *Comité de Obreros y Empleados pro la Gran Bretaña y la Libertad del Mundo*.

During his three weeks in Chile and Peru, Fairbanks found time to prepare a long report for the State Department on the desperate need for an American "Secretary of Information" to organize a counterblast to the overwhelming outpourings of Dr. Goebbels. Douglas pressed in urgent terms for the formation of an organization equivalent to the British Ministry of Information. When the time came to form the Office of War Information it was perhaps appropriate that so many of Douglas' colleagues on the aid-the-Allies committee lent their talents to it.

This frequent compilation of lengthy memoranda on every conceivable topic is a constant Fairbanks' trait. He will sit down and mull over some idea, check its implications with experts, produce a paper on the subject, and fire off copies to all the myriad acquaintances who might be in a position to do something about it. The example of the common citizenship plan has already been noted. There will be many others, covering themes as varied as the necessity for devising a formal uniform for American diplomats, a new production code for the film industry, the encouragement of international trade and the organization of relief work, the institution of an international Legion of Honor under the auspices of the United Nations, and a paper on the twentieth-century role of the British monarchy. Some of them are impractical, but none of them have been completely ignored. Their consideration, in due context, will give further insight into the gadfly methods he employs in his one-man campaign to improve understanding between the countries on both sides of the Atlantic he knows so well.

His sponsors were pleased with the results of his South American tour. On his return Sumner Welles told a press conference: "The trip Mr. Fairbanks has undertaken has been eminently successful in every way. I think he has carried out his mission with the utmost measure of discretion, tact and ability. I think he has been a very useful representative on a trip of that kind at this moment. I could not speak in terms sufficiently high of the admirable work and excellent impression he created."

The State Department arranged for him to make a nation-wide radio report of his impressions, in which he gave due warning of the dangers inherent in the Latin-American situation. One chain of newspapers did not join in the general approval. Under the heading "Soldiers Three" they commented: "Robert Montgomery, one of the few young movie actors with conspicuous versatility and intelligence, has suddenly bobbed up a full-fledged naval officer attached to the American Embassy in London. Douglas Fairbanks, Jr., has returned from a tour of Latin America as some kind of goodwill representative of the President. It's easy to start this sort of thing, but hard to follow through. What, for instance, are the White House plans for the Marx Brothers?"

However, the President was well satisfied. "Dear Douglas," he wrote on July 16, 1941: "From every source I have heard nothing but words of praise and commendation of the way you conducted yourself on your trip and I am sure it will do a great deal of good. With every good wish to you and Mrs. Fairbanks, always sincerely, Franklin D. Roosevelt."

The same day Douglas wrote to the Bensons from Westridge: "I came out here to do my first film in fifteen months. I just did not have the time to make one before, nor have I the time to make one now really, but the wolf is at the door, expenses have been heavy and bills must be paid." There were still many complications attendant upon his father's will, which had been in the hands of lawyers for over a year and a half.

The film was the Dumas story of *The Corsican Brothers*, directed by

Gregory Ratoff, in which Fairbanks, for the first time as sole star, appeared in a production wholly in the tradition of his father's costume melodramas. Perhaps as a result it grossed more than any film he had so far made.

Before leaving Washington he had checked with the Navy to inquire if and when they might need him for active duty. He felt that he had exploited himself to the full for the aid-the-Allies committee and the government, and the time had come to stop talking and get out and do something.

His position in Hollywood was not a happy one. In a letter to the Bensons, Mary Lee gave some idea of his difficulties in that touchy and curious community: "Douglas feels very foolish standing in front of cameras when he knows there is so much to be done in the world. After the picture we pack up and go East for the duration. Just what his work will be I don't know, but if he doesn't get away from here I think he'll pull his hair out one by one. We returned to California to find a hot-bed of petty gossip. That Douglas has the guts to give up his beautiful home and the sunshine of California, his career and the money he is missing, and go forth to do his bit is really a thorn in their sides."

Between shooting scenes he was taking correspondence courses on naval law, naval intelligence, and administration and was attending parades at San Pedro. The fertile flood of memoranda continued to flow. One letter to Sumner Welles on July 29, 1941, is not without point as an indication of Fairbanks' international outlook, in view of developments five years later. Lord Halifax had just stayed at Westridge. "We spoke at some length of the war and of the peace to come. I told him several of my ideas which I've been working on for the better part of a year. He was so interested that he asked me to write him a memorandum on it that he could take back to London with him."

This advocated an international army to maintain internal order after the war was over, an international fleet based on the same principles, and an international general staff who would be empowered to disband or reduce national armies according to local necessity, and continued: "The right of appeal of minorities or individuals against their governments must be guaranteed under the authority of a tribunal outside Europe, whose decisions would be backed by the international force. No government to be allowed, except by common consent through an international economic council to impose tariffs exceeding 10 per cent in value. All means of transportation and communication to be subject to international regulations, including canals and rivers which are of international importance as trade channels. Financial help from America to enable Argentina, Brazil, Chile and other Latin-American countries to assemble and keep a reserve of the raw materials Europe will need. The American nations must be prepared to grant credits in cash or in kind to any country which subscribes to these conditions and is able to prove upon demand that it is living up to its professions. By holding out the hand of instant help to a world literally starving, as will be armistice Europe, providing from its war-collected surpluses such elementary needs as wheat, meat and raw materials for industry, and denying itself of its own free will the right to keep out Europe's products by infinite tariff walls, the American continent will bring Europe into recognition of the first principles of neighborliness and democracy."

Welles, who appreciated Fairbanks' enthusiasms, replied gravely, with a hint of tongue-in-cheek, a week later: "It is obvious that you have given thoughtful consideration to the many complex problems involved in a lasting peace settlement. . . . This subject . . . is being studied carefully and continuously by a special division in the department. . . . I have sent your letter to that division for consideration and therefore I shall not comment on the details of your plan."

By then Douglas had evolved a more personal proposal. Shortly after his return to the States, the President had appointed Colonel William Donovan as Co-ordinator of Information. Douglas wrote to Sumner Welles again suggesting that in view of the creation of the new department he might be assigned by the Navy, the Department of State, or the President to act in the capacity of observer-cum-co-ordinator between America and the other democratic countries. "As you know, I have a great many personal contacts in many of these countries, and I might be of some use in helping to present a solid propaganda front between the democracies of the world. If among us all we could agree on certain fundamental moral, cultural and political issues, it may be possible not only to hasten the conclusion of the war but also to pave the way for great co-operation after the peace." It was an idea that did not turn out to his advantage.

So many people are prone to describe Fairbanks as a socially successful snob that it is interesting to study his comments in another letter he sent during this period to Con Benson, by then a group captain in the R.A.F.: "You ask me . . . for news of the so-called 400 in New York. When you added that you imagined they would not be playing the game you were quite right. Some of them are, of course, but the majority are not, and the main tragedy is that they are being assisted in their nonchalant revelries and detached behavior by rich refugees who have come from all over. The regular New Yorkers are, for the most part, terrified out of their wits and would sooner talk about anything but the war. Many of the Mayfair crowd have gone down very badly, people we all know who are seen nightly cavorting about, either spending money like drunken sailors or sponging on their hosts' hospitality beyond the limit of good manners, and assuming that frightful air of superiority which Mayfair and Park Avenue have developed to such a fine art."

Two of the friends from his Mayfair days to whom the description did not apply were on their way to stay at Westridge. Lord Louis Mountbatten, as he then was, fresh from his exploits in the destroyer *Kelly*, had come to the States to take over command of the aircraft carrier *Illustrious* at Newport News. His wife, Edwina, was making a trip across Canada and the United States for the St. John and Red Cross organizations. Lord Louis had gone to Pearl Harbor to lecture to the American fleet there on the use of antiaircraft on board ships and antiaircraft precautions at sea. The Fairbankses had seen them in New York and invited them to rejoin forces at their California home. Lady Edwina arrived first, and when her husband reached Los Angeles they stayed quietly for about a fortnight. It was their first sight of Hollywood since spending part of their honeymoon at Pickfair nineteen years earlier.

Mountbatten paid one visit to the San Diego naval air station and the North Island naval base. On the instruction of the commandant of the 11th Naval District, Douglas, resplendent in his uniform as a junior-grade lieutenant, accompanied him as a sort of honorary A.D.C. However, he displeased many of his Hollywood friends by insisting that anyone who was entitled to a reserve uniform should dig it out of moth balls for a formal dinner in his guests' honor.

After two intensive years of war, Mountbatten was delighted to relax in the Westridge swimming pool every day. At night he and Douglas would sometimes go to the local fun-fair and shoot the chutes and roundabouts, with Lord Louis shouting his delight. Their daughter, Patricia, was with them, and the only formal dance of the visit was her first, almost a coming-out party.

As he sat beside the swimming pool one morning, Mountbatten received the cable from Mr. Churchill recalling him to London to succeed Admiral of the Fleet Sir Roger Keyes in charge of Combined Operations. While not revealing the exact nature of the appointment to his host, Lord Louis made it clear that he was being recalled for an exciting job. Douglas immediately asked if there was any possibility of his joining him in any operations with which he might be connected. Mountbatten promised to remember this request.

In the middle of making *The Corsican Brothers* Douglas had received an official envelope from Washington, saying that the Navy Department required him to report for duty as soon as he could wind up his affairs. He arranged with his associates to sell out his interests in the film—which deprived him of any share in its considerable profits —to relinquish his position as associate producer, to crowd in the scenes he had to complete, and leave them to attend to the administrative and creative side. He and Mary Lee closed Westridge at the end of September and left for Washington. For most of the next four years the house was let to Cary Grant and his wife, the former Barbara Hutton.

The Fairbankses had been invited by President Roosevelt to spend their last weekend before Douglas joined the Navy at the White House. Robert Sherwood was a fellow guest and remembers the occasion: "The President had us in for cocktails before dinner. It was always a very pleasant interlude. The President sat and made the cocktails, with the tray on his desk, working over the process as though it was some form of alchemy, measuring things out. He made a very bad martini, but you had to like it because he was the President. This was a sort of farewell to Douglas, and the President and Harry Hopkins were teasing him, saying: 'Oh, Doug, we hate to see you go, the U-boat sinkings this week are higher than ever. We never know when the *Tirpitz* is coming out and of course we don't have a ship now that we think could stand up against her.' Finally Doug, not realizing that he was being had on, said: 'Well, you're certainly building up my morale.' It was a wonderful example of Roosevelt's ability to put people completely at their ease. You forgot that you were in an august presence and joked and laughed as if it was a private home."

Douglas had repeated to the President his plan for a liaison appointment with the Department of Information under Colonel Donovan. The request had been referred to the State Department, which was favorably disposed, and the Navy Department, which was not. A very senior officer who, because he later became a friend and admirer of Fairbanks', shall remain nameless, initialed the memorandum: "This is just an idea for a junketing trip. The young man in question would do more harm than good. The best thing for Fairbanks would be to get in some sea service in order to make a naval officer out of him."

During the last week of October Douglas reported for active sea duty with the Navy at Charlestown Navy Yard in Boston, where he was greeted by Ensign Franklin D. Roosevelt, Jr., whose destroyer had just docked. A few days later he rang up Genie Chester: "I was living up in the country, on a party line," she told her friends, "and about two o'clock in the morning the phone rang—it was Douglas. He was sailing in about half an hour and he had called up to say good-by. It was sweet—but he woke up the whole countryside."

13

A MODERN WAR is many wars. Behind the infantryman crawling through the mud, the naval rating frozen to his oerlikon gun during long hours closed up at action stations, and a bomber's tail-end-Charlie hunched in his plastic chicken coop lies the battle of wits of the boffins, the intelligence staffs, and the clandestine raiders who seek to confuse the enemy and penetrate his secrets.

Deception was a major weapon in the conflict. It was equally effective on land or sea or in the air. In the early years of the war, during the North African campaign, reliance was placed on the relatively primitive methods of optical illusion. Regiments of tanks simulated out of balloon fabric would appear and disappear overnight in the wastes of sand, drawing enemy formations after them. Mock airfields were built and the silhouettes of fighters projected on clouds to confuse attacking bombers. The first elaboration was the equipment of a couple of trucks with wireless transmitters and receivers, which would work up a flood of fake messages suggesting the concentration of a large number of troops, threatening attacks which existed only in the minds of the operators. With the perfection of radar a whole new field was opened up, giving particular scope to naval and air warfare. Strips of silver paper dropped from a single plane could simulate a whole fleet of bombers, a lone motor torpedo boat could be made to look on the enemy's radar screen like a battleship. Special loud-speaker units were perfected which enabled three or four light craft to reproduce the sounds of a major amphibious operation, while on land a similarly equipped truck could duplicate the noise of an armored regiment moving into position for a night attack. A single bomber could drop scores of dummy parachutists, some life-size and some only a foot high, with everything to scale, which looked from a distance like a major airborne attack spread over half the landscape. Security and censorship let pass the calculated leak or "lost" the fake document designed to disperse a whole order of battle. There was no limit to the ingenuity the Allies displayed in this grim game of deceit.

When Combined Operations Headquarters was formed in London, a special department was devoted entirely to devising means of strategic and tactical deception. Their successful use in a primitive form was one of the positive results of the otherwise disastrous Dieppe operation. Developed on an increasing scale in the Mediterranean theater, particularly in the Sicily, Salerno, and South of France land-ings, their most conspicuous triumph came with the invasion of Nor-mandy. While the main invasion forces stormed ashore between Le Havre and Cherbourg, mass deception measures operated from light surface craft and fighters kept a whole German army group pinned down in the Pas-de-Calais to parry what the Germans expected to be the main attack, and thus prevented half a million men from rendering decisive assistance to their desperate colleagues round the beachhead.

These tactical diversion groups specialized in immobilizing strong enemy forces by minimum means. Their problem was to make a pea-shooter prevail successfully over a battery of howitzers. Running enor-mous risks, their only true defense was bluff. Like many honest men, Douglas Fairbanks displayed an unsuspected aptitude for this mixture of mayhem and mystery.

When he was demobilized after five years of war he received this citation, signed by James Forrestal, the Secretary of the Navy: "Com-mander Fairbanks assisted materially in the original development of tactical deception and diversionary warfare, conducting research and developing the operating procedure of numerous special devices. He recruited and organized volunteer technicians in the first 'beach-jumper' unit with a special school for their training. He was highly instrumental in enrolling the interest of navy departmental agencies, in furthering the project and bringing it to the proper state of develop-ment so that it later became a positive contribution to the success of Allied operations against the enemy in all theaters of war. Commander Fairbanks discharged his responsibilities with unusual initiative and skill, thereby reflecting great credit upon himself and the United States Naval Service."

Such generous recognition formed a marked contrast to the experi-ence of his early months in the service. The American Navy yields nothing to the Royal Navy in the rigidity of its discipline and its in-sistence on anonymity. The general atmosphere among its regular officers was one of wary hostility to this new junior-grade lieutenant. Here was a volunteer from the publicity-mad and somewhat uncouth world of the cinema, a man whose public activities had been making headlines for a couple of years, who seemed by devious and uncomprehended means to have a totally unwarranted entrée into the White House and the Commander-in-Chief. It could only be supposed that Fairbanks had some ulterior motive in joining the service, either for purposes of self-aggrandizement or for other obscure, but certainly suspicious, reasons.

The reaction was instinctive rather than organized, but it permeated from admirals down to junior officers, with whom the net result was to see how he would take some fairly severe hazing. Fairbanks' first orders were to report for watch duties under instruction in the battleship U.S.S. *Mississippi,* flagship of the Atlantic Fleet based on Iceland. The process started in the supply ship in which he took passage to Argentia in Newfoundland. He was quartered in the petty officers' mess aft and put on double watch-keeping duties, although other neophytes half a dozen years his junior were given officers' bunks and assigned purely nominal tasks. Douglas found it all a somewhat childish piece of horseplay and kept his temper. The night they arrived in Argentia, the captain admitted that it had been a put-up job, adding that Douglas had taken it very well. "Why shouldn't I?" said Fairbanks with a shrug.

Although America was not yet in the war, the ships of her Atlantic Fleet were escorting Britain-bound convoys out to the six-hundred-mile limit and beyond. During the second part of his passage to Reykjavik, Douglas was given his introduction to active service conditions in a destroyer which met a full Atlantic gale. For two days the ship, its gyrocompass out of action, battered by heavy seas and rolling fifty-seven degrees, shrouded in fog which prevented the taking of bearings, lost contact with the convoy. Security regulations prohibited outgoing wireless messages, and the ship's officers were obliged to read incoming reports that the ship was missing. Seasick, drenched, and miserable, Douglas thought back on his long months of work with the aid-the-Allies committee and said to himself, "My God, I am partly responsible for this, and now look what I've got myself into."

When the destroyer put into Reykjavik at the end of the patrol Douglas reported to the U.S.S. *Mississippi.* Unfortunately for his perfectly sincere desire to submerge himself in the anonymity of the naval service, his appearance soon attracted the notice of the press correspondents who had accompanied the American troops there. His arrival was duly reported on the front page of scores of newspapers in the States. Officers with twenty and thirty years' experience behind them reacted sourly to the spectacle of a junior-grade lieutenant being photographed for the newspapers. "Have you hired yourself a press agent?" he was asked by one outraged captain.

This hang-over of his movie celebrity was to dog Douglas for months, and the caustic disapproval to which he was subjected made him feel sometimes that he had been disloyal in joining the Navy at all. Fortunately, the *Mississippi*'s executive officer, Captain Jerauld Wright, took him seriously, put him in command of one of the gun turrets, and helped to raise his morale. Ten years later, when Wright had become a vice-admiral, commanding all United States naval forces in the Atlantic from his headquarters in London, the two were able to renew their friendship. The fitness report—equivalent to the Royal Navy's flimsy —Wright signed when Douglas left the *Mississippi* two months later was balm to his frustration: "I believe that Lt. (j.g.) Fairbanks will make an excellent naval officer. He has taken a keen interest in all naval matters and has done an excellent job in every task assigned him. He is intelligent, energetic, and conscientious, has an attractive personality and is sure to have a following in any assigned duty. I would be very pleased to have him aboard permanently."

Douglas also acquired unexpected prestige with the captain, Penn L. Carroll. In those days every reservist had a way of cocking his cap on the side, which a regular officer would not do, and showing a lip of handkerchief in his pocket, a practice reserved for admirals. One very windy day Douglas had to report on the bridge and to keep his cap on at all crammed it square on his head. As he was moving off he heard the captain say: "There's the best goddamn reservist that's reported on board this ship in a long time, the first s.o.b. who's had his hat on straight."

Nevertheless, Douglas was still hankering after the sort of naval-cum-diplomatic liaison appointment he had suggested to the President and Sumner Welles. He remained in touch with Roosevelt, and while aboard the *Mississippi* sent a long report about various aspects of the naval service. He recommended that there should be one doctor in every destroyer instead of one in every five, reported that the majority of officers and men wanted some liberalization of the liquor prohibition, and commented on the Negro problem, the difficulties involved in cipher procedure with the British, due to the difference of methods, the problem of the co-ordination of ammunition supply—differences in size and equipment, making it impossible to assist the British ships with ammunition and ordnance repairs—and ended with a recommendation that British Navy battle dress be adopted in the American Navy. This was probably too unorthodox even for the President, and there is no evidence in the Roosevelt papers that the letter received any reply.

A fortnight later an event occurred which removed all ambitions but that of active service from Douglas' mind. He was on watch on the *Mississippi* as assistant communications officer, breaking down signals on the decoding machine. Most of them were routine. Then the machine, banging away like a typewriter, disgorged one message reading: "Air raid on Pearl Harbor, this is not a drill." Douglas thought, "Well, this is just another thing, it doesn't concern us," put it in the waste-basket and went on. Two messages later he did what might be called a "slow take."

"What the hell was that?" he said aloud, fished it out of the waste-basket—and ran to the captain's cabin. The news created a tremendous storm of excitement. The crews in the Atlantic Fleet had felt themselves forgotten men as far as the American public was concerned. They had been fighting a war for four or five months, ships had been sunk, men had been killed, they had served under regular war-time conditions attached to the British Home Fleet and were an integral part of the war. Yet, as far as the American people was concerned, nothing was happening at all. The fact that they were actually in the war to which they felt they belonged raised the sailors' morale sky-high. There were cheers and shouts and bangs on bulkheads, celebrations and congratulations. Then came a signal from the British flagship: "Welcome to the party."

The *Mississippi* was summoned back to Norfolk, Virginia, en route to the Pacific, to make good the losses of Pearl Harbor. Douglas received orders to report to the Navy Department in Washington, but before he left the profession he had abandoned provided one last ordeal. He was officer of the watch when the crew was given a preview of a new film. It was the last he had made, *The Corsican Brothers.* "Go to it, Doug," and "Kill him, sailor," the men cheered and catcalled as the actor fought himself in his dual role on the screen. "I had no way of escaping," says Douglas. "I was on duty and I had to take it. I was interested too, because I had never seen the film myself. I had left before it was finished. It was my last contact with my professional self for years."

Back in Washington he found time to send a short note to the Bensons: "As a belated Christmas present I have sent through the good offices of your Embassy a check for five hundred dollars. I am sorry it isn't more, but all income except my lieutenant's pay and a bit of savings is now stopped for the duration."

His father's estate was still in the hands of the lawyers, and he had insisted that the whole of Mary Lee's divorce settlement should go into a trust fund for their children. His own high earnings just before the war had gone largely to support his many voluntary activities. The best years, financially, of his career have always had to balance out the intervening accumulations of debt.

Douglas was first appointed to the office of the Chief of the Bureau of Ordnance under a reserve captain named Lewis Strauss, in later years head of the apocalyptic Atomic Energy Commission. They have remained close friends ever since. As his next assignment with the public relations director, Douglas edited a series of books for the troops called *Know Your Allies,* and renewed his friendship with Adlai Stevenson, who had been drawn into the government as an adviser to the Secretary of the Navy Colonel Knox, to maintain liaison with the Department of State.

Word of Douglas' presence in Washington reached the ears of a meticulous Congressman. He inquired of the Secretary of the Navy why he was in Washington and not at sea. Was Fairbanks, he wanted to know, being shown favoritism, or had he been handed a quick post-Pearl Harbor commission for exploitation purposes?

Far from being flattered by this disproportionate notoriety, Douglas was appalled, and saw all his plans for an interesting, anonymous war go out of the window. The Bureau of Naval Personnel satisfied the legislator that Douglas had been in a couple of actions and in the Navy for about a year, but he was then called on the carpet by a senior officer, who spent a good fifteen minutes lecturing him on the evils of maintaining a press agent while in the service.

When the admiral stopped for breath, Douglas gave his word-of-honor assurance that not only did he fully agree but that the very thought had never even occurred to him. As the admiral seemed quite astounded at this intelligence, Douglas further persuaded him that were he actually looking for publicity, he would have stayed in his prewar job, where its glare was perpetual and blinding. After a sympathetic nod, the admiral told him that his presence ashore, however deserved, or whatever the importance of his duties, was an embarrassment to the Navy and that he was to be ordered back to sea immediately.

He spent three weeks on mine-sweeping and sub-chasing duties out of Staten Island in New York Harbor. His commanding officer, Lieutenant Commander C. H. Koopman of the U.S.S. *Goldcrest,* took such a liking to his new lieutenant that he sent in a fitness report giving him the maximum possible marks in every one of the fourteen points of character on the list. As this was a manifest impossibility, not even approached by John Paul Jones or Admiral Mahan, the Navy suspected collusion, hauled Douglas back to Washington, and reassigned him to Task Force 39, in European waters.

Before leaving, Douglas just had time to accept the President's invitation to join a few friends at the White House to listen to one of Roosevelt's radio "fireside" chats.

Robert Sherwood remembers the occasion well: "At the end of the speech they played the national anthem, so all of us in the room rose to our feet. I was standing next to Doug, and when we left the room he came up to me and said: 'Anybody seeing you standing at attention would know that you must have been in a Highland regiment.' Which indeed I had, in the first war. I was in the Black Watch. 'How did you know?' I asked. He laughed and answered: 'The way you had your thumb right on the seam of the kilt, where the pleats begin.'"

Mary Lee and two-year-old Daphne had been able to stay with Douglas in Washington and New York. Now they returned to Box-wood Farm as Douglas flew across the Atlantic in a bomber. As the junior officer aboard, he was put in the bomb bay and spent fourteen hours hoping the doors would not fly open.

Arriving in Prestwick, no one knew the whereabouts of the flagship U.S.S. *Washington*, and Douglas was able to spend a few pleasant days in London finding out that the battleship was at Scapa Flow. The squadron was engaged in the "White Patrol" off Norway and northern Iceland, guarding against another sortie into the Atlantic shipping lanes like the foray of the German battleship *Bismarck*.

In the new command he found again that his presence was vaguely resented. "What's he doing here?" or "Is he just on here for the ride?" or "There's a catch to this somewhere!" was the attitude. He recounted his training and experience up to that time to unbelieving or suspicious ears. Paying almost fanatic attention to regulations on dress, routine, and duties, he volunteered for extra chores in order to establish evidence of his zeal. At one point he was assistant staff gunnery officer, assistant communications officer, assistant flag signal officer, and combat intelligence officer—all at the same time. It taught him never to volunteer for anything.

He had by that time built up a dual reputation. Among the ratings and his brother officers he had succeeded in being accepted as a perfectly matter-of-fact fellow, as obedient, as conscientious, as lazy, as scared, as seasick, and as tolerably efficient as they. But to the admiral, Robert Giffen, his too anxious efforts to prove his qualifications for being absorbed into the service merely meant that he wanted more war than he was getting. As a result, he was detached as a "special observer" to the aircraft carrier U.S.S. *Wasp*, which at the beginning of May 1942 made the dramatic run into the Mediterranean with Spitfires for Malta.

While the carrier was loading the planes in the Clyde, Douglas remembered his colleague Will Fyffe, the famous Scottish character actor. They had appeared together in *Rulers of the Sea* and played many a practical joke on each other. Fairbanks had had to rescue Will Fyffe from a burning building in the film. The stocky Scot weighed a good two hundred pounds, and Douglas knew he had a herculean task before him. When the signal was given he struggled and strained to raise Fyffe from the ground. He tugged and pulled without avail, with Frank Lloyd, the director, shouting, "Come on, Doug, come on." Fairbanks was on the point of giving up when he discovered that Fyffe had himself tied by a rope round the waist to a stanchion on the floor.

Now he wanted Will to come and sing for the crew. He got on the telephone in the Central Hotel in Glasgow and asked, "Have you ever heard of Will Fyffe?" The operator said, "Of course, I have."

"I don't know where he lives," Douglas said. "He's in Scotland and it's a big country. Will you find him?" Inside an hour the operator had located him at the other end of Scotland. "Will," said Douglas, "I cannot tell you exactly where I am, but I would like very much for you to sing. If you would take the train to Glasgow I will meet you, will you do that?" "Certainly, Duggie," Fyffe said. He made his way there at his own expense. Douglas met him and took him to the ship, and he sang in the hangar deck, without an accompanist, the day before they sailed.

At the end of June, just after his promotion to lieutenant, Douglas was detached to the U.S. cruiser *Wichita* for the disastrous P.Q.17 convoy to Murmansk, when twenty-three out of the thirty-four merchant ships were sunk.

A week before the *Wichita* sailed, King George VI paid a visit of inspection to Scapa Flow and came on board the U.S.S. *Washington*. A widely circulated news picture showed the King shaking hands with Fairbanks as he inspected the ship's company. What had occurred was that the King was just about to be taken down the line of officers and have them presented to him, when he spied Douglas. The King walked straight over to him, leaving the other officers, and at the moment the picture was being taken was saying: "Well, what are you doing up here? I haven't seen you since we played golf at Sunningdale before the war." Then the King had to start at the head of the line and come down again. Douglas was teased terribly. The gesture had been most pleasing, but at the same time the worst thing that could have happened to him, to be singled out just as he had succeeded in submerging himself in the service.

From now on he was, in fact, accepted, and although from time to time during the war his status as a celebrity caused one or two awkward moments, he was left free to concentrate on the work to which he now turned.

On his return from detached duty, Admiral Giffen, to Fairbanks' unexpressed discomfiture, greeted him heartily, congratulated him on his "warrior spirit," boasted to the staff how he kept volunteering for special jobs, and that, by God, he gave 'em to him, and, by God, that's the kind of young fella to have aboard, and, by God, there'd be some more good cruises and scraps along soon which, by God, he'd see Fairbanks got in on. One admiral in Washington even went so far as to say that the best thing that could happen was for some celebrity like Fairbanks to be either severely wounded or killed, because it would show that there was no favoritism in the naval service.

Douglas compiled the official report on both these operations. The first was relatively uneventful, in spite of the potential dangers. But the forty-seven Spitfires the *Wasp* launched saved Malta.

As the carrier turned back toward Gibraltar and safety, this message was received from the defenders: "Almost continuous air battle has been in progress since 0830 and the delivery of aircraft. After rapidly refueling they have been in the air many times. We have lost three Spitfires and the enemy has had thirty of his aircraft destroyed or damaged. We are most grateful to you all."

The Murmansk convoy was another matter. Fairbanks' recollection of one of the worst and least publicized naval disasters of the war still remains vivid in his mind:

"*Wichita* was one of two American and two British cruisers giving close support to the convoy and there were further heavy units covering us from long range. German submarine and air attacks started in earnest on July 4 and by the evening we had lost four merchant ships. It was American Independence Day, but with all hell breaking loose round us I shall never forget the signal from the captain of one of the British cruisers, H.M.S. *London* to Captain Hill in the *Wichita:* 'Never let it be said that we are bad sports and do not make every effort to help you celebrate your national holiday.'

"We were by this time well east of Bear Island, at continuous battle stations in the midnight sun. The Admiralty in London had received reports that the German battleship *Tirpitz* was out with the *Scheer* and *Hipper* and the cruiser force received peremptory orders to withdraw to the westward at high speed, leaving the convoy to scatter and reach Murmansk as best it could. Our reaction was one of stunned shock. We felt there must have been some error in transmitting the signal.

"The Americans were particularly bitter, cursing the British for what they believed to be running away in the face of a good battle which we had a chance of surviving. We resented leaving the defenseless merchant ships to straggle at nine and ten knots through the icy water, which we knew from experience would not permit survival for more than a very limited time. Two of our *Wichita* observation pilots had already died before we could fish them out of the drink. Our anger was made more intense by the philosophic and good-natured spirit in which the merchant ships received the order and saw us turn tail. Only when we were clear of the immediate battle and steaming back in line ahead for Scapa Flow were we able to compare notes with the British cruisers and found that they were as bitter and angry as we were.

"I recall another exchange of signals between *London* and *Wichita* in which we were informed that the Germans had claimed us as sunk and that therefore we must be a ghost ship. Captain Hill replied: 'We are so numb we cannot tell but feel positions must be reversed as we have been attending your wake all day.'

"In the officers' mess at Scapa, after rather too many beakers, there was much mutual recrimination and many hard words were passed. These were finally resolved in cursing the Admiralty and their inability to judge a tactical situation from a lot of pins on a board more than a thousand miles away. It was considered to be a pusillanimous defeat and a shocking error of judgment."

Mary Lee heard a radio report that an American heavy cruiser had been sunk and was at her wit's end. Even a friend at the Navy Department in Washington was prevented by security regulations from giving her any information. In London, Lord Louis Mountbatten, divining her misery, found time amidst his hectic high-command duties to send a cable saying: "All our friends are well."

14

MOUNTBATTEN HAD NOT FORGOTTEN the promise he had given Douglas a year earlier in California. He had been building up Combined Operations headquarters for six months and had just received an offer from the United States Chiefs of Staff to make American officers available to his command. In the end a considerable number were assigned to him, providing the first example of an Anglo-American, inter-service, inter-Allied headquarters, which subsequently served as a model for the Supreme Commands of the later war years.

One of the first officers for whom he asked was Fairbanks, who in July 1942 was given a cover appointment in the headquarters of the commander, U. S. naval forces in Europe, in London, and then joined Lieutenant the Earl of Antrim in the Chemical Warfare and Deception Department which was just being organized at Combined Operations headquarters in Richmond Terrace. Their directive was to devise means of deceiving the enemy as to the exact point at which the landings involved in the reconquest of Europe were to be made. Mountbatten wanted Fairbanks to help create the department and subsequently pass on the techniques to the American forces.

Many minds were working on deception tactics and equipment, and the problem now was to adapt them specifically to amphibious warfare. Douglas' chief contribution was the knowledge of sound effects he had acquired during his years in films, together with all the tricks of camouflage and illusion which are an integral part of the shadowy world of the cinema. The dummy parachutists in graduated sizes was another of his ideas. The group carried out their experiments with sound, radar, dummies, and phony wireless chatter with embryo units at the secret Combined Operations headquarters at Achnacarry Castle, the haunted family seat of the ancient Cameron clan near Ballantrae in Scotland, commuting between there and London for more planning.

As part of his experience, Fairbanks was initiated into all the operational assaults pending at the time. He had a hand in the planning of the Dieppe raid and his well-known figure had been seen so frequently around Combined Operations headquarters that one or two of the American newspapermen in London reported that he had actually taken part in the operation. Douglas was in fact at sea, carrying out a deception operation on the flank, and did not see the reports. It was Mountbatten who again found time in the turmoil following the disaster to send another cable to an anxious Mary Lee in Virginia, saying: "Just saw a friend of yours who is in fine shape and sends his love."

A few days later Mountbatten called him in and said: "Douglas, we've had some losses and there is a shortage of landing craft and officers. I want to send you on an amphibious landing course so that when you go back to your own Navy you can show them how the naval end of the commandos operates. We need the men and the boats so badly that the only course you can take is an operational one." Fairbanks had just had a year of active sea service and was rather enjoying his staff work and seeing his friends in London again. In his moment of hesitation Mountbatten jumped up and said: "I knew you'd be keen about it, it's just the thing for you." He spent the next six weeks at Warsash, attached to the landing-craft flotillas of the H.M.S. *Tormentor*. He was the only American officer there and acted as a member of the unit. They carried out several "pajama raids" on the enemy coast—so called because of the condition in which they usually found the defenders—and stood by for a nuisance operation to destroy German gun emplacements in the Channel Islands, a plan which Douglas had himself worked out at headquarters. In the end the weather caused its postponement.

His most awkward moment came one evening when he was duty officer and had to deal with a rating who had returned aboard after too enthusiastic a session at a public house. As an officer of another Navy, Douglas had absolutely no jurisdiction, so he asked the chief petty officer what he should do. "You've got the men's regard and the men's respect and that's as good as any authority round here," the chief told him. So Douglas had the rating up, put him on captain's report, and that was the end of the matter. It was probably just as well that the man was too befuddled to realize that he could have objected to the whole procedure.

One more pleasant ceremony he was able to attend was an invitation to visit the Douglas Hospital at Southampton, one of the three he had been financing since war broke out. Lady Morvyth Benson was there to greet him, and he was duly photographed with the patients, who gave him a rousing welcome. It was the first time they realized who their benefactor had been.

While in London, Douglas renewed many of his political contacts. He frequently saw Averell Harriman, who had been sent to Britain to expedite the Lend-Lease program, met several members of the European governments in exile, stayed for weekends with Anthony Eden and the Mountbattens, and spent much time with two of his former colleagues on the aid-the-Allies committee, Herbert Agar and John G. Winant, then the American Ambassador to Britain, to whom he was able to report many impressions for transmission to Secretary Hull.

Of his old friends, he found to his delight that Irving Asher, by then a major in the U. S. Signal Corps, had also been posted to London and was using some of the frozen pounds of his film career to occupy a luxurious suite at Claridge's Hotel, where Douglas stayed whenever he passed through London. It became a haunt of many famous names. King George II of Greece, who was also living in the hotel, was a frequent guest for cocktails. It so happened that the name of their favorite floor-waiter was King, and one evening, when George II, the Duke of Kent, and Mountbatten were all present, Asher found something missing in the bar and called out, "Oh! King." To his horror the King of Greece turned around, came over, and said: "Yes? What is it?" He turned aside Asher's confused explanations and apologies by saying: "How was I to know? I always expect Americans to say 'Hi, King.'" It was a very successful party, and far from taking offense, the King, when he returned to his country, took his namesake with him to act as major-domo in the royal palace in Athens.

Asher has another favorite story about Fairbanks. They were sleeping at Claridge's one night during an air raid, and Douglas, who was just back from one of his Combined Operations jaunts in the Channel, slept soundly through the wail of sirens and the crump of bombs. When the all clear sounded, two air-raid wardens in the street started talking about the raid and Douglas woke up. Crawling, with a muttered grumble, out of his bed to the window, he called out in a stage British accent: "I say, you chaps, couldn't you make less noise?" Asher was convulsed. "Where did you get that 'old chap' stuff?" he asked. "I didn't want them to think it was an American complaining," answered Douglas.

The suite at Claridge's also served as background to tragedy. The Duke of Kent, who had been appointed Inspector General of the Royal Air Force, resented the fact that he was confined to purely nominal and representational duties. He wanted to do something more active but had found no one in the British Services prepared to expose a member of the royal family. In the course of one conversation on the subject with Douglas, he inquired whether the American forces might be prepared to allow him to play a more active role. Irving Asher put Fairbanks in touch with the U. S. Air Force commanding general, "Tooey" Spaatz. Douglas told him that the Duke would like to act in some liaison capacity between the two air forces and arranged for the two of them to meet unobtrusively in his suite. Douglas then took the Duke and the general to the Bon Viveur Restaurant and left them to discuss the problem. General Spaatz made the suggestion that if the Duke were to visit the R.A.F. station in Iceland, he would be made welcome at the American air base and would be able to meet some of the flying personnel. Spaatz would then put in an official request for the Duke to act in a permanent liaison capacity. On his way there the Duke's plane crashed in Scotland and he was killed. At the funeral service in Windsor Chapel, Douglas was the only foreigner invited in a personal capacity.

At the end of 1942 Fairbanks returned to the States to report to Admiral H. Kent Hewitt, in command of the Amphibious Force,

Atlantic Fleet, at Hampton Roads, Norfolk, Virginia. His job was to organize, on a hitherto unimagined scale, "beachjumper" units to put into practice all the deception tactics developed at Combined Operations. He did not start off on the best foot, as he chose to arrive in British naval battle dress, an innovation only excused when it was realized that if that was the way their Allies were going to be dressed, they had better get used to its appearance, in case the British were mistaken for the enemy. This taste for the unorthodox did not commend itself to some of his superiors in the intelligence and planning staffs in Washington, who listened at first with studied indifference to his account of the possibilities of deception units.

There was, indeed, some suggestion that he was under a slight cloud. Just before he left London, Mountbatten had told him that he was so well known by sight that he was something of a security risk, and for that reason had not been sent to Gibraltar with his landing-craft flotilla to take any part in the North African landings. However, Douglas was completely undeterred and applied himself with renewed zeal to working up and organizing the new units.

Fortunately he acquired the firm support of Admiral Hewitt, and it was Douglas who drew up the paper for the American Joint Chiefs of Staff which was in the end grudgingly accepted as the directive for the deception units. He was sent around the country to universities like the Massachusetts Institute of Technology and Notre Dame to interview promising young students due to be called up in the Navy, particularly those with technical qualifications. They were asked to volunteer their services without being told the nature of their duties. In the course of time the unit acquired about four hundred ratings and over seventy officers and, although a full captain was put in charge, Douglas remained responsible to the admiral for the development of its tactics. It was at this time that he was first recommended for promotion to lieutenant commander, but naval tenderness to any suggestions from outside sources of favoritism were to delay the acquisition of his half stripe for the best part of a year.

Mary Lee came down to live in a small cottage in Norfolk. Douglas would be up every morning at two-thirty to be on the beaches by 3

A.M. and carry out mock maneuvers before dawn, which simulated the forthcoming invasion of Sicily.

During his naval service Douglas was able to keep in spasmodic touch with his diplomatic activities. He had been a useful unofficial channel of communication between Combined Operations and certain interested parties in Washington, but he preferred to restrict himself to the limitations of his rank. On his return he did pay one visit to the White House while he was stationed at Norfolk, to be greeted cheerily by the President with the old chestnut: "Well, have they made you captain of the heads yet?" The contact was purely social.

The fact that he had genuine gun smoke and salt water on his buttons and braid had somewhat quieted the caustic comments in the Navy Department, and Douglas preferred not to expose himself. However, he did see Cordell Hull and was told of certain political objectives that were being discussed at the time concerning the Middle East, and current problems with Generals de Gaulle and Giraud and the status of the Vichy Government. "Now, if in the course of your duties you should see so-and-so," Mr. Hull would say, "this is the sort of thing we're working on. Let us know your reactions." It was made as informal as possible and left entirely to Douglas' own discretion. On his return abroad he continued to send private reports to the Secretary of State, which were always welcome.

At the end of May 1943 the whole command transferred across the Atlantic and set up headquarters in Algiers. In his capacity as special-operations officer on the planning section of Admiral Hewitt's staff, Douglas established contact with "A" force, the British military formation which had so successfully carried out deception tactics during the land fighting in North Africa, and became naval liaison officer with such cloak-and-dagger organizations as the American Office of Strategic Services and the British Special Operations Executive and Special Air Service. This was a world of organized skulduggery—dropping agents, organizing sabotage, and spreading alarm, confusion, and despondency in the enemy-held areas. Its intimate history can never be written, because the few officers with an over-all picture of the whole have been sworn to secrecy by their governments for the rest of their lives. Subordinates, similarly bound by security, only controlled limited operations and were often ignorant of their relationship with the whole. The crews of the planes and small craft who assisted them often had no idea of the identity or business of the passengers they were carrying. Rigid compartmentation of knowledge is the basic condition of successful intelligence and espionage work. The "beachjumper" units were only part of an incredibly complicated whole.

Armed with an "open sesame" document, Douglas went everywhere: "To All Concerned. Lt. D. E. Fairbanks, Jr., U.S.N.R., is the special operations officer in the War Plans Section of my staff, in which capacity he is of course informed on all secret planning. He is in addition to his regular duties charged with arranging for the acquisition of special material and personnel and with the preparation of plans for the execution of special operations. It is particularly requested that those concerned will give him every possible assistance and appreciate that for security reasons he will not always be able to give full explanation of the duties which he is performing. Signed: H. K. Hewitt, Vice-Admiral, U.S.N., Commander, U. S. Naval Forces, North-West African Waters."

"The only way to organize any operation in peace," sighed one indulgent British admiral, "is to include Fairbanks in on it."

Once the North African coast had been cleared, the main purpose of Allied strategic deception was to persuade the enemy that the next landing was more likely to be in Sardinia than Sicily, more likely to be in Greece than Italy, and more likely to be in Macedonia than the South of France. Within that framework the possibility of tactical ruses was unlimited. "Operation Mincemeat"—the "Man Who Never Was," the corpse in a marine uniform—launched from a submarine off the coast of Spain, with his pockets full of fake orders and directions— was part of this plan, and Fairbanks had been one of the few officers initiated into it by the organizer, Lieutenant Commander Ewen Montagu, R.N.V.R. For each successive amphibious assault it was the duty of the deception units to persuade the defenders of the enemy coast that the main blow was due to fall anywhere but the chosen spot, that ancillary landings were due to take place where they were not, and that non-existent reserves were due to be put ashore on the flanks.

Before the Sicily invasion, General George S. Patton invited Douglas as a one-man preview audience of his speech to the troops. During the landings, the first operation of the "beachjumper" units was relatively limited in scope, and Douglas remained in the flagship *Monrovia* with Admiral Hewitt.

He then went in with the third wave of infantry to make a tactical report on the Gela beaches, accompanied by the British liaison officer, Lieutenant Commander Gerald Butler, R.N. They landed on a magnificent and totally unused stretch of beach, although a furlong away the water's edge was a jumbled mass of landing craft, equipment, and troops jostling for space. Waving indignantly at the only visible beachmaster to draw attention to this extraordinary oversight, the two explorers were answered only by peremptory gesticulations that they failed to understand. They therefore set off along the beach to castigate this ignorant incompetent. Before they could begin to register their protests at this manifest mismanagement, their intended victim, who was only an ensign, managed to gasp: "But, sir, you have just walked across a mine field. We have had to rope off that half mile of beach, it is thick with them."

Shortly after the Sicily operations Douglas was given home leave. Visiting Marrakech on the way to England, he came down with fever and was "nursed" by the chief medical officer of the British Army in the aircraft during the flight to London. Recovering slightly, Douglas went on arrival to dine in the country with Laurence Olivier, was taken ill, and sent to the hospital with an attack of jaundice. He finally arrived in Newport, Rhode Island, just in time for the birth of his second daughter, Victoria.

The "beachjumpers" came into their own during the Salerno operation, when the Allies were fighting their way up Italy. In conjunction with Army and Air Force units and a combined naval force of American, British, and Dutch ships, their task was to persuade the Germans that there was going to be a landing north of Naples as well as to the south. For this purpose they were to carry out a series of hit-

and-run operations on the mainland and secure the off-shore islands of Ventotene, Ponza, Procida, Ischia, and Capri. Later they were able to learn that they had been successful in pinning down a Panzer division and several infantry formations which, in the touch-and-go battle of the beachhead, might have succeeded in ejecting the main force.

From now on Douglas took part in a number of their operations himself. He was responsible for their planning at staff level and was detached to advise the senior officer of the various task groups on their execution. Although still junior in rank, he was the only officer in the group with an over-all knowledge of the strategic plan of which they were a part. It was an unusual position, as security usually required that anyone with access to so much secret information should not run the risk of capture by the enemy.

During the preliminary raids up the coast, Douglas went ashore with a small party at Civitavecchia, about fifty miles behind the enemy lines. To add to the verisimilitude of the landing, an Allied air raid had been timed to coincide with the operation. As Douglas crouched in a cellar with some of the local Italians, one of them suddenly startled him with a raucous Brooklyn accent. "I know you," said this unshaven apparition, "you are Douglas Fairbanks"; and then launched into a long tirade about how he had been ruined as an independent cinema owner in New York by the exorbitant prices charged for their films by the United Artists Corporation. In vain Douglas protested that his father must have been the villain, but the torrent of abuse continued and in the end he was only too pleased to beat a retreat, although the enemy had not fired a shot.

The plan for neutralizing the island of Ventotene, cutting the cable with the mainland and establishing a base from which to harass German shipping hugging the coast, had been drawn up by Douglas and co-ordinated through agents. The garrison was expected to consist of royalist Italians, who had indicated their willingness to surrender without a fight. The Allied task group consisted of two Dutch gunboats, the *Sumba* and *Flores*, six American PT boats, eight British MTBs, several British MLs, and the American destroyer *Knight*, the whole under the command of Captain C. L. Andrews, U.S.N. As the small craft swept into the little harbor they found that they had been quite neatly double-crossed. A few Italians called to them from shore when they got in close and everything seemed all right, until Douglas, the captain, and three companions set foot on shore. A German gunboat in the harbor blew up in their faces and the island appeared to do the same. It was not long before they found out that the Italians who were prepared to surrender had been locked up, that there were something like four hundred Germans left on the island, together with quite a number of Italian Fascist troops. Captain Andrews went back in his motorboat to obtain reinforcements from the larger ships, which were attacking other islands in the area.

A brisk fusillade continued through the night, with each side trying to bluff the other about its actual strength. Douglas' small group managed to capture the town jail, releasing all the inmates to fight on their side. Operations were held up for quite a time while an Italian nobleman, who had been incarcerated there by Mussolini for nearly ten years, searched the building for his only remaining eyeglass so that he could function with due dignity as the spokesman.

The Germans retired to the northern end of the island and, with the judicious use of a smoke screen, flares, loud-speakers, and the rest of their paraphernalia, the party was able to maintain its hold on the harbor until reinforcements arrived and settled the issue. Appropriately enough, the other lieutenant who had accompanied Douglas ashore was Henry Ringling North of the famous circus family.

John Steinbeck, the novelist, who landed with them as a war correspondent, found it quite an affray. "A real Dick Tracy stunt," he called it afterward. "They had told us that there were no Germans on the island, so we landed with flashlights lit and yelling to one another and they thought we had an army with us. Hell, the captain and Douglas Fairbanks had nothing but tommy guns and, so help me, they took the whole island. Two very tough citizens they are."

As night fell the following day, a series of lights flashed from the next island to the north, Ponza, which the local Italians interpreted as a signal that the Allied group should proceed there. Having been double-crossed once, Douglas and his "beachjumpers" were in no mood to risk a second experience of the same kind, although the captain of one of the MTBs volunteered to scout the situation. For years afterward, an inaccurate intelligence report led Douglas, and indeed the most senior officers in the Mediterranean command, who have long told the story at his expense, as he has at his own, to believe that an opportunity had been missed of capturing Mussolini. The former Italian dictator had in fact been interned on the island after his arrest by the Badoglio government on July 25, 1943. However, during August he was moved first to the island of Maddalena, off the coast of Sardinia, and then, by the end of the month, to the Abruzzi mountains in Central Italy, whence he was rescued by German parachutists on September 12. The Salerno landing took place at dawn on September 9. It is a pity to spoil a good story, but the dates cannot be reconciled.

The main Salerno battle was now raging and Douglas went over to the mainland to see if he could borrow a few Commandos from his Combined Operations friend Colonel Laycock, who had gone in with them on the northern flank. But the Commandos and Rangers had suffered heavy casualties and, just as Douglas was wondering how he would be able to complete his part of the diversionary operations, in view of the difficulties they had encountered, he received a message that an Italian motor torpedo boat had arrived under a white flag with a communication for him. The Italian officer brought a letter from his commander, the Duke of Aosta, whom Douglas had known ten years earlier as the Duke of Spoleto during his European tour with Fairbanks Senior. Douglas had been able to send a message to the Duke through an Allied agent, and with the unconditional capitulation of the Badoglio government on September 8, Aosta now informed him that he had a flotilla of light craft that he was willing to place at the Allies' disposal.

With this accretion of strength, the operation proceeded. The Italian officer told Fairbanks that the Germans were in process of evacuating the island of Capri, but that if it was not occupied immediately they intended to return within a day or two with sufficient strength to hold it. The force moved up cautiously, in line ahead, led by the destroyer *Knight,* creeping up the coast of the island just as the sun was setting on the third day of the Salerno operation. All the inhabitants were up on the hills waving colored handkerchiefs, like a scene from a musical comedy. As they came into the harbor the last German ship was moving off. They let it go unmolested and the island was captured without firing a shot.

Douglas and Captain Andrews went ashore and were received by the mayor of the town, the head of the Fascist militia, all dressed up in swords, and accepted the formal surrender with the full red-carpet treatment. Having no further operations scheduled for that night, the landing party began investigating Edda Ciano's villa, a few other villas belonging to friends, and then celebrated in a hotel. Some years later the town wanted to put up a plaque to Fairbanks as their liberator, but the Navy said no, it had been liberated by the Allies and no individuals could be named.

A day or two after he had established himself in a particularly sumptuous villa, Douglas had his attention drawn to a small row boat laboriously making its way out from Naples. Sitting in it, with his family, escaping with the help of two husky Neapolitan boatmen, was Benedetto Croce, the philosopher. Fairbanks' last recollection of this idyllic haven was of seeing the attractive sixteen-year-old Croce daughter sitting on a garden wall with one of his American sailors, who was reading to her out of a book, although Douglas knew that none of the Croces spoke a word of English. He went over to them and found that it was a volume of Shakespeare. The sailor had never read it in his life, but was declaiming it at the girl's request because she had always known it in Italian and wanted to hear the music of the original words in English.

While the battle front crawled up toward Naples, the "beachjumpers" carried out a number of harassing raids from their new base, capturing an Italian admiral off a peninsula fortress right outside the city and encouraging the defenders to shoot and disclose the pattern of their harbor defenses. During one of these snap landings Fairbanks found himself in command of a small group of Commandos and Rangers. They had to get over a wall. "Over the top, men," he shouted, and then wondered why nobody moved. In a flash he realized how much like his former self he must have sounded. The troops just looked at him with an eloquence that seemed to say: "We've seen you do it in the pictures, you show us how." But there was no prop man around to cut convenient toe holds and hang vines for him to clamber up. He grinned with as much self-possession as possible and told them to bash in a gate.

He had no need to feel self-conscious. His part in the island operations earned him his first combat decoration, the American Silver Star Medal. "For conspicuous gallantry and intrepidity while attached to a Special Task Group during the amphibious assault on Italy," the citation read. "Efficient and untiring in the performance of duty, Lieutenant Commander [then Lieutenant] Fairbanks rendered valuable service in the formulation of important plans for mixed Allied operations of a highly technical and complex nature, and later, while temporarily assigned to the Staff of a Naval Task Group Commander, accompanied the combat units into action and participated in the successful execution of the planned activities. During the occupation of an island in the area he courageously led a landing party ashore and, although exposed to enemy rifle fire, established essential picket positions, thereby contributing materially to the accomplishment of a vital mission. Lieutenant Commander Fairbanks' valiant conduct under fire and his outstanding skill were in keeping with the highest traditions of the United States Naval Service." He was the first Hollywood actor to receive a medal for courage in actual combat.

Even this did not cure his taste for sartorial eccentricity. Later on, in Naples, one of his friends found him in a typical Fairbanks' uniform—British white summer officer's rig, with long white stockings, white shorts, white shirt, and American shoulderboards—the whole thing entirely out of order. He was one of the most popular men in the city, living in a hotel up on the hill, which had been carefully reserved for officers of the rank of colonel, captain, and above.

Fairbanks was frequently able to mollify ruffled Allied tempers. With his intimate knowledge of both the major Allied countries, he was able to transmit soothing messages between fractious personalities and managed to write back to his contacts in Washington and London suggesting means of dealing with some of the sharper asperities.

He was sent on a visit to Cairo to co-ordinate Mediterranean deception strategy with the Middle East Command. While there, he was conducted over the factory for tactical camouflage and deception devices run by Major Jasper Maskelyne, better known in peacetime as a member of the famous family of theatrical illusionists.

Douglas also received a request to call on King George II of Greece. Arriving at the villa, he found that he was the only guest, apart from the A.D.C. and chamberlain, Colonel Levidis. The King had for some time been in a dilemma about his relationship with the Western Allies. He gave Douglas a frank account of his difficulties and the contradictory information about future policy in Greece he was receiving through diplomatic and military channels, which never seemed to agree. He outlined future developments as he saw them in the Balkan area and made it clear that he was having difficulty in presenting his views to the proper quarters. He asked his guest to use his personal good offices to see that his feelings were made known in the right places. Douglas sent a long report of the conversation to the President and Cordell Hull, with a copy to Anthony Eden. This is probably the only record made of his intervention, which was not without positive results. Moreover, it was a typical example of the sort of confidential, persuasive role that he has so often been able to play.

The visit to Cairo was also marked by the only wound of his war career. He was at a party in a suite in Shepheards Hotel with Lieutenant Colonel Humphrey Butler, former equerry to the Duke of Kent, Major Max Niven, brother of the film actor, Colonel Philip Astley, ex-husband of Madeleine Carroll, and Lieutenant Colonel Hendrie Oakshott, later a Member of Parliament, when some unduly attentive gesture was resented by the hostess' Alsatian, which leaped forward and sank its teeth firmly in his left buttock.

By the time he returned, the "beachjumpers" were operating in the Adriatic, with British Commandos and Combined Operations small naval units, to support the Yugoslav guerrillas under Marshal Tito. Douglas tells this story against himself. He was on the island of Vis, when the great man was due to come and express his thanks to some of the officers who had supported his campaign. Everyone cleaned up their uniforms, lined up smartly on parade, and waited with pleasurable expectation as Tito arrived with an aide carrying a small box. "Would it be a green and white ribbon or a purple and red one; was it worn around the neck or was it a star?" Douglas was thinking. When Tito finished complimenting them, he said that he wanted to give them each a little souvenir of his gratitude, solemnly put his hand in the box, and presented them with two tins of anchovies apiece.

During another operation in the area one of Fairbanks' best officers was killed right next to him. They were standing shoulder to shoulder talking, and Douglas, turning around, found that the top of his companion's head had been blown off and caught him as he fell. Douglas did not have so much as a scratch or a speck of dust on him.

After playing their part in the capture of Corsica, the "beachjumpers" set up joint headquarters with the American PT boats and British light craft in Calvi and Bastia. The next objective was Elba. During a briefing trip to Algiers, Fairbanks had his request for air transport back to his unit forestalled with the query: "Are we carting Fairbanks over to look for his Corsican brother?" The air forces got back this crushing rebuke from the chief of the combined navies in the Mediterranean, Admiral Sir John Cunningham: "I know of no more urgent business in Corsica than that we commissioned Commander Fairbanks to do."

The amphibious force was under the command of the British Rear Admiral (later Vice-Admiral) Sir Thomas Troubridge. The diversionary operations covered the northern part of the island, while the main assault went in from the south four hours later. The "beachjumpers" executed their operation successfully, with a minimum of losses, considering their job was to stir up trouble and pull the defense over to that side. But the French Bataillons de Choc they put ashore suffered terrible casualties. Douglas conceived a great admiration for their commander, General de Lattre de Tassigny. "I've never seen a tougher disciplinarian and martinet than he was," he says. "One man was sent to the Chad for three years because de Lattre objected to his coming on parade without shaving after this operation." For his part in the capture of Elba, Douglas was subsequently awarded the *Croix de guerre,* with palm.

Many of the original "beachjumpers" had by this time been transferred to other theaters. Their equipment and specialized knowledge made them important members of the complicated and successful diversionary operations in the English Channel which pinned down German reinforcements during the Normandy invasion. Others were already operating in the Pacific, where they suffered heavy casualties in the Philippines.

Techniques had been perfected and the whole pattern of deception had become a vastly complex affair. The invasion of the South of France involved a plan covering almost the whole Mediterranean from the Balearic Islands off the coast of Spain to Salonica on the eastern extremity of Greece.

The "beachjumpers" themselves formed only a small part, as a special operations unit, of a larger amphibious task group, which was itself only one factor in a web of activity which included agents, the local underground in the German-occupied areas, feints and fake build-ups of invasion forces. The enemy command was led to believe that a major landing was to be made either in Greece, at the head of the Adriatic, on the southeastern coast of France near the Spanish frontier, or on the French Riviera, where the blow finally fell. The tactical deception plan narrowed down to operations on both sides of the main invasion beaches at St. Tropez. The Germans were known to have a hard shell of defense with very few mobile reserves. The object was to prevent troops in any one sector of the coast from going to the aid of any other.

Prewar memories intruded themselves into Douglas' planning. The first part of the operation involved a feint between Nice and Cannes, a stretch of coast he knew well. He found himself trying to remember the villas and homes of people that he knew so that Allied gunfire would not hit them. "Here's so-and-so's place," he would say to himself, "must leave that, but here's an old bridge that needs to be rebuilt anyway; at this time of day there'll be nobody in the post office."

The force was then to cross the front of the main armada and stage a demonstration between Marseilles and Toulon. It was a highly complicated operation and involved the largest single task group ever assigned to such a purpose. One group of small ships from Calvi in Corsica, another group from Bastia, two British transports, a beacon ship, two British gunboats that had spent most of their lives up the Yangtze River and had sailed round the world to the Mediterranean, an American destroyer from Naples, all had to converge. Their feints had to be co-ordinated with the French underground in the south to lend credence to the deception and weave it into the whole general plan. The unfortunate situation had to be faced of obliging the citizens of Toulon and Marseilles to rise up for the day of liberation, with the full knowledge that unless they took care of themselves they would be caught and victimized, because the Allied forces were not going in there. Air, ground, and sea forces were all co-ordinated and were to commence operations a few hours before the main landing.

Fairbanks, in the gunboat *Aphis,* with her sister ship, the *Scarab,* four royal naval motor launches and twelve American PT boats in one group, put ashore the French Bataillons de Choc at the Point des Deux Frères between Nice and Cannes. The troops advanced over an uncharted mine field and suffered nearly fifty per cent casualties, but they cut the vital coastal supply road from Italy.

Proceeding west at high speed, refueling on the way, the ships joined up with the rest of the force, led by the U.S.S. *Endicott,* commanded by Lieutenant Commander John D. Bulkeley, who had won a Congressional Medal of Honor for evacuating General MacArthur from the Philippines.

Over Toulon and Marseilles the plan included a mock air raid with three planes, mock radio traffic, carefully scripted, between the aircraft and two of the MTBs, naming whole squadrons by their call signs, reporting imaginary air battles, dropping the silver strips known as "window," and juggling with the radar, to convince the Germans that a huge air fleet was over the area. Dummy parachutists dropped behind Aix and Toulon and intermittent showers of 4.5-inch rockets from the ships had the German defenses in an uproar.

When the smaller vessels went close inshore to create their own brand of alarm in the Baie de la Ciotat, the *Endicott* withdrew, with the senior officer of the combined task group, to return to the main force. What happened next is best told in the terms of the recommendation for Fairbanks' combat Legion of Merit:

"On receiving a call at 0540 from a disabled A.S.R.C. of the group that it was under attack by two enemy ships, Lieutenant Commander Fairbanks immediately returned his unit to the area and first engaged the enemy at 10,000 yards, opening fire at 0610. Ordering the MLs to screen the gunboats to seaward, he closed the range to less than 4,000 yards while the enemy fire became increasingly accurate and intense. It was then seen that the enemy forces were two destroyer-corvette type ships, one a former Italian vessel [the *Capriolo*], and the other a large converted yacht [the *Kemal Allah*], each mounting three radar-controlled 4.7-inch guns and capable of at least thirty knots. Finally, with electric power gone, radio antenna shot away, with some of his main batteries temporarily immobilized by heat and age, his own maximum speed limited to eleven knots, and German shells continually straddling and near-missing his ships, he successively deployed the unit behind a smoke screen and emerged in a new tactically superior position as U.S.S. *Endicott* returned in answer to earlier radio calls to the scene of action. As the units under Lieutenant Commander Fairbanks once more closed with the enemy, he succeeded in directing the scoring of the first direct crippling hit on the superior Germans and prevented their retreat. After more intense exchange of fire by 0740 both enemy ships had been sunk.

"Approximately forty-five of the enemy were killed and 120 survivors taken prisoner. The survivors were rescued by ships of the group, and all units withdrew. Minor shrapnel and blast damage were sustained by the Allied ships but there were no fatal casualties to Allied personnel.

"The success of the operation as judged by subsequent intelligence reports was to a considerable degree due to the conception and thorough development of the special plans produced and to a considerable extent executed with considerable heroism by Lieutenant Commander Fairbanks."

His own comment?—"I was never so scared in all my life," but his part in this multinational operation resulted in the award of the British Distinguished Service Cross and the French *Légion d'honneur.*

That was the end of Fairbanks' shooting war. With a well-deserved new reputation, he was recalled to Washington for staff duties with the Navy Department.

"It appeared to me that he was constantly trying to contribute the maximum toward winning the war, and making good as a naval officer, while avoiding any appearance of capitalizing in any way on either his own or his father's reputation as an actor," Admiral Hewitt said of him many years later. "Fairbanks' service throughout was distinguished and a credit to himself and to his country. I was happy to have him with me."

15

WOULD JAPAN HAVE SURRENDERED without invasion or the dropping of the atom bomb? If she had done so in time, would Russia have obtained control of Manchuria and then succeeded in bringing about the communization of China? These are subjects for endless speculation and form part of a fascinating pattern of events with which Fairbanks was intimately associated after his return from overseas service to the Navy Department in Washington. He was the author of a spectacular scheme for obtaining the intercession of the Empress Dowager with Emperor Hirohito to end the war, a plan brought to an untimely end when President Roosevelt died the day before Fairbanks was due to present it to him for final approval. Undeterred, Fairbanks then drew up a document which was accepted in all its main premises as the Potsdam Declaration on Japan. Its purpose was the same as the abortive cloak-and-dagger scheme—to maintain the institution of the Japanese monarchy as a channel of authority for the surrender.

Fairbanks' first contact with Japanese affairs can probably be traced to a pony. Douglas Senior had been a close acquaintance of Prince

Konoye, one of the most traveled of the Westernized members of the Japanese ruling caste, and had entertained Emperor Hirohito, when, as Crown Prince, he visited the United States shortly after World War I. Young Douglas was at this time the proud possessor of a cow pony, one of the few presents his father had ever given him. He adored the animal, rode it out to local ranches, organized juvenile rodeos, and fancied himself as a cowboy. The Crown Prince admired the pony, and Fairbanks Senior, always quick in gesture, took it away from his son and presented it to the Prince.

The Fairbankses connection with Japan was not quite as tenuous as that. Senior visited the country two or three times, was received by the imperial family, played golf with Hirohito and Konoye, and was *persona grata* among the more sporting, celebrity-conscious group of the court. Moreover, the films of both father and son had always enjoyed great popularity there. It gave the name of Fairbanks a wartime *entrée* which very nearly bore fruit.

On his return to Washington in August 1944, Fairbanks installed his family in a rented house in Massachusetts Avenue. He and Mary Lee also resumed their habits of joint entertainment at her Boxwood Farm home in Virginia. The guest roster quickly resumed its interrupted list of famous names. The Duke and Duchess of Windsor graced one of the first weekends. John M. Schiff, the banker, members of the Vanderbilt and Astor families, Walter Lippmann and Arthur Krock, the political pundits, half a dozen admirals and scores of other figures visited this quiet retreat.

Douglas had been attached to the Strategic Plans Division of the Navy Department under a captain to whom he took an enormous liking—"Dopey" Dupre. His basic duties involved planning on a global scale the sort of operation he had devised with such success in the Mediterranean. It was necessary to establish informal liaison with the State Department on the political implications of his recommendations, and in his irrepressible way he was soon wearing his usual six hats. When he was not trying to get interservice co-operation for his plans, he was contacting old friends in the British, French, and other Allied forces and putting his spoke in on their behalf on subcommittees of the Joint and Combined Chiefs of Staff, commenting and reporting on political postwar planning and spending part of his time in the Psychological Warfare Division.

He soon attracted again the steely and disapproving glances of very senior regular officers, who did not even allow his combat record to soften their dislike of his gift for insinuating himself into the most secret conclaves, and what they still suspected was a flair for personal publicity. His invitations to the White House were renewed, and on several occasions he gave President Roosevelt personal accounts of his European observations, commenting freely on any personalities who came up in the conversation. He acquired a reputation for "knowing the boss too well," and was warned by the Navy Department that if he wanted to keep his job and not be transferred to some atoll in the Pacific, he had better stick to Navy business. It would do him no good with his two-and-a-half stripes, he was told, to exploit access to the President, denied even to admirals except through formal appointment. In self-defense he had to lie low, although he was still occasionally let into the White House through the back door.

The gathering momentum of the Pacific war was increasingly colored by the nightmare of the appalling casualties likely to be involved in an invasion of the Japanese homeland. The Philippine, Iwo Jima, and Okinawa campaigns, where Japanese soldiers, who had to be exterminated to the last man, had inflicted tremendous losses on American troops, had successively underlined this foreboding. At the same time it was becoming clear that Japan's armed forces were being rapidly sapped of their strength and that victory was only a matter of time.

The highly organized and successful interception and decoding of Japanese wireless traffic, reports from agents, the flow of information through neutral countries and the Vatican told an incontrovertible story of the swift erosion of Japan's industrial capacity and her ability to defend herself. The need to end the war was becoming an increasingly open subject of conversation in Tokyo, especially among the group of ousted politicians and more enlightened court officials who had long been kept out of power by the Tojo military clique. The problem of how to take advantage of this swing in opinion became a matter of urgent concern to the American administration and Chiefs of Staff.

None of the protagonists in what follows, with the exception of Fleet Admiral King, naval Commander-in-Chief, and the Secretary of the Navy, James Forrestal, knew of the gigantic effort being made to develop an atom bomb. Nor should it be forgotten that the first atomic explosion only took place at Los Alamos on July 16, 1945, three weeks before the first bomb was dropped on Hiroshima. Even in the stratosphere of strategy, the possible effect and the very efficacy of the bomb was a matter for conjecture, and the question still remains whether its use was either necessary or desirable. Alternative plans might have served the same purpose without any of the subsequent historical repercussions.

By the spring of 1945 Secretary Forrestal, on his return from a visit to Iwo Jima, had recalled to his department one of the United States Navy's Japanese experts, Captain Ellis M. Zacharias, a forceful officer whose independent ideas on the strategy of the Pacific war had caused him to be banished to San Diego in California as Chief of Staff of the 11th Naval District. Zacharias was given the task of devising a plan to take advantage of the increasing peace sentiment in Japan and bring about a termination of hostilities by other than military means. He was made privy to the top secret clauses of the Yalta Agreement, one of which provided for the cession to Russia of the Kurile Islands as an encouragement to Russian participation in the war against Japan.

Such was the wealth of evidence tending to show that the United States could successfully "go it alone" in the Pacific that Zacharias, in his first report to Forrestal, urged that the Soviet Government be released from its obligation to join in the war against Japan in order to avoid the danger of future Communist domination of the area. This report was supported by Forrestal and energetically advocated by Admiral King, who was, however, overruled by the other Joint Chiefs of Staff.

That was the first setback. It now remained to be seen what steps could be taken to bring about the capitulation of Japan before the time arrived for Russian participation in the Far Eastern war. The problem was to establish firm contact with the right elements in Japan, and obtain authoritative surrender terms for communication to them from the Allied governments. Douglas Fairbanks, in spite of his relatively junior rank, was one of a small group of officers and State Department officials who now applied themselves feverishly to this task, and he devised an intricate plan to take advantage of the contacts who would respond to the influence of his name.

The Japanese Emperor had put out feelers through Tatsuo Doi, the Catholic Archbishop of Tokyo, and Pope Pius XII was himself prepared to act as an intermediary in ascertaining Allied terms for formal peace negotiations. This information reached the American Government from a special mission of the Office of Strategic Services in Italy in contact with Pietro, Cardinal Fumasoni-Biondi, head of the *Congregazione di Propaganda Fide,* the Vatican's own intelligence service. However, the American State Department advised against this particular line of approach on the ground that the American public would object to any peace negotiated through the mediation of the Roman Catholic Church. It also appears that a similar message was sent through the good offices of the Soviet Government, but this was never delivered, and the fact that it had been sent at all was only discovered after the war was over.

The second line of approach was through a Swedish diplomat, from whom information had come that there was about to be a reshuffle in the Japanese cabinet. His report was proved accurate when, on April 5, the Emperor dismissed General Koiso and appointed in his place Admiral Suzuki, whose principal task was to ascertain possible peace terms. This change opened up a possible third line of approach, as General Hiroshi Oshima, the Japanese Ambassador to Germany, who had been captured when the Allies burst over the Rhine, declared himself willing to meet any of Admiral Suzuki's representatives as an intermediary. This was frustrated when the Army denied the Navy sufficient access to the general in his prisoner-of-war camp.

Fairbanks had for weeks been working on the establishment of a tenuous line of communication with those elements in Japan likely to bring about a *coup d'état*. One of the central personages was the Empress Dowager, a woman of great character and indomitable will, still capable of bringing influence to bear on the Emperor. For weeks Douglas had been studying intelligence dossiers, taking advantage of the possibilities of communication, both through the Vatican and neutral sources, and finally presented a plan which required the landing of an emissary from a submarine on Japanese soil. Such fragments of this story as have leaked out have suggested that Fairbanks himself was to make this journey. That, in fact, was not the case, as the intention was to use a Japanese-American Nisei, for the purpose. Moreover, this step was partly in the nature of a diversionary operation, designed to inform the contacts in Tokyo that the time had come to act.

The chain of contact was established, and messages were passed to two or three former members of the cabinet ousted by General Tojo. They were known to be part of a small group around the Empress Dowager, and in guarded terms they let it be known through neutral go-betweens that in certain circumstances they would be prepared to act.

The plan was to get everything in readiness for a palace revolution and let those on the spot organize as best they could the means of communication. The Emperor was to speak on the radio and order the cessation of hostilities, in the expectation that the great masses of the armed forces would obey his command as a god before the politicians could counter it or do away with the Emperor.

Although he was encouraged by Captain Dupre, Fairbanks' scheme got short shift from the Navy high command, who wanted to have nothing to do with "such cloak-and-dagger nonsense." Douglas reverted to back-door methods. First of all he went around the corner to another Navy Department building in Constitution Avenue where his old Hollywood friend, Gene Markey, was sitting on Secretary Forrestal's staff, resplendent in the four rings of a reserve captain, coordinating the Navy's film services. Markey made it possible for Douglas to present his plan direct to Forrestal, who, although greatly interested in it, did not feel that he could make any recommendations without the backing of his service chiefs. They, needless to state, returned the dossier with terse comments of disapproval.

In the meantime, Douglas, lobbying around in his usual fashion, in defiance of all chains of command, had discussed his scheme with Mr. Joseph Grew, for many years previous to the war the American Ambassador to Japan. Grew was one of the chief protagonists of ending the war by diplomatic means and shared the predominant State Department opinion that the best way to accomplish this was to maintain the Emperor on his throne and permit the Japanese to retain something of their traditional form of government. The former Ambassador introduced Douglas to Eugene Dooman, a senior foreign-service officer, who had for years been one of his top assistants in the Tokyo Embassy. Dooman was now head of the State Department's Japanese desk and chairman of a State-Navy-War Departments committee formulating surrender policies. Dooman warmed to the Fairbanks' charm and, while giving expert advice on some of the difficulties inherent in the plan, promised his support. Even so, the essential cooperation of the Navy was not forthcoming.

Evidence was mounting that the need for some such step was becoming urgent. Encouraged by Dooman, Captain Dupre, and those of his friends and naval colleagues who considered the scheme eminently feasible, Douglas decided to present it directly to the President for approval. He still had access to the White House, and not long before had been engaged in trying unsuccessfully to soften some of President Roosevelt's prejudices toward General de Gaulle's intransigence and the role to be played by French troops in the reoccupation of Indo-China.

Fairbanks now decided to try his luck again. He got in touch with the President and asked if he could see him informally. The answer came back that the President was about to leave for Warm Springs, Georgia, but that he would be back on April 13 and would be glad to see him if he would come in the side door at a given time. The President had been studying the plan submitted by Dooman through Secretary Hull, was very much interested, and wanted to hear more.

The evening before the interview was to take place, Douglas and

Mary Lee went to a cocktail party at the house of former Governor William Vanderbilt, with Senator Warren Austin, who later became the first head of the American delegation to the United Nations. It was with martini in hand that the company heard the shocking news of the President's sudden death.

That was the end of the matter. Fairbanks made an effort to keep it alive, but the whole momentum of activity in the Navy Department was by now concentrated on the infinite logistical details involved in the invasion of Japan. "We did have everything established, we did know our Japanese personalities, and there were enough people on a high level who believed in it for us to have gone ahead if the President had given his blessing," Fairbanks says. Ironically, late in May an intelligence report, confirmed in full when the Allies occupied Japan, said the Supreme War Guidance Council, Japan's highest authority, had accepted a resolution to seek ways and means of ending the war.

Douglas had the compensation of leaving his mark on the document which the Japanese finally accepted as the basis of the surrender terms —the Potsdam Declaration. Under Dooman's influence, he had aligned himself with the group who saw in the retention of the Emperor the only guarantee of orderly transition from war to peace as opposed to those who wanted to have him shot as a war criminal. Mr. Grew had instructed Dooman to endeavor to reconcile these two schools of thought and produce an agreed statement of policy which the United States Government could propose as an Allied proclamation to the people of Japan. A preliminary version was used by President Truman in a broadcast on V-E Day, but this, although speaking in general terms of the Allies' benevolent intentions toward the Japanese people, made no reference to the vital point of the retention of the monarchy.

In the meantime Fairbanks had produced his own draft, entitled "Proclamation by the United States, United Kingdom and Chinese Heads of State," which was approved by Secretary Hull and Mr. Grew, who showed it to President Truman on May 28. The President said he would accept it, providing Mr. Grew obtained the concurrence of the Army and Navy. Secretaries Stimson and Forrestal passed it, as did General Marshall, head of the Joint Chiefs of Staff. This was the document which Mr. Stimson took with him to Potsdam and showed to Mr. Churchill. Its text was cabled to Generalissimo Chiang Kai-shek for his approval, and it emerged practically unchanged as the Potsdam Declaration on Japan. The operative paragraph included the words: ". . . [the establishment] of a responsible government of a character representative of the Japanese people. This may include a constitutional monarchy under the present dynasty. . . ."

In case the identification of a movie star with such a document of state should appear too implausible, the testimony given by Mr. Dooman in December 1951 before the Committee on the Judiciary, United States Senate, 82nd Congress is conclusive:

Mr. Dooman: This paper, then, was taken by Mr. Stimson to Potsdam. I arrived myself at Potsdam on the 13th of July, and I was told by Mr. McCloy, who was then there, that Mr. Stimson was in active discussion with Mr. Churchill with regard to that document. . . . It was then telegraphed to General Chiang Kai-shek, and on July 26 it was promulgated then as the Potsdam Proclamation to Japan, and it was on the basis of that document that Japan surrendered.

May I also add, for the benefit of—I do not want to take credit that really belongs to somebody else, but I would like to put on record here that the preamble to the Potsdam Proclamation was taken from a document prepared by Douglas Fairbanks, who was then in the Navy Department in the Psychological Warfare Department.

The Chairman: Douglas Fairbanks?

Mr. Dooman: Douglas Fairbanks. I would like to make acknowledgement, if I could, of his contribution to a paper which, after all, is part of history.

Mr. Sourwine: You are referring to the movie actor?

Mr. Dooman: The movie actor.

Mr. Sourwine: Father or son?

Mr. Dooman: Son.

Mr. Sourwine: Douglas Fairbanks, Jr.?

Mr. Dooman: Yes.

The naval high command had always been less than enthusiastic about all this extracurricular activity on the part of a junior officer. At the beginning of 1945 it had been suggested to Douglas that he should join Lord Mountbatten's South-East Asia Command in a liaison capacity. A recurrence of the amoebic dysentery he had picked up in Italy, complicated by pneumonia, had prevented this. Douglas spent six weeks in Bethesda Naval Hospital, and in Palm Beach, Florida, on convalescent leave in February and March. In August, anxious to remove such a gadfly, the Navy issued peremptory orders for him to proceed to the Far East to take up this appointment.

He was to stay with Mountbatten for the invasion of Singapore, proceed to Chungking and then to Okinawa, remaining there for the invasion of Japan, where he was to supervise the various cover and deception plans in a similar manner to his period of service in the Mediterranean. Before leaving, he was promoted to full commander.

He was enjoying his last weekend leave when his mother called up on the telephone and said: "Douglas, did you listen to the radio this morning?" "Why, no," he replied. "They've just dropped some new bomb on Japan," Mrs. Whiting insisted. "Oh," said Douglas, "just another big blockbuster, I expect. The papers always have to write something sensational. Take no notice."

His mother was quite content to take his word and called all her friends, saying: "Well, Douglas knows everything and he says pay no attention. It's just the papers being sensational."

Even much more senior officers had yet to grasp the full impact of what had just happened or the swift sequence of events which was to follow. The first bomb was dropped on Hiroshima on August 6, the second on Nagasaki on August 9. Japan surrendered on August 14. One of the last letters of introduction which Douglas picked up before his trip was dated August 8. It was from Admiral of the Fleet Sir James Somerville, with the British Admiralty delegation in Washington, to Admiral Sir Arthur Power, Commander-in-Chief East Indies Fleet: "Dear Arthur: This letter is to introduce Commander Douglas Fairbanks, U.S.N.R., whose name is probably familiar to you. . . . Fairbanks is being sent down as an observer for forthcoming operations. . . . He wants to get in touch with Peter Fleming and the cloak-and-dagger people. Fairbanks is 'in' on nearly all these parties. Good luck to you, good hunting and best wishes for Zipper. Yours, James."

Neither "Zipper" nor Fairbanks' trip ever materialized. The war was over. So, although he had kissed his family good-by, said farewell to his friends, he was recalled to Washington.

Shortly after V-J Day a start was made with the demobilization of reserve officers with the longest terms of service. Commissioned long before Pearl Harbor and with two American gallantry citations, Fairbanks was near the top of the list. Peace had come so suddenly that he had made no plans at all. It was even being suggested that he should stay on in the Navy with still further increase in rank. The possibility of some form of government service added to his uncertainty. He had been away from his highly volatile profession for more than four years, had maintained very little contact with it, and was very dubious about the possibility of a comeback. He felt the best thing to do was to volunteer to stay another six months in the Navy while the situation sorted itself out.

Rather plaintively, he wrote to Lady Morvyth Benson: "Could Con tell me if there would be any companies seeking or wanting United States directors on their boards. I am available for as many as possible"; sending similar notes to such other friends as Winthrop Aldrich, John Schiff, and Lewis Strauss.

His doubts about his future were increased one day just after the war ended, when he shared a taxi with a naval captain he had never seen before. Douglas sat quietly staring out of the window when he felt, with a sort of sixth sense, that the captain was scrutinizing him closely. Anticipating what was coming, he became flustered, began humming, looking at his watch, fingering his tie, and otherwise showing his nervousness. The captain looked away as if to trace back in his memory where he had seen that face before. Obviously, said Fairbanks to himself, he is warm but has not quite got it. At length, the suspense got too much and Fairbanks turned, smiling slightly as if to say: "I know what you're wondering about. Why not ask?"

The look succeeded. "I'm sorry, but I've been trying to place your face," the captain said. "I've seen you somewhere before. What *is* your name?" Douglas tried to tell him as quietly and modestly as possible. "Fairbanks," he said, "Douglas Fairbanks—Junior." The captain continued to stare for a while, then solemnly shook his head as if in defeat. "No," he confessed, "I'm wrong. I thought I knew you. Thought you were someone else—a fella on my ship—name of Griffen."

To a newspaperman who wanted to write up his war career, Fairbanks said, "Look, sure I've done a job, but so have a few thousand other guys who didn't happen to be well-known beforehand; you go write about them. I didn't get into this for publicity, and I don't want to be cast with those who did."

His immediate seniors had liked him well. In the fitness report covering the first part of his Washington duties, Rear Admiral Thebaud, Chief of Naval Intelligence, wrote: "An excellent officer of pleasing personality and qualities, which have well equipped him for duties involving planning and execution of operations of a special nature. His ability to co-operate with others and to command their respect is of a high order. He is intelligent, loyal and capable, very much the gentleman."

Douglas turned again to his indefatigable memorandum writing. For Admiral Thebaud he produced a plan for the Navy to maintain openings for reserve officers as honorary assistant naval attachés if residing abroad. Then he took part in the formation of a new organization called Reserve Officers' Naval Services, with the co-operation of the Navy Department, as a means of "stimulating interest in the armed services and improving the status of reserve officers to ensure their maximum effective utilization by the government." With him as founder, members and national officers figured Rear Admiral Lewis Strauss, Lieutenant Commander Roger Firestone of the tire people, and Gene Markey.

Even his long-abandoned *alma mater* felt the weight of his pen. He wrote to Darryl Zanuck in Hollywood suggesting that an *ad hoc* committee should be set up with representatives of the motion-picture producers, of the Academy of Motion Picture Arts and Sciences, and the Cultural Relations Division of the Department of State, to sit as an advisory body on films exported to foreign countries, giving their approval only to those properly representative of the American way of life. He attracted some criticism for remarks at a Picture Pioneers' dinner in New York, in which he urged that the industry, as the pulpit that preaches to the largest world audience, put the world's interest foremost in film production and not depend entirely on box-office considerations.

Perhaps the most typical brain child of this period was a long paper he drew up on the institution of a United States Federal Award for Achievement, based principally on the French *Légion d'honneur* with its international appeal, together with the methods of presentation and selection of the British Orders of Knighthood. This is the Fairbanks' brand of romanticism in full flower, and at its most unacceptable to a large number of his staunchly egalitarian compatriots. He had produced a similar scheme many years earlier, at the request of Cordell Hull, which, surprising as it may seem, formed the basis for the institution of the Legion of Merit in August 1942. However, this remained a military decoration, and Fairbanks hankered after its extension to the civilian field, with other embellishments.

Between June and November 1945 he distributed to such recipients as Fleet Admiral Leahy and Adlai Stevenson, among many others, a memorandum with this preamble: ". . . The United States is the only major power in the world which does not recognize the distinguished service of its citizens except in times of war. It is an anachronism that the world's most powerful nation, dedicated to peace and the democratic way of life, acknowledges only those services contributing to a national war effort and leaves to private civilian organizations or institutions the duty of rewarding services to peace and the general welfare."

In the course of a detailed study on the administrative aspects of such an award, with examples of the procedure followed in other countries, he remarked: "It has been proven by time that most men will serve for one of three motives: money, power or honor. Only the latter remains unrecognized by the United States. . . . It is generally acknowledged that whereas the most distinguished military leaders retain their rank and status for life, other servants of the people are not similarly rewarded. It is proposed that:

"All former Presidents of the United States retain the courtesy title of 'Mr. President' for life (as in France), that they be given the title of 'Honorary Special Adviser to the President,' be granted the life-time honor of a seat in the Senate, the right to speak from the Senate floor (but without a vote) and be given the insignia of the highest degree of honor proposed.

"All former Cabinet members and Secretaries of government departments retain the courtesy title of 'Mr. Secretary' for life, be given the title of 'Honorary Special Adviser to the President' and be given the insignia in the highest degree of the Honor.

"All former Presidents of the Senate and Majority-Minority Leaders of the Senate retain the courtesy title of 'Senator' or 'Honourable' for life, be given the right to speak from the Senate floor (without a vote) and be given the insignia of whatever degree the Committee believes appropriate.

"All former Speakers and Majority and Minority Leaders of the House of Representatives to be given similar honors.

"All United States Ambassadors and Ministers on the date of their appointments to receive the insignia of a lesser degree of the Honor proposed above, so that, should their assignments prove successful, they may, in due course, be promoted.

"All Governors of States or Territories to be eligible for the appropriate insignia of the Honor proposed.

"All Military, Naval, and Air Force officers of Five-Star Rank and their nominees to be given the courtesy appointment of 'Honorary Aide to the President' and to wear the aiguillettes on all appropriate occasions."

The appendix to the letter to Admiral Leahy was pure Fairbanks. It recommended, *inter alia,* that American diplomatic representatives abroad should wear a uniform. "It ill becomes a nation of our eminence to oblige representatives and envoys abroad to dress as if they were waiters," he wrote. Further suggestions were designed to encourage postwar recruiting and the maintenance of popular interest in the armed forces. He proposed that Army and Navy personnel in full-dress uniform should be stationed as sentries outside the Lincoln, Washington, and Jefferson memorials and the War and Navy departments.

Specially selected underclassmen from the United States naval and military academies were to be on duty throughout the year at the White House, dressed in traditional full-dress uniform. Inter-service personnel were to be assigned duties in important and historic places throughout the country, such as the Statue of Liberty, Grant's Tomb, Mount Vernon, Independence Hall, and the entrance to the Golden Gate. "Dignified and impressive ceremony, including the participation of bands, should accompany changes of the sentry guard in the manner of similar activities in Paris, London, Rome, Stockholm, Brussels, Moscow, and Ottawa."

Douglas still advocates these ideas actively and any sympathizer receives a copy.

One weekend in September he and Mary Lee stole enough time, with Daphne and Victoria, to visit his childhood haunts of Watch Hill, finally fulfilling his father's prediction of six years earlier. The large Sully mansion had become a summer boardinghouse, the fields round it a housing estate. The big sunroom, with its glass veranda, where his father and mother had been married, was now filled with rocking chairs and old people dozing away their holiday. The rock on which he had slid as a child, which he had remembered as a miniature mountain, was now covered with moss and seemed little bigger than an armchair. Walking around, he remembered hidden niches and cupboards of which the owners, who had been puzzled at the reason for his visit and only half accepted his explanation, were entirely ignorant. Behind one boarded-up alcove he found old pieces of sculpture and plaster models of Greek statuary which had once contributed to the Victorian splendor of the whole. As he left he signed the register: "After twenty-four years, the ghost returns to Kenneth Ridge."

Most of his last months with the Navy were connected with the more nebulous forms of postwar planning, particularly concerning Europe. There was one plan for the restoration of the monarchy on a democratic basis in Germany, the removal of the capital to Munich, and the institution of a federal system on the United States model for Greater Germany. Another for reconstituting the economic unity of the Danubian Federation, while avoiding its former political aberrations and, always, the problem of Germany *vis-à-vis* Russia and the Balkans. In January 1946 he was informed that he would be placed on inactive duty within a month, and made arrangements for the paper work to be completed at the 11th Naval District at San Diego, so that the family could return to the Pacific Palisades home they had not seen for over four years.

To his surprise, he had discovered that there was still a lively demand for his services in the film industry, and he had already had several tentative talks with representatives of RKO. However, his home-coming was hardly triumphant. Hollywood had been deluged with returning heroes, and their Byzantine welcomes had been overdone and done too often. Several actors and executives had returned well before the end of the war, and Douglas was probably the last name of note. By this time it was strictly business as usual, and he found even his best friends making embarrassed excuses for their failure to organize a more boisterous welcome. "We think you're great," they would remark. "But let me give you some advice; you must get out of uniform as soon as possible; people don't like seeing you in it."

Hollywood is a community which resents those who break away from it, because the majority do not. Those that did were counted on to come back at the height of their glory so that a great to-do could be made of them, but if they came back too late, then the best thing for them was to hide their light under a bushel. Yet here was Fairbanks, who had always tried to represent the best side of the community to which he belonged, who had defended it around the world as not being as bad as people thought, and now found it had remained just as it was. Before he left he had been criticized for taking part in public affairs, but once the war had started and he was discovered to be at sea, everyone said: "Bravo, he's one of our boys." Then, because he had not timed his return to a nicety, it dissolved into anticlimax.

A few days before he took off his uniform for the last time at the beginning of February, he attended a big party given by Sonja Henie. Dodging diffidently behind the massed flowers, he was spotted by his first wife, Joan Crawford, with whom he has always remained on friendly terms. She came rushing over to him, while Douglas awaited, with pleasurable anticipation, at least one word of welcome. Her first words were: "Darling, of course you're so behind the news, aren't you? I suppose you haven't even heard that I'm no longer with M-G-M. I'm with Warner Brothers now."

The warrior was home.

16

WHEN DOUGLAS FAIRBANKS accepted the handsome fee which tempted him back to Hollywood to appear in *Sinbad the Sailor*, with Maureen O'Hara, there was nothing to indicate whether his comeback attempt would be successful or not. Return to civilian life found him in a quandary. Acting in films had long since lost most of its savor, but it provided him with the only source of income sufficient to support the outside interests which had become his chief preoccupation in life. He had, in the end, received little more than half the inheritance named in his father's will. A large proportion of this had been spent on financing his voluntary public activities, supporting his family on a junior officer's pay, subscribing to war charities, and in the expenses incidental to maintaining the contacts and social life which formed his essential background. Although his father had been dead six years, there were continuing problems with the lawyers and the estate was not yet finally settled. Senior's holdings in the United Artists Corporation had long since been disposed of by agreement between the other beneficiaries of the will. During his naval service, Douglas had left his uncle Robert with a tacit power of attorney to deal with such matters, and found, on his return to the industry, that the only springboard for his continued career were his own somewhat rusty talents.

He might have been more optimistic had he known how eager the RKO studio had been to obtain his services. About halfway through the shooting of the film, he was having a snack lunch with one of the senior executives, when this worthy, in an expansive mood, slapped his thigh and said: "Well, we certainly had you for a sucker." "How do you mean?" asked Douglas. "If you had stuck out for two weeks and not been so keen to accept our offer, we were prepared not only to double it but to give you a percentage of the profits," he was told.

However, the studio had given him veto powers on the story, sets, cast, costumes, and almost everything else to do with the picture. Douglas decided to stylize the role almost to the point of ballet and followed the precedent of his father in calling on expert advice. To ensure the authenticity of the costumes, he enlisted the services of Dwight Franklin, late of New York's Metropolitan Museum. One day on the set Franklin took a faded photograph out of his wallet, which showed him with Fairbanks Senior in his *Black Pirate* role, recalling that the father had said he would get in touch with him whenever he was ready to do a picture of the *Sinbad* period. Franklin had forgotten the conversation until the cable came from the son over twenty years later.

It was a strenuous film to make, requiring a host of acrobatic feats, and Douglas had to go into strict physical training to prepare himself for it. "You must be in the pink, Douglas," said one interviewer, who saw him bounding about the set. "No," he replied; "I'm really in the red, that's why I'm back in pictures." Asked how it felt to have grease paint on again, he answered: "Excluding the wearing apparel and the pay check, it's the same utter confusion." This had indeed been compounded when forty-two thousand fan letters, which had accumulated during the war, were transferred to the RKO offices for indexing and the dispatch of appreciative signed photographs to those who had not forgotten him. The night watchman saw the sacks of correspondence and, under a misapprehension, burned the lot as rubbish.

When the film was released it grossed more than any Douglas has ever made and was one of the highest earners of any Hollywood production in 1946. Its reception restored his professional reputation even if it did not produce commensurate rewards for his pocket, but he was sufficiently pleased to be accepted where he had left off five years earlier not to quibble.

Westridge had been reopened, and the Fairbankses soon acquired the reputation of providing the best and most exclusive entertainment in the film colony. Their parties, steering an unerring course through the garrison-town-type hierarchy of Hollywood, varied between formal and slightly solemn dinners for senior executives and producers, uproarious routs with such neighbors and bosom cronies as David Niven, and mass gatherings of the elite to greet visiting notables. To each they contrived to give something of a country-house-party atmosphere, rigidly shielded from the normal publicity brawl.

The first overt sign of his return to the happy hunting ground of persuasion and lobbying of the great came in February 1946, when he was one of the signatories of a petition to President Truman to take the lead in organizing a true world government. The list included such names as Albert Einstein, Thomas Mann, Sinclair Lewis, and many others.

During his last months in uniform he had resumed contact with his old internationalist ally, Clark Eichelberger. Many of the names in the Committee to Defend America, with whom they had worked to such good purpose, were coming together again in its postwar successor, the American Association for the United Nations. Over the years it has been the most active body engaged in interpreting the work of this world organization to the American public and eliciting their sympathies in its support. The day he left the Navy, Douglas was invited to become one of its national vice-presidents.

Although a purely voluntary organization it has, by reason of the prestige of many of its members, acquired a quasi-official status and has served on many occasions both to influence American legislators in support of United Nations policies and to interpret the mood of the American public to the international delegates and secretariat at United Nations headquarters in New York.

Fairbanks re-established contact with Senator Warren Austin, first head of the United States delegation to the U.N., made speeches, wrote articles and attended several U.N. Assembly meetings. On one such occasion he was given a formal reception. The public at large had begun to hear of his interesting wartime experiences for the first time. He used this renewal of popularity to stimulate interest in the U.N. and American participation in world affairs generally. The campaign took up a great deal of his time, as it meant traveling constantly across

America, with people flying out to see him in California, organizing chapters all over the country, and building up a large membership. In addition, there was much work behind the scenes on U.N. studies, carrying forward on a civilian level some of the postwar plans on which he had been engaged while still in the Navy.

He also became interested to a lesser extent in a number of other organizations, allowing his name to be exploited on a welfare scheme for the American Indians, for whom he still retained his boyhood interest, and helping Mrs. Eleanor Roosevelt in her work on behalf of European refugees. He became a sponsor of the War Memorial in Washington Cathedral and a patron of the Pacific War Memorial, which extended all over the Pacific. As a result of his South American venture before the war, he had several formalities to perform from time to time in connection with the Pan-American Union, and he made occasional appearances on behalf of the Red Cross and similar organizations.

Over the course of time he became intimately involved in the operations of E.C.A.—the Marshall Plan—administered by Paul Hoffman. Douglas was never an actual employee of the organization, but as the two were very close and good friends they saw a great deal of each other. Douglas stayed with Hoffman when he went to Washington, and they would sit far into the night, exchanging ideas on international relief, rehabilitation, and finance. When Douglas went abroad he served, as far as he was able, as a private reporter on the economic situation in the various countries in which the Marshall Plan operated. His purpose was to recommend ways and means by which the American taxpayer could be relieved of some of the expense and how the countries who were benefited could stand on their own feet and develop their export trade.

Fairbanks quickly reverted to the pattern of his life during the years leading up to the war. Acting and film production only formed a small part of activities. His Pacific Palisades home was always thronged with guests, his correspondence assumed production-line proportions, and his frequent visits to Washington and the East always found him lobbying on some international issue or pleading some good cause.

During the debate on the loan to Britain in 1946 he prepared a memorandum of arguments in its favor, based on discussions with administration leaders, which was distributed to members of Congress. In a series of talks with Leslie Biffle, Secretary of the Senate, he discussed the best means of persuading wavering legislators and had copies of his paper put in the hands of every member of the Senate committee discussing the proposed loan. In an echo of the prewar campaigns of its predecessor, the American Association for the United Nations printed thousands of copies of his arguments, under the title *Dollars for Peace,* and distributed them to members, with the request that they should write to their representatives advocating the passage of the necessary bill.

But over the next three years Douglas devoted the greatest proportion of his free time to his work for the CARE organization, that prime example of legendary American philanthropy which during its existence has sent more than $150,000,000 worth of food parcels and rehabilitation equipment to those countries struggling in the bitter aftermath of war. It was an association which earned him much recognition abroad, and then petered out in somewhat acrimonious fashion when some of its board members and executives felt that he had received more credit than was his due. The part Fairbanks played is very typical of the free-lance enthusiasm he brings to projects of this nature, and the criticisms he attracted are equally typical.

One evening during 1946 he was sitting over dinner at Westridge with a few close friends, when the subject came up of the fine meal they had just enjoyed compared with the short commons to which so many European citizens had been reduced in the first chaos of peace. Douglas, immediately full of enthusiasm, started jotting down notes for a scheme which would enable individual Americans to send food shipments to their less fortunate European cousins. He felt that the need was not for another official foreign relief measure, sponsored by the American Government at the taxpayers' expense, but a person-to-person scheme to forge individual links between citizens on both sides of the Atlantic.

The next day he developed the idea into one of his long memoranda, suggesting the formation of an organization to be called Food for Friends, and sent copies to the President, friends in the State Department, and other prominent acquaintances whom he felt might back the idea. In due course his letter filtered through channels to Arthur C. Ringland, who was head of the State Department's Advisory Committee on Voluntary Foreign Aid. This had been set up during the war to approve and issue operating licenses to organizations engaged in foreign aid, and still retained a registration control in order to co-ordinate their activities, avoid duplication, and ensure that the American people were not imposed upon by spurious agencies. Ringland replied to Fairbanks, approving wholeheartedly of his suggestion, but informing him that there was already an organization in being, carrying out very much the type of work he had in mind, and offering to effect their introduction.

This was called CARE, the Co-operative for American Remittances to Europe, and had been formed for the specific purpose of sending food parcels by an association of twenty-six different foundations—the various war relief societies, labor unions, and the welfare organizations of various religious denominations. Paul Comly French, a member of the Society of Friends and a former newspaperman, was soon appointed executive director, with offices at 50 Broad Street in New York. CARE had concentrated in the first instance on acquiring surplus U. S. Army ten-in-one ration packs, and then, as the supply situation eased, evolved a series of "parcels" based on the diet of the recipient country. The organization had been granted freight facilities in military transports and was slowly perfecting a system whereby individual donors in the States named the beneficiary, who signed a receipt acknowledging delivery.

Because of the number of unscrupulous firms springing up to profit from the urgent desire to help relatives in Europe, CARE's directors established a guaranteed delivery standard for their packages, and set up missions in European countries so that American personnel could control their delivery and minimize pilferage, diversion, and black marketeering. The system worked admirably, but operations were still on a modest scale. There was a much larger requirement to be filled.

People without friends or relatives in Europe also wanted to help and were asking if CARE's personnel overseas could not find them a "friend in need." This was the basis of Fairbanks' own plan, which was forwarded to the CARE directors just as they were discussing the means of raising funds for such "general relief packages."

In the spring of 1947 Richard Reuter, the deputy executive director of CARE, flew to California to discuss with Douglas the best manner in which he could co-operate with the committee. At their first meeting he found himself plunged in the full frenzy of a typical Fairbanks working week.

"As I came on to the lot, a stunt man by the name of Sharpe was jumping off a balcony. After doing this three or four times they got the cameras set and the action laid out, then Doug went up the stairs and jumped off the balcony a couple of times. He came into his little trailer dressing-room-cum-office, we chatted for about five minutes, when the director interrupted us: 'Mr. Fairbanks, we're just showing some rushes; would you like to see them?' So he said, 'Well yes, I'd like to see them, come on along, Dick.' Off we went to see the rushes and then ducked back to the trailer.

" 'Now, where were we on that,' said Fairbanks, so we recaptured the picture of the European food situation, by which time they were ready to take another shot of a dueling sequence. This went on for another half hour to forty minutes. Doug came back, perspiring rather freely from a fairly active session. We got back to the discussion, and as he was changing his costume for the final take of the afternoon we chatted some more and recapitulated the earlier conversation. I finally left, having, I suppose, all told had twenty to thirty minutes with him, much interrupted, in the middle of producing a Hollywood film. The next morning I went out to see Mrs. Fairbanks at Westridge. We chatted about what seemed to have been accomplished the night before and agreed on how I should present things to Douglas during the afternoon. That went on for five or six days."

It became clear that Douglas would never be free to exercise any executive function, but that he could give invaluable assistance in publicity and fund-raising drives. His contacts in Washington and

Europe would enable many difficulties to be smoothed over. It was agreed that he should form a separate subsidiary committee for this purpose, of which he would be the chairman. This was christened the "Share through CARE Committee," and Douglas invited a number of prominent public figures, including Mrs. Vincent Astor, Cole Porter, Dr. Robert Millikan, the scientist, Colby M. Chester, Henry Luce, Quentin Reynolds, and William Randolph Hearst, Jr., to act as sponsors. For the next three years Douglas stumped the United States, inveigled his movie colleagues into making broadcasts extolling the work of CARE, drummed up contributions, and toured European capitals making token presentations of parcels. Apart from the cost of one journey of an hour and a half from New York to Philadelphia, he paid all the expenses involved in these extensive trips out of his own pocket.

Quite apart from the humanitarian aspect of the work, Douglas was particularly interested in the opportunity it provided for enhancing American prestige in Europe, as a political weapon, amidst the Communist threat of the troubled postwar years, and as a means of presenting European problems to his own countrymen.

"It was the first time we ever had a fund-raising arm of CARE," says Reuter. "I'm not sure how much any of us really understood the difference in the pattern that we were setting up. What we were doing unconsciously, but somewhat consciously on my part at any rate, was to form an independent group that would be responsible for raising funds to purchase CARE packages. I think it's something we've never quite evaluated, but there is no doubt that it was a turning point in our pattern of operation. The 'Share through CARE Committee' was a title chosen in an attempt to get the CARE name tied to it, to avoid the confusion that would arise if the Fairbanks committee was appealing for funds for, say, 'Food for Friends,' which would then be used through the CARE channel."

The film this slightly dazed visitor had seen in production was a new venture on Fairbanks' part. With the reception of *Sinbad* providing evidence of his undiminished popularity as a star and the box office enjoying a postwar boom, Douglas had decided to make one further bid to establish himself as an actor-producer. Living quietly in Hollywood, retired on a pension, was the man who had been his father's general manager for more than a score of years, Clarence Ericksen. At the first invitation to renew his loyalty to the family, Ericksen agreed to join Douglas in the formation of a new producing firm, the Fairbanks Company, to work with Universal International Studios, who were to provide the production and distribution facilities.

Two films were planned in the first instance, *The Exile*, a fantasy based on a story by Cosmo Hamilton, to which Douglas had owned the rights for eight years, concerning the fortunes of Britain's King Charles II during the days of Cromwell's Commonwealth, and *The Fighting O'Flynn,* from a novel by Justin Huntly McCarthy, about an Irish soldier of fortune who more or less singlehandedly repels Napoleon's attempt to invade Ireland in 1797. The original story dealt with the siege of Londonderry in 1689 by the forces of King James II, and a stage version was produced in 1903 by Sir H. Beerbohm Tree. The film script transposed the action to the later period, chiefly as a means of saving money on the costumes.

The wheel had come full circle, both productions were in the tradition of the senior Fairbanks in his prime. To seal this revival the cameraman in *The Fighting O'Flynn* was Arthur Edeson, who had photographed *The Thief of Bagdad, Robin Hood,* and *The Three Musketeers* twenty-five long years earlier.

Another man who helped to keep the family tradition alive was Dave Sharpe, the stunt man who had caught Richard Reuter's eye and who had helped to work out so many of Senior's seemingly effortless acrobatic feats. He had since often served in the same capacity with Douglas. Every leap and turn in the action sequences of a Fairbanks film is a carefully systematized piece of choreography. Sharpe himself was a gifted athlete. In 1925 he had been national A.A.U. tumbling champion. With his knowledge of every gymnasium twist and turn, he would study a film script, work with the set designers, plot the action, and measure with a stop watch the exact time to be taken up by each sequence. Chairs, tables, props, plate-glass doors made out of sugar, would be constructed with tolerance of a fraction of an inch, to ensure that dangerous backward leaps could be made to look effortless and rendered perfectly safe by repeated practice. On the set he was a complete dictator, adopting a sergeant-major attitude to the star which made directors blanch. "For twenty years the guy's been treating me like a dog," Douglas used to say.

In *The Fighting O'Flynn* Douglas had to pole vault from roof top to roof top, slide down a castle buttress, and ride a barrel being hauled up by block and tackle several stories from the ground. The pole-vault stunt was practiced for three weeks before it was filmed, with heavy mats on the ground to guard against injury from a slip. Sliding down the buttress required another technique, like riding a surfboard in breakers. Fairbanks practiced that for another twenty days with a dummy and then made a dozen practice slides with his co-star, Helena Carter, before the scene was photographed. Scientific preparation precluded most of the danger. Even so, when the barrel reached the beam at the top and shattered, a flying stave might have injured him as he hung on. The devices of illusion are endless. The secret of some of the more spectacular leaps is a concealed trampolin which can send a man soaring six feet in the air as if in flight.

Fairbanks contributed his services in these two films on a profit-sharing basis. They cost just over a million dollars apiece. Both were well received by the critics and should have earned a considerable sum. *The Exile* was greeted as amusing nonsense. Photographed in sepia, it was released about the same time as the *Forever Amber* film and acquired the slightly mocking nickname of "Forever Dark Brown." Some American papers called *The Fighting O'Flynn* the best film Fairbanks had ever made, and even the *Irish Press* in Dublin, mollified perhaps by the presence in the cast of the Abbey Theatre's Arthur Shields and J. M. Kerrigan, was enthusiastic: "Through the smoke of me clay pipe I watched a million men spend an unsuccessful hour making sundry attempts on the life or lives of Fairbanks Junior, the bould Oirisch rover. They might as well try to catch a leprechaun on Burgh Quay by throwing salt on his tail."

Unfortunately, their release coincided with the first mushroom growth of the television habit, the thinning of war-fattened pocketbooks, and the business recession of 1947–48. Films were expected to break even, at least, in the United States and make their profit abroad, but just at that point the increase in the British film tax nullified that hope. Over the years they have recouped their cost by a handsome margin, but at the time Universal International preferred to see which way the wind was blowing before continuing the collaboration. Hollywood is as sensitive to box-office appeal as litmus paper to vinegar, and when a star's films reach the stage where they are just about meeting expenses, studio executives start to hedge on featuring him in other productions.

In between these two films Douglas had picked up some ready cash by lending himself to 20th Century-Fox to make *Lady in Ermine,* directed by Ernst Lubitsch. His co-star was Betty Grable. Fairbanks, who admits himself that he is a hopeless dancer, had to make the musical sequences thirty seconds at a time, and even then each shot had to be repeated a score of times before they could get it right. It was the last film Lubitsch made. The little German genius was already a very sick man, and he died ten days before it was completed, the remainder being supervised by Otto Preminger.

Although the critics were lukewarm, Lubitsch had not lost his touch, and Fairbanks found it a refreshing experience to be under such subtle and gifted authority. Just before he died he went over the script of *The Fighting O'Flynn* for Douglas, adding numerous marginal notes and suggestions on its production, of which full use was made. Lubitsch had a premonition of his death. A few days before the end came he said to Douglas: "This will be my best epitaph."

Fairbanks' Hollywood career had reached its last crisis, at least, to date. He had borrowed money, deferred his own fees, and put the last remnant of his own capital into the arrangement with Universal International. The war had drained him of his last reserves. Although he had earned very substantial sums during his life, he had very little to show for it. One way or another, the money was always going out to various causes, not at a profligate rate, but the selected few would engage much of his attention. All the traveling and subsistence came out of his own pocket, as he refused to allow any of the organizations for which he was working to pay his expenses. The problem of production was one of finance. For a star to sink his own money in a company is always a dangerous thing to do. With costs going up and returns going down, it meant that he was getting very extended indeed.

The Fairbanks now had a third daughter, Melissa. While her two elder sisters are dark and take more after Mary Lee, Melissa has grown up a blond imp, famous among her father's friends for her irrepressible *boutades*. Douglas is a devoted and exemplary father, determined that his children should have the best of everything. But he applies very strict standards to their upbringing, anxious that they should remain totally unspoiled. Genie Chester remembers an occasion when she drove with Douglas, Daphne, and Victoria to see them off on a trip to Europe by transatlantic liner from New York. They nosed the car up to the dock gate and when the guard saw Douglas he let them drive right alongside. "Why are they letting us drive right up?" Daphne asked. "On account of your father," Genie told her. But Douglas gave her a severe look and said afterward, "I don't want them to ever think that I'm different from anybody else, or that I get things because I'm known"—and that has always been the rule.

The Fairbanks had their large handsome house, which they had bought many years earlier and converted at a time when things were not too expensive. Westridge had been a bargain, but the problem was to maintain it. The whole atmosphere in the film colony is one of such constant economic pressure to keep up appearances that if anyone falls behind they are just left on the road and the parade passes them by. This Douglas knew only too well. He knew the tricks of the trade, the subtleties of negotiation, and the ruthless nature of the competition. He had been brought up in the midst of it, but it no longer amused him to fight on those terms.

The solution of course was, and always has been, to sign a long-term contract with one of the major studios with a guaranteed income for a certain period. He preferred to take his chances and be his own master, doing things his own way and making his own mistakes, rather than be subject to somebody else's whims. He no longer wanted to play parts of which he did not approve or did not want to do at a particular time, or which would prevent him from engaging in the public duties which he enjoyed.

It was a vicious circle, because he continued to be suspect in both camps. On the government and public side, his acceptance would be more orthodox if he would only abandon his profession and devote himself full time to serious pursuits, detaching himself from a freakish medium which was looked on askance by people in other walks of life. At the same time it was recognized that it provided a very good springboard for attracting public attention to any project, irrespective of what he might be able to do privately. The theatrical world, distributors, exhibitors, and the film-producing companies had reverted to their prewar attitude, implying in so many words that he should not continue with his public life. The more he detached himself the less he was identified with the movie colony. The competition was too fierce and the public declines to consider its theatrical heroes in any but familiar terms. They do not like to regard actors as working private citizens, and prefer to think of them in a romantic, shadowy form.

It was pointed out to Douglas time and again that he was trying to mix incompatibles. He would counter that he had been doing that for many years and there had still been films like *The Prisoner of Zenda, The Corsican Brothers,* and *Sinbad,* which had nevertheless turned out to be successful. But the argument would continue, yes, but they were infrequent, there would be one winner and too many lean years before another one appeared. Economic success would only be assured by full-time concentration on one job. He was told that he had become, as a personality, too detached from the ordinary run of theatergoers, and seemed to belong to another quite different group, so different in fact that they could not identify themselves with him. He no longer had what they liked to feel was the common touch, at least as far as the theater was concerned.

Douglas took all this to heart, realizing that the only easy solution was to surrender himself completely to his profession and tie up with one of the bigger companies permanently. That he was not prepared to do. He resolved to take his chances economically, make such income as he could by various means, either by investing in other people's films, producing when he could, or interesting himself in other businesses. He joined the board of the Pathé organization, a holding company of Robert Young, the railway magnate. It had certain film and laboratory interests, together with holdings in real estate, mining, and railways. Douglas remained a director for about a year, but was traveling around so much that he could not attend their meetings regularly. Young asked him to stay, but Douglas felt that he was not doing a good enough job by merely putting in an appearance at one out of every five or six board meetings, and he resigned. Another friend, Winthrop Aldrich, both then and at various times since, has discussed with Douglas means of working outside the film industry, with sufficient income and leisure to permit the continuance of his voluntary work, but nothing has crystallized.

In spite of these accumulating difficulties, he continued to devote all the time he could spare to outside activities. The first major appeal entrusted to his "Share through CARE Committee" was a scheme to mark the wedding of Princess Elizabeth with a gift of one hundred thousand CARE parcels, to be distributed at her discretion to needy or deserving households in Britain.

This was an idea Douglas himself had put forward at an early stage in their discussions. In August 1947 Richard Reuter wrote to Fairbanks to say that CARE had received authorization from the British Foreign Office, and inviting the "Share through CARE Committee" to sponsor the drive for contributions. The campaign was a spectacular success and Paul Comly French, in his annual report, paid generous tribute to it.

Douglas was really a one-man committee, traveling thousands of miles, making scores of speeches and personal appearances, putting on a weekly radio show on a national network, with Hollywood stars and such public figures as Herbert Hoover, all of whom gave their time without any payment. Don Sharpe, Fairbanks' radio and television agent since before the war, played a major part, badgering stars to participate, getting scripts written, and producing the shows, all without fee. Fairbanks also used his influence at government level to smooth out administrative problems of shipping and distribution in America and the European countries.

During the spring of 1948 Fairbanks conducted further CARE fund-raising drives for the mass shipment of parcels to France and Italy. In June it was announced that he had been appointed to the Olympic Games committee by its president, Avery Brundage. He helped to raise fifteen thousand dollars in the film industry to send Southern California athletes to Olympic trials in the East during June and July, and an additional $30,000 to help defray the cost of sending the winners to the Olympic Games in London in August.

By that time, Douglas himself had decided to pay his first postwar visit to Europe. As a way out of his Hollywood impasse he wanted to study again the possibilities of film production in England, renew his friendships on the other side of the Atlantic, and extend the whole range of his activities. His program included publicity appearances to boost the two films he had just made, speeches, broadcasts, ceremonies in half a dozen capitals on behalf of CARE, representation in Paris with Mrs. Eleanor Roosevelt of the American United Nations Association at a conference of sister bodies, timed to coincide with the Assembly meeting of that year, and discussions with leading European figures on political, economic, and military subjects. These he summarized for the State and Navy Departments on his return. It was also Mary Lee's first visit to Europe since a quick tour many years before the war, and something of a delayed honeymoon for them both.

Their reception in London was heart-warming. Douglas had been giving Mary Lee such glowing accounts of its delights and hospitality that he was afraid the reality might be an anticlimax. He need not have worried. All his English friends had rallied around, and their hotel room was banked with flowers for Mary Lee, whom most of them had yet to meet. The Bensons gave them a welcome party at the house of Mrs. Freddie Guest, attended by the Duchess of Kent, and a continuous round of invitations, dinners, and receptions confirmed to them that they had a second home. Such indeed it has become.

They dined with Herbert Morrison, accompanied Mrs. Roosevelt at the unveiling of the plaque commemorating the President in Westminster Abbey, attended the opening of Parliament, after they returned from a tour of the Continent. In Paris, Douglas had attended the opening of the United Nations Assembly, was the guest of an old Hollywood friend, Julian Huxley, at the Unesco conference, and made a token gift of CARE parcels at a public ceremony to the veteran French trade-union leader and minister, Léon Jouhaux. In Italy he and Mary Lee were received in audience by the Pope. During the conversation with His Holiness, talking about President Roosevelt, the war, and relief work, Douglas did not know whether to be surprised or pleased when he was asked what his business interests were. The Pope knew of his public activities but had overlooked his career as a film actor.

In Rome, Douglas distributed more CARE parcels, with attendant publicity, in the slum quarters of Trastevere and the Catacombs, and received the belated award of the Italian Cross of War and Military Valor. His sponsor, the Duke of Aosta, had by then left Italy with the fall of the monarchy, but the wording of the citation referred obliquely to their curious co-operation at the Salerno landings five years earlier.

He was also responsible for two effective anti-Communist propaganda episodes. CARE was being accused in the left-wing Italian press of sending empty packages. The mayors of two northern industrial towns even refused to welcome the friendship train which had been sent from the United States, loaded with gifts, proclaiming that CARE and the train were specious American propaganda. The Italian radio offered Fairbanks an opportunity to broadcast a refutation, so he went on the air to announce that he was shipping both the mayors a large consignment of CARE packages for the needy people in their cities. "The mayors couldn't refuse the packages," Fairbanks says. "They had to accept them and help distribute them. That soon put a stop to the rumors that the scheme was just a propaganda stunt."

Stopping off at Bologna to lunch at the world-famous Papagallo Restaurant, he succeeded in breaking up a whole Communist parade of twenty-five thousand demonstrators single-handed. He was recognized at the table, and the news of his presence spread to the surrounding streets. Soon a crowd of people were pressing their noses against the glass windows, to be joined by the members of the procession as they passed, laying down their banners. The entire demonstration was broken up, the streets in all directions of all sides became filled with cheering crowds, yelling "Viva America, Viva Douglas." They rolled up their Communist slogans and nearly overturned Fairbanks' car in sheer enthusiasm as he left. Two detachments of Carabinieri had been called out to control them. It was a very amusing switch, and very Italian.

When Douglas and Mary Lee returned to London the Bensons lent them their charming Queen Anne house in Cowley Street, near the Houses of Parliament, and the Fairbanks stayed in England for another month. The day of the American presidential election they were lunching with Winston Churchill. Douglas, in common with many of his countrymen, thought that the Republican candidate, Thomas Dewey, was going to win. However, his host was perfectly sure that President Truman would be re-elected and proved to be right.

Fairbanks was sitting between Mr. Churchill and Field Marshal Lord Montgomery, who at that time was about to pay a short visit to the United States. Douglas tried to persuade him to travel as far as California and stay at Westridge, but the austere field marshal felt that the atmosphere of Hollywood would be little to his taste. Douglas explained at some length that it was, in fact, a quiet suburban existence, that the house was secluded, that there would be no need for him to attend "wild" parties or see any but chosen friends and acquaintances, and that he would be able to live his accustomed retired life. At this point, Mr. Churchill, who had not appeared to be paying any attention to the conversation while talking to the Duchess of Buccleuch on his right, turned around and growled: "It all sounds bloody dull to me."

Douglas also renewed contact with Alexander Korda, and agreed to return the following year to make a film for him. Back in the States, he was able to give a firsthand account of the work of CARE in Europe to the devoted and hard-working office staff in New York, and made an extensive tour of the larger Eastern cities to raise more funds. "It was the best boost in morale we could have had," Richard Reuter comments. "At this period we were very appreciative of the help Fairbanks did provide. It was of real inspiration to the staff and of the greatest assistance in interpreting the program to the American people." Unfortunately this was an opinion which was not to endure, and the signal circumstance which now followed was one of the reasons.

17

FAIRBANKS WAS ENJOYING what, in his hectic life, was almost a rest, at his Pacific Palisades home when, on March 28, 1949, he received a telegram from Sir Oliver Franks, the British Ambassador in Washington, advising him that he had been made an honorary Knight Commander of the Order of the British Empire. Although he had as house guests one of his staunchest British admirers, Lady Morvyth Benson, with her daughter Jill, he did not dare show them the message, as he was convinced it was a practical joke on the part of one of the many people who had for years poked caustic fun at his public activities.

Other British friends had hinted to him unofficially that he was due to receive some acknowledgment from the British Government of all his untiring work over the years to foster goodwill and friendship between the two countries. He had heard indirectly that Lord Halifax, Lord and Lady Mountbatten, Ernest Bevin, and a few others had been sponsoring such a suggestion. He was given to understand that this might result in something like an honorary O.B.E., but it seemed more likely that his connection, through the Douglas Hospitals, with the work of the St. John Organization would be signalized by conferring on him one of its ranks. Douglas was perfectly reconciled to the idea of receiving perhaps a piece of parchment couched in appreciative terms, and now here was this telegram. Surely there could not have been a leak somewhere and some wag had decided to play the fool.

He rang up his friend Sir Robert Hadow, the British Consul in Los Angeles. They had first met in Buenos Aires when President Roosevelt sent Douglas on his mission to South America. Had Sir Robert had word of this? No, but he would call back.

In half an hour came the reply: "That's what my cable says. Many congratulations."

"Hadn't we better check with Washington?" Douglas asked. "The cable company must have made a mistake and put a 'K' instead of a 'C' or an 'O' or an 'M'."

There had been no error in transmission. The first message was in order. Even then Douglas could hardly control his emotions as he told his wife and friends the news. For such a romanticist and sentimentalist it was a major event. He was more deeply touched than by anything that had ever happened to him. "It was a most tremendously gratifying and emotionally moving moment, as symbolic things often are in life," he says.

The "statement of services" which had been drawn up in London by the Foreign Office in recommending the award delved deep into the Fairbanks career. Although it has often been assumed that his work for CARE was the principal consideration, this only formed one of the thirteen paragraphs in the document.

This referred to his support for the British War Relief Society and the Douglas Hospitals, and the care of British orphans in the United States during the war; his share in the formation of the William Allen White and Fight for Freedom committees, the propaganda films and the subsequent neglect of his profession to act as pro-Allied propagandist; his report to Lord Halifax at the conclusion of his mission to South America; his naval service, when "he was frequently assigned duties and responsibilities which required Anglo-American action"; his advocacy of the British loan, the settlement of Lend-Lease and the Marshall Plan, and his work for the dozen or more bodies fostering Anglo-American and international understanding with which he is connected. The many friends who contributed their knowledge of his activities to this compilation made sure that no part of the impressive record was omitted.

The normal procedure would have been for Fairbanks to receive the insignia of the order from the British Ambassador in Washington, but at the time Sir Oliver Franks was engaged in an extensive tour of the United States, and Douglas was due to return to Europe to make the Korda film and pay a further round of visits on behalf of the CARE organization. It became impossible to agree on a date, as the only time that the Ambassador was to be in Washington clashed with Douglas' transatlantic booking.

There was one possible solution to the impasse, which to Douglas seemed the ultimate pleasure. He hoped that in some way it might be arranged for him when in London to receive the award from King George VI in person. Nothing could be more completely in character. Here was the little boy who had marched up and down outside Buckingham Palace, the avid collector of toy soldiers, the lover of ceremony who wants to see an honor guard mounted at every American national shrine, the incurable romantic whose sense of history and tradition envisages a rose-hued world of mass knight errantry, cast in real life in the sort of role his family had made their screen hallmark. The oil and water currents of his career, seemingly in defiance of physical laws, were merged. It is easy to mock such an attitude, but the award represented a real milestone. He had proved himself. He was appreciated. He was a real person who had done real things and acknowledgment was about to be made.

He sent discreet inquiries to two or three friends in England, who replied that as far as they knew his request was impossible, that this was something done only on rare occasions and with very special people, usually senior Allied officers. No foreign civilian had ever received the insignia from the sovereign. However, they hinted that they would see what could be done. There was no law forbidding the procedure, but it was a breach of custom.

When Douglas arrived in London in the middle of June, he got in touch with the Foreign Office and the Lord Chamberlain's office. After a few days he was told that the King had agreed to make an exception. Douglas was to be given a private audience after the next regular investiture on July 12. The night before, he was a guest at the famous party at the residence of Lewis Douglas, the American Ambassador, when Princess Margaret danced the cancan with Sharman Douglas. He had only a few hours' sleep before going to Buckingham Palace.

His audience took place after the morning investiture. The arrangements were almost furtive. He was instructed what to wear and when to be there. He was not allowed to take his wife or family, a great disappointment to Mary Lee, although she was able to wait outside. Douglas arrived through a side entrance and was shown into the office

of Sir Michael Adeane, the King's secretary, where he was told that
his interview would last three or four minutes, that the King would
present him with his decoration and indicate when he should leave,
that he should then bow, take two steps backward, and that would be
all. He waited until a bell rang and was escorted down endless corri-
dors and galleries to a large room, where King George VI sat in the
far corner.

The King rose and came over with the insignia, saying: "You wanted
me to give this to you personally, didn't you?" Douglas replied: "Sir,
I am very appreciative that you have." "Well, I wanted to give it to
you too; we are very grateful and very touched at your being such a
friend for so long."

After the presentation there was a pause, the King saying: "That's
that, isn't it?" Douglas, almost too overwhelmed to speak, remarked
on the beauty of the decoration, adding nervously and half facetiously:
"I feel I should keep it on all the time now; I must look up every
opportunity to wear it."

In spite of Douglas' protestations that he should leave, the King then
invited him to have a cigarette, saying: "No, no, stay, it's all right;
I'm done for the morning, sit down." They started to talk of politics,
Anglo-American affairs, the late Duke of Kent, doctors, and the King's
leg, which was already giving him trouble. There was time for three
cigarettes and a small glass of sherry from a decanter on the desk.
Finally Douglas realized that the King, a shy man, was not going to
dismiss him and it was up to him to excuse himself. The interview
had lasted forty minutes instead of the stipulated three or four, and
the manner of his leaving later became a joke between them. Douglas
did not know whether he should back all the way out, and ended by
going sideways, a sort of crab crawl, the length of the room.

Two days later Douglas and Mary Lee received an invitation to
one of the first full-dress court balls to be held since the war. There
the King and Queen came up to them, and before they could stutter
their thanks and appreciation, the King remarked: "You said you'd
like to have a good reason for wearing what I gave you and I thought
that this would be the best and earliest time." The gesture was so

charming that it left Douglas at a loss to reply. Then the Queen sent for him to dance with her and told him how her husband had talked of his audience and how much pleasure the award had given them both, saying that it had meant a great deal to them personally.

Nothing has so confused Douglas Fairbanks' present status as this award. It is surprising how many Americans assumed that in accepting it he automatically became a British subject. Others become mildly apoplectic when they ring up his office or home and hear an over-enthusiastic secretary reply: "Sir Douglas" is doing this or that. Some confusion even reigns in Britain, and the lady in waiting to a very royal personage indeed once started a letter to him "Dear Sir Douglas. . . ."

It is, of course, quite wrong to address him thus. He is no more Sir Douglas than President Eisenhower is Sir Dwight, nor are any of the other seventy-odd Americans who have received honorary knighthood in recognition of their services to Anglo-American relations and the Allied cause. Most of these are service figures who held high appointments in the first and second world wars, and Douglas is one of the few members of the civil division of the order. None of them have received the accolade—the symbolic touching on the shoulder by the sovereign's sword, which accompanies the patent of knighthood granted a British subject.

Membership in an order of chivalry is one thing and the accolade another; they go together but they are separate. There is a historical reason for the duality. In the days of the Crusades a man could be made a member of an order of chivalry and become a knight of that order, but he could not swear fealty to a foreign sovereign if he still owed loyalty to his own feudal monarch or baron, who may not have been participating in that particular part of the Crusades. The accolade had only indirectly to do with becoming a member of the order. It meant that the knight accepted the bond to the sovereign, that the king, as liege lord, could then call on him as his subject to present himself with his sword and armor and fight the king's wars. The romantic days of chivalry are past, but the accolade still has this implication in law. In an honorary knighthood the arms are the same, the diploma is the same, everything is the same, except that a foreign citizen is absolved from being considered subject to the sovereign's call to arms.

Fairbanks has gone a step farther than most of his fellow American honorary knights in devising a coat of arms, which has been acknowledged by the College of Arms. It consists of a shield showing the two hemispheres of the globe, representing the New World and the Old, linked by a golden ribbon denoting friendship. On the crest an American eagle, resting on a knight's helmet, holds in its beak the spur of knighthood. Circling the shield is the rose-pink and pearl-gray ribbon of the Order of the British Empire with the cross of the order below. The motto he has adopted—*Fides Conatus et Fidelitas*—means "Faith, Effort and Loyalty."

Cyril Hankinson, the editor of *Debrett's Peerage,* also elicited Douglas' help in obtaining the personal details of all the American members of the orders of knighthood, whose names are now included in the roster of that august volume.

Within a year his work on behalf of international understanding, particularly his efforts with the CARE organization, had brought him recognition in other European countries. The Dutch Government made him a Commander of the Royal Order of Orange-Nassau; he became an officer of the Royal Order of the Crown of Belgium; while during a visit to Athens, King Paul of Greece, in recognition of his friendship and assistance to his brother, when King George II was in exile, invested him with the rank of Knight Grand Officer of the Royal Order of King George I of Greece. This is the family order, the second highest the country can bestow. Italy has also awarded him the Republican Order of the Star of Italian Solidarity. In recognition of his work for the organization over many years, he has recently been promoted a Knight of Grace of the Most Venerable Order of the Hospital of St. John of Jerusalem.

It would be too much to expect his republican countrymen to approve unreservedly of this glittering array. Most American, and many of his British, friends tend to poke gentle fun at the unashamed pride Fairbanks takes in displaying these marks of appreciation. Much of it is envy, some of it is mild astonishment that someone whose public position seems so assured should need to remind himself and others of it with such punctilious frequency. The recorded opinions of some of his closest friends may help to explain why so many people in the United States fail to take him entirely seriously: "There are two fellows named Douglas Fairbanks," says one of the people who knows him best. "There's one who is a highly estimable, public-spirited fellow, who's had a distinguished career, short, up and down, but still a laudable career in pictures, a fellow who has gone out of his way to do many kind things to many people and who has a true sense of public service. This figure has no relationship with another Douglas Fairbanks who has an especially designed chest for his medals, who will wear a sword at the drop of a handkerchief, who will do all the other silly things that we fail to understand. I think he must have a basic feeling of insecurity, so that he has to keep reassuring himself about his position."

Another tells a revealing anecdote: "He belonged to a British club in Los Angeles and insisted that I come as a guest one night and become a member. He told me I had to wear miniatures of my decorations. I told him I had none and was not going to wear them if I had—but he insisted. 'Black tie,' he said, 'and you must wear your miniatures.' He went all over, I don't know how he did it, he got miniatures of the decorations I had, he remembered them better than I did, sent them along and made me pin them on. 'Now I know why you belong to this club,' I told him, 'because we can come here and wear our decorations.' It's an innocent enough foible, it's a wonderful thing, it's childlike. I always say he should have lived in the days when he could wear lace cuffs, because he loves that, he just loves to be a grandee."

An older man, who has known Douglas since he was a child, has this to say: "I always feel I want to take him over my knee and spank him, except that he's gotten to be quite a big boy now. He loves to dress up in outlandish costumes. He suddenly arrived in Hollywood and started wearing kilts in the evening. Well now, you just don't do that, and someone very cruel said: 'What tartan is he wearing, the

Ulman?' He should grow up a little bit and stop going to fancy dress parties.

"Before America entered the war, when he was in uniform in California after he'd been called up by the Naval Reserve, one of the first orders that the Navy issued was that officers were not to wear swords. In fact, they were encouraged to hand them in for our scrap-metal drive. Douglas arrived at Darryl Zanuck's one night for a dinner party with his boat cape on and his sword. His excuse was that he'd been to a drill at the armory. Well, I know that no one in the whole of California, if they went to a drill hall, would have a sword. But he thought it looked like Lord Nelson or something.

"That is the ham in him, unfortunately; that is possibly what he's inherited from his father's business, showing off and climbing the highest building—it's an exhibition complex. People who know him as well as I do are embarrassed when he does these things, embarrassed for him. People who don't know him, I should think, would never forgive him. He knows all this; he's been told it by his close friends. It doesn't help him any. I should think the important people with whom he surrounds himself, who accept him, would be put off by this behavior."

A contemporary enlarges on the theme: "He's been absolutely obsessed, as long as I've known him, with being with the top wherever he is. If it's in New York it must be an Astor, a Vanderbilt or somebody. If it's in Hollywood it has to be the so-called royal society of Hollywood—of which by birth and probably by achievement he's a natural member. They've maintained the social atmosphere round their house, and the same thing in England, which doesn't mean he wouldn't be terribly nice to the bobby or the old valet or the friend he hadn't seen for fifteen years who's now a terrible bore. He puts up with more bores than anybody I've ever known, and he has a great personal sweetness; it's impossible to be near him and not be aware of it, but there still is this terrific drive to give the biggest dinner party and have more titles, more jewels, or if it's Hollywood, to entertain the current big-name visitor.

"If it's self-aggrandizement, it isn't attractive, but I don't think that is the motive. He has a strange compulsion to reassure himself passively that he is Doug, the great Doug Junior. Not that he ever gives you the impression that he thinks he's that, but he must have constantly to remind himself of it. Otherwise I don't see why this guy who has a million friends and is acknowledged in all four corners of the globe to be a dear friend and a tremendously likable character should wear a Navy cloak, or a sword, or his full medals—that represents some insufficiency in his background or his life or his own conception of himself. He doesn't need to do those things."

Now, although these are the sort of stories and anecdotes that are told whenever his name is brought up in conversation, they represent a mood rather than the strict facts. The British United Services Club in Los Angeles, which exists principally for expatriates, does insist on formal attire at its functions, and it would be impolite not to conform. The kilt episode is less than accurate. He has never worn this gift from a Scots friend in the evening, but he did put it on as a joke two Sundays in a row after tennis at Westridge, to amuse his friends, and the story has got out of hand.

He does have a penchant for bizarre attire and has a puckish wardrobe of cowboy shirts, blue jeans, Austrian *lederhosen,* and modified battle dress for sports wear. On the other hand, the fact that he will not avoid an opportunity for appearing in full regalia should not be allowed to obscure the equally pertinent fact that it would be equally eccentric not to wear his decorations when the formal invitation to any function so specifies.

It will probably never be possible for him to escape entirely from his original environment. In almost every aspect of public affairs with which he has become increasingly identified, his original introduction was as a film celebrity. This has been his passport, and with it he brought the quirks of behavior that belong to his background. However professional an actor's approach to his work, there is a psychological satisfaction in appearing in costume and assuming another personality. The fact that over the course of the years Fairbanks has been considered by his friends to seek unnecessary opportunities of wearing his naval uniform or his many decorations is only part of the mental process by which he has sought to transform himself into the figure he has become, Douglas Fairbanks, the useful citizen. These marks of progress in the realm of actuality have been for him tangible evidence of his separation from the fantasy world in which he grew up and which forms his *alter ego*.

Gilbert Miller, as American as the other friends just quoted, takes a much more charitable view: "I think that Douglas' honors are well bestowed because they represent a great deal of work. I think some people feel that there's a certain *naïveté* about Douglas' liking for decorations. To me it's all part of the very attractive, extremely youthful quality he has—it's very refreshing. But when it comes to a serious thing, there's nothing immature about Douglas. I really value his friendship a great deal; at my time of life it's very pleasant to have a young friend who's so serious. He's a great talker on all subjects, but the funny thing about Douglas is that people think he's a playboy. He's one of the most serious people I know. He goes into things very profoundly. An examination of Douglas' official record, what he's done in public life, both for charity and representing the United States Government, makes very impressive reading."

One of the most resounding testimonies comes from his old naval colleague, Admiral Lewis Strauss, Chairman of the Atomic Energy Commission: "Every time we meet we swear eternal allegiance. I am proud of our relationship. He keeps me in touch with romanticism. Although he grew up in the artificial atmosphere of the film colony, he is one of the most valuable citizens we have in the United States. It burns me up that Britain and other countries should have recognized his acts so handsomely and that we have given him nothing."

Those who know him less well forget, perhaps, how unique it is for an actor to achieve any position outside his profession at all. Subconsciously Fairbanks needs these tangible reminders of the path he has trodden. He is always meeting people who consider him only in terms of his original environment and think that half the stories of his war service and public activities are publicity stunts like many another Hollywood invention. More than most men it is essential to him, say, to display the pre-Pearl Harbor campaign ribbon when he wears his uniform at Naval Reserve and service functions.

His wartime combat awards meant more to him in terms of self-justification than to a great many of his fellow fighting men. Each of his civilian decorations represents a recognized milestone in the by no means easy path he has chosen to follow. He still remembers with pleasure the change in the attitude of an American general in Vienna, during one of his CARE trips, who had made it fairly clear that he did not consider film actors overly impressive types and was visibly taken aback by the kaleidoscope of color on Fairbanks' chest at a service reception.

Apart from combat and campaign decorations, there are practically no tangible honors of the European type to which citizens of the Great Republic may aspire. Americans debunk far more readily than they reward. This is doubtless good democracy, but it is something of an enemy to reputation.

It is a curious phenomenon that the Briton who is a Francophile is regarded in his own country as a man of praiseworthy attainments, whereas the American whose activities seem to denote Anglophilia or liking for some other European country is regarded as a citizen whose attitude borders on disloyalty. It must, one assumes, be a throwback to the unhappy memories so many Americans have of their countries of origin.

Many of the causes Fairbanks has espoused—wartime aid to the Western Allies and advocacy of closer Anglo-American union—have been violent political issues in the States. Many of his services on behalf of the American Government belong to the intangible fringe of diplomatic activity which does not appear on the record. Yet his very acceptance in European circles is due to his outstanding qualities as a representative of America. "I am probably more American abroad than I am at home," he says, flipping ruefully over some recent press cutting which describes him as more British than the British.

As we shall see, his unpublicized association with leading members of the postwar American administrations has been at least as close and effective as his ties with President Roosevelt. The fact remains that the prewar pattern of greater general acceptance in Europe, and in Britain in particular, has been repeated since the war and has, to a large extent, influenced the geographical distribution of his activities. A minor event during 1949 underlined the contrast. His rebuff by New York's Racquet Club has already been noted. His name has been before the equally exclusive Brook Club for many years, but in spite of the countless supporting signatures he has not at this writing been elected. There is a bias against his professional identity and a feeling that he is too closely associated with things abroad, a combination which does not conspire to make him an ideal member. Yet in London there is no such prejudice, and in spite of long waiting lists his election, when proposed to both Buck's and White's, notoriously selective clubs, was put through in a matter of weeks.

The general American attitude did not fail to affect the members of the CARE organization. His work on their behalf continued until the end of 1950. The most publicized aspect of his activities continued to be the distribution of token packages in the various European countries—France, Belgium, and Holland and then Italy, Greece, and Austria. To these he added his usual quota of speeches, official receptions, and free-lance lobbying. In Vienna he was asked to make a propaganda speech outlining American policy in Austria in the Cold War, and in Greece toured the guerrilla areas with the American General James Van Fleet in a morale-boosting visit to the forces engaged in throwing back the Communist invaders from across the Yugoslav border.

However, his relationship with the organization had taken an awkward turn. Some of the executive personnel and board members, while appreciating the tireless expenditure of his time and own money on their behalf, had been distinctly put out at the sudden rash of awards with which he had been presented. It seemed to them that he was receiving an undue degree of credit, which had not taken into sufficient account the devoted routine work of the main organization and its territorial representatives.

For his second European tour on their behalf it had been agreed that the name of his own committee should be shortened to "The CARE

Committee" as a means of identifying him more closely with its operations. This led to press reports referring to him as CARE chairman, CARE head, CARE director, CARE president, and the like, and there were complaints in the New York headquarters that Douglas had not always been as specific as he might in defining his exact status in conversation.

During a ceremony in London in November 1949, at St. John's House, Collingham Gardens, Douglas presented some token packages to Countess Mountbatten, in her capacity of Superintendent-in-Chief of the Order of St. John. In her speech of thanks, his old friend did him an ill turn by concluding her remarks, saying: "Fairbanks is CARE and CARE is Fairbanks." This was too much for the resident London representative who, in common with many of his colleagues in Europe, did not perhaps appreciate the vast amount of work Fairbanks had done behind the scenes for the organization and did not always understand why it was necessary for Douglas to help him carry a token package at one of these ceremonies. He wrote an infuriated protest to New York. Fuel was added to this flame shortly afterward when, in her column in the New York *Journal-American* on February 7, 1950, Louella Parsons quoted a letter she said she had received from Douglas in Bad Gastein, Austria, where he was taking a short holiday, reading: "In my capacity as chairman of CARE we will visit Vienna. . . ."

This clipping was brought to the attention of the executive director, Paul Comly French, who wrote to Douglas to say that the confusion concerning his functions had now become too great and that the name of his committee was to be changed back to its original longer form. A copy of this was sent to all the representatives in Europe, and from then on Douglas obtained little further co-operation from them. He also had reservations about the manner of continuing the work of CARE. The original purpose now seemed to be largely fulfilled, with the general improvement in conditions in Europe, and at the end of 1950 he sent in a rather tart letter of resignation.

However, the State Department had been sufficiently appreciative of the work he had done to ask him to become foundation sponsor of a new organization then being formed for relief work in Korea. He agreed to serve in the same voluntary fund-raising capacity as for CARE, but when the formation of American Relief for Korea was announced he was named as its national chairman. Until the organization was wound up in 1954 he somehow managed to find time, even when in England, to function actively as its executive head. Twenty-four million pounds' weight of clothing, blankets, and comforts were sent to the suffering civilians in that war-torn peninsula. In recognition of his efforts he was made by President Syngman Rhee in 1953 an honorary citizen of Korea.

The film Fairbanks had agreed to make for Alexander Korda during the late summer of 1949 was called *State Secret*. Filmed on location in the Dolomites under the direction of Sidney Gilliat, it was a civilized and superior thriller, which critics compared approvingly with Carol Reed's *The Third Man* and Alfred Hitchcock's classic *The Lady Vanishes*.

Douglas found it very enjoyable but extremely hard work. He was ill during the two months on location in Italy, running temperatures of 102 and 103 degrees, with the heat and all the mountain climbing involved pulling him down. When he got back to London to finish off the interiors in the late autumn he had lost about a stone in weight and was looking and feeling terrible. The family stayed through the winter in England and the children were put in school.

The accumulation of tension, work, and public duties had reduced him to a condition of nervous exhaustion, and he decided to take one of his rare holidays. Moving his family to Bad Gastein, he tried to relax by taking the cure. At first he felt worse, retired to bed, and started painting again to pass the time. Then, with a little skiing, exercise, and more of the baths, he suddenly started to feel very well indeed, well enough to undertake his combined CARE, Marshall Plan, and fact-finding trip to Vienna, the occasion reported by Louella Parsons. This was interrupted by a report that his second daughter, Victoria, was seriously ill, with a temperature of 104 degrees. The local doctor in Bad Gastein would not believe that penicillin had proved anything yet and refused to administer it. When he finally agreed to use it there was none available, and a supply had to be obtained from the American Army medical stores.

Flying back, Salzburg airfield fogged in, and Douglas and Mary Lee had to return to Vienna and go by train. Mary Lee was already distraught with worry, and when the train stopped in the middle of the night at the Russian Zone border for passengers to show their visas, she was convinced the end had come and that they were all going to be sent to Siberia. Douglas, in the upper bunk, failed to take quite such a serious view of the situation. He found the sight of the little blond Slav soldier, who could not read anyway, looking at their passports upside down in a solemn attempt to check their bona fides so amusing that he collapsed with laughter and was able to offer his wife no comfort at all. However, all was well, and when they rejoined their family Victoria soon recovered.

Although the Fairbanks remain transatlantic commuters, the center of gravity of their life in recent years has moved to London. The idea of continuing with his own production in California became economically impossible, the costs were too high and the gamble was too great. He did not want to risk any further outlay until he saw some return from the two films already on the market. The objection he had to signing a contract and solving all his financial problems still obtained; he stubbornly refused, preferring to adapt his life to suit the times and reduce his actual operations rather than submit to other people's dictates, even though they might be wiser than his.

During 1950 they acquired their present house in The Boltons, although its redecoration and furnishing, and their constant travels, prevented them from taking up residence there until 1952. Until November 1950 they rented a furnished house in Mayfair's Hill Street. Douglas filled in his time by playing the lead in a modest little fantasy called *Mr. Drake's Duck* for an independent producing group headed by Daniel Angel. It was the last full-length feature film in which he has played to date.

It was at the Hill Street house that the Fairbanks first entertained the future Queen Elizabeth II. On his return to England, Douglas had been quietly accepted again into the royal family circle. He and Mary Lee were on particularly intimate terms with the widowed Duchess of Kent, and through her had met again the young heiress to the throne and her husband. Those who rightly base their affection for the members of the royal family on the fact that they so closely reflect the habits and manner of life of their subjects can imagine the pleasure with which its ladies accepted the discreet gifts of nylon stockings which the Fairbanks brought back for them from each visit to the States.

Most members of the royal family are ardent film fans, particularly its younger generation. One evening Douglas learned from Princess Margaret how much she and her sister and the Duke of Edinburgh had enjoyed *The Third Man* and its unique zither background music. Anton Karas, who had composed and played it, was appearing in London at the time, and when Douglas suggested that he might be able to get him around one night, the Princess said she would love to hear him. A small dinner party was arranged for the two princesses and the Duke and, as an added attraction, Douglas asked Noel Coward to join them and sing some of his songs after dinner. The visit was completely private and there was no publicity. If there had been, the Fairbanks might have been spared some of the furore which greeted another similar occasion two years later.

Returning to the United States for six months, the Fairbanks were back in England in the late spring of 1951 for three months to take formal possession of the house in The Boltons. Douglas made every attempt during this period to pursue his professional career in Hollywood, but the only response he obtained was some lavish entertainment and a series of lectures about the impossibility of his attempt to combine two lives. Two projects on which he spent much time and money, *Knights of the Round Table* and *Elephant Walk*, were made subsequently by other companies. It became clear that film production in Britain provided the only possible outlet, and they arranged to let Westridge until the situation clarified.

18

DURING THE POSTWAR YEARS Douglas had succeeded in striking up a very warm relationship with President Truman. It was not
as intimate as his acquaintance with President Roosevelt, but still very
cordial. Every time he was in Washington he called at the White
House, and the original fifteen-minute appointment would always
stretch itself to half or three-quarters of an hour, while they chatted
about everything under the sun, reviewing the world situation, poring
over maps and books, sometimes reminiscing about Fairbanks Senior
and life in general, and then turning back to politics again.

"I think that with the passage of time he will be regarded as one
of the greatest presidents," says Douglas. "He tripped up and lost
prestige in the States by unnecessary outbursts, like standing up for
his daughter, barking at critics and other petty little things. In many
ways he was just Mr. Average-man-in-the-street, but he had tremendous
guts. He knew my affection for F.D.R. and shared this adulation for
his predecessor, and often confessed that he was embarrassed to be
called by the same title. He felt that there was only one Mr. President
and that was F.D.R., and at best he was only a stand-in and an unfortunate substitute. He was always extremely modest about it, and I
found him absolutely enchanting.

"He had an amazing talent for detaching himself from petty an-
noyances and seeing the world picture in the most mature way im-
aginable. He had statistics at his finger tips about the exact degree of
undernourishment in India and the possibilities in the Far East of
applying what was to be known as Point Four—three years before
Point Four had become a reality we were already discussing it. He
had clear ideas about the European refugee situation, the possible
threat of Russia and scores of other subjects. Actually his pro-British
sympathies were probably keener and more honestly pro-British than
F.D.R.'s were. Harry Truman is a very able politician. He doesn't have
F.D.R.'s genius, but he is a man of tremendous character, absolute

honesty and the highest integrity, with a blind loyalty to his personal and official friends. A friend was a friend, whether it was a nation or a person."

The President also thought well of Fairbanks. "The thing I like about young Douglas," he told one of his senior American ambassadors, "is that in all the times I've seen him, he's never asked me for anything for himself. I'm a politician, and it's my business to give things to people who ask for them. He never does; sometimes I wish he would."

That does not mean that Douglas was not ready to champion a friend. At one period Lewis Douglas, then U.S. Ambassador in London, was being subjected to a great deal of press criticism in America for becoming "too pro-British." The President admitted to Fairbanks that he was under strong pressure from some advisers to replace the Ambassador but that "he was still the boss and under no constitutional obligation to accept such advice." Fairbanks interceded vehemently, pointing out that Lewis Douglas not only enjoyed an *entrée* in British politics such as had been accorded to very few of his predecessors, but interpreted the American scene better than had been the case for some years. President Truman soon made it clear to all that the Ambassador was to stay in his post as long as he wished.

On various occasions Douglas received hints from members of the Truman administration that he had his choice of three ambassadorships, which were not named but indicated as being important, or a post as a presidential assistant. He reacted with no particular enthusiasm, as he was conscious that the income problem would enter into it. He had associates and partners, family and obligations, that could not be ignored or reconciled with static responsibilities. He had never considered himself a party man as such and always preferred to regard himself as a free-lance. This, he felt, was the capacity in which he could be most use.

He maintained his contacts in Washington at the highest level. Whenever he returned from Europe he would see General Vandenberg of the Air Force, General Bradley, his friends in the Navy Department, or Paul Hoffman. With each he had many conversations about conditions in the European countries he had visited, but his chief channel as adviser and informant was Admiral Sidney Souers, one of the most influential and quietly self-effacing men in the capital.

Souers, descended from a Louisiana French family, was a St. Louis businessman who served during the war in the U. S. Navy and was one of the few reservists to attain admiral's rank. Douglas had first met him in 1944 when Souers was Assistant Chief of Naval Intelligence for Plans. In 1946, at the request of President Truman, Souers formed and became the first head of the Central Intelligence Agency and then, a year later, organized and became the first executive secretary of its superior instance, the National Security Council. He remained in that position until 1950, continuing as its *éminence grise* and special consultant to President Truman until the Republicans took office in 1953. The National Security Council, an entirely new departure in American political life, was devised as the President's policy-making body in international affairs. It has become perhaps the most powerful and effective component of the executive arm of the U. S. Government. It will perhaps come as a surprise to those Americans who regard Fairbanks as an amiable semi-expatriate, whose chief activity has been to sponsor European interests in the United States, to learn how highly Souers thought of his services to this body.

For six years, from 1946–52, Souers would see Douglas or receive lengthy written reports from him a score of times a year: "I found Douglas very helpful and had him advise me on matters of psychological strategy. He was always interested in the welfare of the United States, and as he traveled abroad he made reports to me periodically from all parts of Europe. They were based upon intimate associations, and were always of a character which, if acted upon, would tend to better the relations of our country with these other countries.

"I always assumed that a volunteer of that sort never went out with instructions, because if he did, he himself would be an agent, and I tried to protect Douglas' position abroad. He would have been in a different category as an agent of the U.S. in his dealings with these other countries or the prominent people in them. So while we would have general discussions before each trip, I always tried to maintain his status as a volunteer, who simply would make suggestions as he went around the foreign dignitaries of ideas which might be helpful to us.

"He has done a lot to cement Anglo-American relations, but at no time did I ever have the feeling in doing so he was ever anything but a good United States citizen and that the U.S. came first. He felt that U.S. interests were best protected by close Anglo-American relations, and there was no question of a conflict of loyalties, even though his relationship with the British was very good and very close. To show him too close to the British angle is not fair to him as a U.S. citizen, because he is both. And that's why I think he can be so valuable.

"He was able to talk frankly at all times, and then have his views and the information made available directly, or almost directly, through me, to the President of the United States. He was highly respected and constructive, because his approach to all problems is constructive. I always passed on his views to the President as they stood, because he thought highly of Douglas as a patriotic American and thought he was a good, smart, fine fellow, despite the fact that he was the son of a great man. He was also an outstanding man himself and he always welcomed the actual report. I usually gave it to him without summarizing or condensing it in any way. I would talk about it with him a few minutes and he always welcomed its receipt."

These reports would touch on the most diverse subjects—the effect of individual American diplomatic *démarches* in the various European countries and the degree of acceptance of her representatives; penetrating summaries of foreign reaction to world events, constructive criticisms of current propaganda campaigns and suggestions for improving this important weapon in the Cold War; economic information, and, always, the running verbal interchange of fact and opinion with the highest dignitaries in each country. Most of the latter, of course, has never been put on record, but the participants always knew that Fairbanks could be relied upon to use the information they gave him only to the best advantage. The unique confidence thus reposed in him makes it impossible to refer in greater detail to this aspect of his work, as otherwise the basic premise of its continuance would be removed. Fairbanks operates at a very high level, and as this is his greatest service, it is only proper that his capacity to do so should not be diminished by a breach in security.

One example can be given of his constant endeavor to placate Anglo-American asperities, in the personal part he played during the awkward period while the problem of the Allied naval command in the Mediterranean was being debated. Fairbanks knew both Admiral Lord Mountbatten and Admiral Carney well. General Lord Ismay, another close friend, who had recently been appointed the first secretary-general of the North Atlantic Treaty Organization, had several discussions on the subject with Douglas and invited him to help, unofficially, in bridging some of the gaps. Certain American officials felt that Britain was in Egypt and the Sudan for purely selfish interests, indulging in her usual "infamous colonizing act." The British considered that the Middle East was one of the most vital sectors in the world for Anglo-American co-operation and that the responsibility must be shared if an Allied command was to function effectively.

Douglas went to work interpreting not only the American view to Mountbatten and to government officials in London, but also, through the U.S. naval attaché in London, Rear Admiral Neil Dietrich, the U.S. Ambassador and members of his staff, the reasons for the seeming intransigence of the British. Whenever he had opportunity he would discuss the matter with Anthony Eden and check, through Admiral Sidney Souers in Washington, with President Truman, and with Admiral Forrest Sherman, at that time U.S. Naval Chief of Staff, and the head of the Intelligence Division, Admiral Felix Johnson. In the end, relations between the two Mediterranean admirals became extremely cordial, and although it would be idle to pretend that Fairbanks made any but a minor contribution, it was another example of the honest-broker role he delights in playing.

It is incorrect to assume that he has spent a disproportionate amount of his time propagandizing Britain in the United States. Although his activities in reverse have not been so publicized they are, in the aggregate, about equal. He admires Britain's political stability and flexibility, the country's gentleness and strength, consciously moving forward by reminding themselves of their past roots. On the other hand, he would like to see British acceptance or adoption of America's social liberality and equality, technical ingenuity, mass resourcefulness and vitality. He feels that the political ideal of both these communities, stemming from the same source, lies between the two extremes. He shares the belief that if they found a basic *modus vivendi* they could be a great and constructive force for peaceful progress, greater than any other which might challenge or threaten them. He has written, spoken, talked, and worked in Britain to present and promote the best and generally most admirable facets of American life and ideas, and it has always seemed easier to persuade the British public of American virtues than to present the British case in the United States.

The U. S. Government has frequently requested his unofficial or, as the case might be, official assistance, in persuading or influencing the British on various points of mutual interest. He in no way envisages an exclusively Anglo-American world. This would not only be impracticable but, with America so heterogeneous in origin, unacceptable. Nevertheless, the main thread of his ceaseless round of work still joins the two countries he has made his home. The variety of his more overt activities is prodigious.

In December 1950 he was elected to the National Board of Directors of the United States branch of the English-Speaking Union, and when King George VI died, Douglas was one of the original sponsors, with William Griffin, its chairman, and, incidentally, another honorary K.B.E., of the American King George VI Memorial Fund. This has no direct connection with the British fund of the same name, and has been set up to endow "Rhodes Scholarships in reverse" at American technical colleges. The intention is to place fifty scholars a year, with bursaries of three thousand dollars to cover their return fare, subsistence, and sufficient excursions around the United States to see something of the life of the people. The sum of five hundred thousand dollars has already been raised.

After one of the meetings Douglas addressed on behalf of the English-Speaking Union, he was being besieged by autograph hunters.

Griffin knew he had spent a very busy day and must have been tired. So he sought out Mrs. Fairbanks and said: "Mary Lee, don't you think we ought to break this thing up and bring Douglas home?"—"What is he doing, Bill?"—"He's giving out autographs."—"Oh!" said Mary Lee, "don't do that; Douglas says that once people stop asking for his autograph he's through."

Griffin is a warm admirer of Fairbanks. The two first met through Lord Wakehurst, a great friend of them both, who was at that time Chairman of the Commonwealth branch of the E.S.U. and later became Governor of Northern Ireland. Lord Wakehurst is also Prior of the Order of St. John of Jerusalem, another of the organizations to whose work Douglas devotes much of his time. In true Fairbanks fashion, his interest was further intrigued by its historical origins. He has from time to time made suggestions that its scope should be extended to other countries, with its members forming an international confraternity, to revive something of the ancient spirit of chivalry in which it was founded.

He is actively interested in the possibility of establishing the order in the United States. At first it was not feasible, as the main features of its activities were already duplicated in the U.S. by other organizations. But there is considerable American interest in maintaining the organization's hospital in Jerusalem, which has existed for nine hundred odd years and is now threatened with extinction. Its maintenance is important because of the political position in the Middle East, where Westerners are no longer regarded with great admiration and where the rivalries are so intense. Douglas is one of those who feels it advisable, particularly from the standpoint of Christian duty and philanthropy, to keep the flag of the order flying over an establishment which stands above politics, race, or religion and exists only to help the unfortunate. The hospital, which was badly damaged during the Jewish-Arab war, has to be rebuilt, and it has at its command the finest doctors in the world for eye diseases. Arrangements involve negotiation with the University of Beirut, the Israeli Government, the Jordan Government, in all of which Douglas has played his part. Now he is seeking a charter from the State Department for the incorporation of the St. John organization in the United States, otherwise Americans cannot contribute and deduct that contribution from their income tax.

In January 1951 he was host at Westridge to Lord and Lady Wakehurst. With Douglas' romantic conception of the work and scope of the St. John organization, it is possible to guess the origin of a long memorandum which reached several of his friends and court officials a fortnight later. Nominally the work of an anonymous committee, it was called "Notes on the Future Functioning of the British Monarchy," and it has served as a basis of discussion, even as high as the Privy Council, ever since.

"In order for the British Monarchy to become a more positive institution, both at home and abroad, and still remain aloof from the ebbs and tides of party politics, it must enlarge its mystic meaning," was the theme. "This element, which has been its best value in the recent past, could evolve even more formidably in the future. The greater exploitation of what the monarchy has come to mean since the birth of the Arthurian Legends (i.e. the Fount of all Honor, the Guarantor of the People's Rights, the Bond that Unites, etc.) is the best of all springboards for the future. For example, it could very well become a sort of 'Papacy of Western Democracy' (anachronistic as that may at first sound), the repository of Western Constitutional progress, the 'Fount of Honor,' not only for British achievements but for contributions of distinction from all Western civilization—regardless of origin, the headship of a vast international fraternity and such other identities as would actively increase its general influence and desirability.

"A form of super-Nobel prize system, for outstanding international contributions to Science, Medicine, Literature, Music and the Arts, Industry, Sociology, could be evolved. The purely British Honors' List would not, of course, be interfered with. It would be an entirely separate and distinct activity, with recommendations for awards being made by recognized groups all over the world. Whereas Nobel prizes are given by the Swedish King on behalf of the Nobel Foundation, these awards could be on behalf of Humanity and Civilization, as represented in their most ancient, yet modern, champion—Britain— and presented by its centuries-old symbol—the Monarch."

It was suggested that the Order of St. John, in view of its international origins, might be a vehicle for this universal honors' list. Various reasons make this impractical, but some of the other suggestions attracted closer attention, particularly this passage (written, it should be recalled, in 1951): "The pre-war Canadian visit and the more recent South African tour show the increasing importance of keeping the Throne more closely identified with the Dominions, as opposed to keeping it exclusively a United Kingdom institution— only nominally belonging to the Commonwealth. The periodic shift of the seat of Imperial authority would tend to link the Dominions ever closer together and to disabuse any possible latent feeling of dependency or inferiority, conceivably leading to ideas of secession."

Like most of the people identified, not necessarily politically but in terms of activity, with the Roosevelt and Truman administrations, Douglas does not enjoy quite the same entrée in Washington now that the Republicans are in power, despite the fact that almost a year before the presidential election he was exchanging letters with General Eisenhower, with whom he has been on cordial terms since the war years in North Africa, urging him to stand and offering his support. On December 20, 1951, before the Eisenhower-for-President boom started, the general wrote Douglas a long, friendly, and thoughtful letter in which he discussed fully and from the heart the position in which he found himself. Although the President does not feel able at the present time to release its text for publication it must in due course find a place in the definitive Eisenhower biography. One phrase which reveals no secrets and reflects pleasantly his opinion of Douglas reads ". . . our country needs dedicated men—among these I include you."

Douglas had also kept in touch with Adlai Stevenson, and received a letter from him a few weeks later, saying: "There is another point with respect to Ike that the newspaper men in Washington do not overlook: the preponderance of isolationists in the leadership of the Senate and the House who would be more powerful politically than the General. How to evaluate these things I don't personally know, and all I am interested in is running for Governor of Illinois again."

On the second point Stevenson was proved wrong, but Douglas came to share his opinion on the first. In the end he took no part in the campaign, as it was indicated that his known internationalist views might prove a liability.

In any case, the time had come to carry out extensive repairs to the Fairbanks' financial fences. During his three months in England in 1951 he had made an investment in a joint production venture with Daniel Angel of *Another Man's Poison,* with Bette Davis. The film found little favor in Britain but did quite well in the States, where it was distributed by United Artists.

During the winter of 1951–52 in the States, Douglas appeared in a radio serial called *The Silent Men* for the National Broadcasting Company and commenced the long and protracted series of negotiations which resulted in his undertaking the production in England of a series of short-story films, partly for British and European cinemas and partly for American television. This was still his main professional interest at the time this book was written. The Fairbankses returned to England in March 1952 to make the first pilot film in this project and have remained in London, with very brief intervals, ever since.

Their first pleasure was to take up residence in their new home in The Boltons. Like Westridge, it had been a bargain. It is too large for most people to manage in London these days, and the previous owner, the Duke of Leeds, had sold them the freehold for £12,500. Restored to mint condition, it is a handsome home.

Within a month they had been burgled twice and had entertained Margaret Truman, the President's daughter, during her visit to England. Douglas wrote to tell her father how he hoped she had enjoyed herself and how delighted they had been to have her. "I appreciate most highly your courtesies to Magie," came the reply, and then, with one of the salty phrases which have made the President such an endearing character: "Of course a letter such as yours swells an old father up like a pizened pup."

The Fairbankses have a genius for quiet, easy hospitality, and it is one of the few homes with a true salon atmosphere left in London. "You would think Douglas was a guest at his own parties," sighs Mary Lee, who has to do most of the work, but his unaffected enjoyment is infectious. He is a human catalyst who can make the most diverse personalities enjoy airing their differences. Many a time he will adopt the viewpoint of one or the other to get the conversational ball rolling and then sit quietly by as the discussion warms up. The amount of air he has cleared over the years in this way must be prodigious.

His friends chaff him about one personal peculiarity, saying he is the only man they have ever known who has not the faintest knowledge of food. "You can put a shoe in front of him and he'll eat it," says one intimate. "He'll tell you he's found a wonderful restaurant, and you go and it's the worst food you've ever had in your life. He has no idea and doesn't care about it at all. He claims he's very observant, follows everything and doesn't miss a trick, but at coffee in the living room I've asked him what he had for dinner and he hasn't the faintest idea. It doesn't interest him at all."

It is a pity, for Mary Lee is a good cook. By August 1952 the newspaper columnists were already referring to her as "the London hostess with the mostes' on the ball," saying she relied on "fish, lobsters, salad and cold salmon, with Virginia ham sent from home, plus real Boston baked beans." Three months later they had another event to talk about.

19

QUEEN ELIZABETH II came to dinner at The Boltons on November 19, 1952. For months afterward newspaper columnists on both sides of the Atlantic speculated how a movie actor had succeeded in effecting this particular piece of social legerdemain. They overlooked the long record of Fairbanks' twenty-year acquaintance with the British royal family, and also the pertinent fact that no one asks the Queen to dinner. She asks herself.

While The Boltons house was being made ready for occupation various members of the royal family would ask the Fairbanks, when they saw them, how the work was progressing. The Queen Mother took a lively interest, as did old Queen Mary, who was always ready with advice about the best antique dealers and how to decorate it. When the work was completed the new Queen, with pleasant memories of her visit to Hill Street before her accession, indicated to the Fairbankses at one of the receptions they attended that she would like to see it some time. Later, her equerry, Group Captain Peter Townsend, intimated to Douglas that a definite suggestion would probably be acceptable. Shortly afterward, Mary Lee had occasion to mention that if Her Majesty would care to see their new house they would be honored to have her do so.

The Queen, in the absence of the Duke of Edinburgh in Malta, suggested alternative dates, one of which was the eve of the anniversary of the royal wedding, by which time the Duke would have returned to London. It was arranged that the dinner party should be restricted to a few intimates and that other mutual friends should be invited in after dinner. The list was submitted to the palace and the form of after-dinner entertainment left to Mary Lee's discretion.

Douglas had learned that the Queen and Princess Margaret were keenly interested in American Negro folk music and a suggestion was made that Cab Calloway and a small group from the production of *Porgy and Bess,* which was playing in London at the time, might be asked to come in and sing. However, Douglas, wise in the ways of the theater "grapevine" system, feared that news of the dinner would be divulged and he canceled the proposal. He was particularly anxious to avoid all publicity and keep the party as private as possible—indeed, even the cook and the butler were not informed of the identity of the guest of honor until an hour before her arrival. The best precaution was to let as few people as possible into the secret, so Douglas wrote a registered note to his father's old friend, Maurice Chevalier, in Paris, asking if he would come in after dinner and sing some of his songs. The great French artist was delighted to agree, on the mutual understanding that the invitation was to be kept strictly confidential.

What had been conceived as a purely private party for old acquaintances of long standing was magnified by the envious, the curious, and the malicious into a social furore of the first order. The suggestion was bruited, by people who knew quite enough about court protocol to recognize its inherent untruth, that the Queen had participated unwillingly in an invitation arranged between Douglas and the Duke of Edinburgh, described as an old wartime colleague in the Mediterranean, although in fact at that time they had hardly met. Newspaper columnists, only too quick to prick bubbles of their own devising, wrote that the Queen had taken offense at finding "a crowd outside the Fairbanks' gate on her arrival," "had sat in stiff annoyance during the whole evening," and "had left as soon as she could." Fairbanks was excoriated on both sides of the Atlantic for perpetrating a major social *gaffe* and was accused of giving the news to the press for personal publicity purposes—a movie actor, it was inferred, could not be expected to know better.

This version was manifestly absurd and wildly inaccurate. The first leak to the press came on the day of the party, when one of the younger and gayer guests was indiscreet enough to mention it to an acquaintance on the staff of a London evening paper. Eighteen months later the reporter in question apologized to Fairbanks for the unfortunate results of his paragraph, although the real offenders were those who subsequently picked up the story and embroidered it out of all recognition.

As a result of this paragraph there were about a dozen people standing outside the house in the pelting rain as the Queen arrived, the inevitable *flâneurs,* who seem to have nothing better to do in life but to gawp at royalty, on or off duty. The Queen spent a happy and relaxed evening among her young friends, all of whom she knew, with the exception of Mary Lee's mother, who was staying in the house and put in a brief appearance before dinner. Far from leaving at the earliest possible moment or even at her normal latest hour of midnight, it was nearly 2.30 A.M. before the Duke of Edinburgh reminded her that they had to get up again at half-past seven.

At midnight one of the press agencies had rung up to confirm the Queen's presence. After obtaining permission, Douglas answered in the affirmative and this report was carried in the social calendar of the London *Times* the next morning.

In the storm of comment that followed, Douglas must have thought sometimes of the old Scots motto that hangs in his private "pub" at Westridge—"Ye canna baith be grand and comfortable." For a man who has spent his whole life in a blaze of publicity, he is extraordinarily sensitive to adverse personal criticisms. This does not apply to critiques of his acting, which he takes in his stride, but when the motives of his private and public activities are questioned he still winces, and this time the general reaction really hurt.

The tight little enclave of Mayfair society, in which he moves freely, but which, all suggestions to the contrary, he does not necessarily admire—his friendships are much broader and more personal—chose to behave at its most waspish. A very prominent ambassadress was said to be outraged that the Queen had chosen to dine privately in an American household before honoring her own. In fact, the Queen had accepted invitations to several private English houses since her accession, and these had been reported without any adverse comment resulting. In the Fairbanks' case, envy and, presumably, total ignorance of the background that had made it possible, reinforced the suggestion that the Queen had been more or less tricked into attending the dinner, and for several months Douglas found himself cold-shouldered. It is extraordinary how an attitude of this sort can spread. His name was studiously omitted from the list of those attending the social and charitable functions reported on by the snob magazines and many of his own compatriots, especially the less well-disposed newspaper columnists and a number of his old California colleagues, sought to justify two baffled decades of prejudice at his social success and public activities by inferring that he had overstepped the mark and had at long last received his deserved quietus.

Certain members of the "Mayfair Set" would nod and pass on while it was believed he had lost royal favor, and then switched to warm and hearty greetings and exchanges when the rumors reversed themselves. This attitude did not catch Fairbanks unawares. It was too like his varying reception in Hollywood where even old friendships availed him nothing if his films had not been successful, but where he was swamped with social and business proposals if the latest box-office reports were encouraging. New York and Washington are no less sensitive to changing winds and the presumed evidence of influence than is London. Full awareness of these fickle judgments has not embittered

Douglas, but it did wound his natural good feeling, and has made him more suspicious about the loyalties of all but the most responsible of his friends and contacts.

"In London's bridge games a Fairbanks is a name for a hand full of kings and queens," wrote one New York wit. Most of his colleagues preferred the bludgeon. Their error lay in supposing that actors and royalty have nothing in common. On the contrary, the anonymous mass adulation to which they are both subjected provides a background of mutual experience. Nor should the compliment thus bestowed on Fairbanks lend credence to the opinion that he is motivated by snobbery. Both he and his father acquired that type of celebrity which is as much sought after as seeking.

Much play has always been made on Fairbanks' alleged predilection for friends in "society." In fact, he has relatively few. Whether in London, New York, Philadelphia, Washington, Paris, Rome, or wherever it may be, "society" as such is not anything of which he is particularly fond or which he admires very much. He does have certain friends who fall into this category, but for the most part they represent only part of a general pattern. He has no great respect for those who neither toil nor spin; he has worked too hard himself. He does share his father's taste for historical freaks, unusual personalities, scoundrels, wits, or those who, for some reason or another, have a specialized knowledge or ability concerned with something he is interested in. But his real friends are a motley, unpigeonholed group, with no definable class, nationality, or interest—beyond the qualities of good fellowship and loyalty.

His position was soon restored by deliberate gestures on the part of the royal family, particularly the continued staunch friendship of the Duchess of Kent and the unwavering loyalty of the Mountbattens. In the following winter, when the Fairbankses attended the wedding in Edinburgh of the Earl of Dalkeith, son of their old friends the Buccleuchs, to Miss Jane MacNeill, they were still sufficiently shaken by the pounding they had received to keep away from their fellow guests, the Queen and the Duke of Edinburgh. However, Prince Philip saw them, pushed his way through the crowd to shake their hands, and said in a loud voice, for all those around to hear: "What's all this; are you trying to avoid me?"

The Fairbankses were also the only non-official American couple to receive an invitation from the Queen, through the Lord Chamberlain, to attend her Coronation in Westminster Abbey. At the reception in Buckingham Palace, the Queen and the Duke seemed to make a deliberate point of first walking past the Fairbankses and then turning back to come and talk to them for several minutes. The other members of the royal family followed suit.

Today their prestige is largely restored, although as recently as the spring of 1954 one American columnist chose to report that "Fairbanks and the royal family have cooled," ignoring the fact that they dined with Princess Margaret a few evenings later and that the Queen and the Duke of Edinburgh were twelve thousand miles away in Australia.

Fairbanks is singularly sensitive to these slights, and harbors a sense of injustice against certain acquaintances and sections of the press in both Britain and America. As a result of the public flurry over his social activities, he and Mary Lee have somewhat restricted the hospitality for which they had become known. Aside from the exigencies of his arduous working schedule, they have for the past eighteen months limited themselves to a quiet dinner of a few friends about once a month. At a dance given in the summer of 1954 at the American Embassy, Douglas felt obliged to decline the Ambassador's suggestion that he dance with Princess Margaret. He explained his fear of a revival of the now familiar caustic comments and kept himself in the background during the whole evening. He has become almost over self-conscious about his position and has taken temporary refuge in the vast amount of work involved in his latest production venture.

The autumn of 1952 saw the inception of the television film enterprise which is now Fairbanks' chief professional interest. The provision of entertainment for the myriad home screens which have become almost an essential article of furniture in every American household, and are becoming to almost an equal extent a new social factor in the European countries, is a problem which Hollywood has yet to solve.

The principal duty of the major film studios continues to be the supply of programs to the cinema distributors who provide the income for the whole industry. Although in due course some form of combination with the television giant is the only solution to its insatiable demands and the new crisis of competition in the movie world, no one has yet worked out the exact pattern of that co-operation.

Of those who have sought to adapt the old technique to the new medium, Douglas Fairbanks is one of the leaders. His excursions into straight film production since the war had, with one or two exceptions, not been particularly successful, but the possibility of making shorter feature films, each telling a coherent story and lasting about thirty minutes, in order to meet the exigencies of television programs, seemed to provide an outlet. Physical facilities limit the number of "live" shows that can be rehearsed and produced for a single or repeat performance on television. The filming of a show makes it possible to present any number of repeats. There will shortly be something of the order of a thousand transmitters across the vast expanse of the United States, the majority linked in networks, but a considerable proportion independent. Many of them have been obliged to fill their programs by showing old films, the only productions the studios are prepared to release for the purpose. The gap can only be made good, to the satisfaction of viewers, by making films exclusively for television showing, and this is what Fairbanks, together with several competitors, set out to do.

For him there was yet another consideration. During the course of his close contact and many conversations with Paul Hoffman, he had talked of the possibility of making such films in Europe. It was agreed that the easiest place to begin would be in England. They would provide employment in a British industry hag-ridden with recurrent crises, make use of vacant studio space, call on a vast reserve of acting talent, and help to implement the fundamental conception of the Marshall Plan—the encouragement of "Trade not Aid" between the countries of the Western world. Handsome sums in dollars would accrue to the British treasury, and would in their turn serve to pay for British imports from the United States. To Fairbanks the operation presented a practical example of the ideals of Anglo-American co-operation he had always cherished.

The problems of financing and production were and continue to be extremely complicated. American television being run on an entirely commercial basis, the first essential was to find a suitable sponsor. After negotiations lasting over a year, Douglas finally reached an agreement with Philip Liebmann, president of Rheingold Beer, to back a large part of the project. The National Broadcasting Company provided the rest of the finance and national distribution.

A major television "series" in the United States usually consists of thirty-nine programs, covering nine months of the year. Although the sums expended on advertising by such corporations in America are vast, the money is spent with a keen eye on results, and the cost of the organization providing the entertainment has to be pared down to the last penny. Moreover, the possibilities of return are infinitely more limited than the chance fortunes that may be earned by films that find favor in cinemas. Each television film has to be made to a set budget, and although their residual earnings, when sold subsequently to other sponsors, provide additional income, this will always remain at a modest level.

Very few major film studios now produce as many as thirty-nine features a year. The Fairbanks television films, and others of their type, are only a third the length, but many of the problems remain the same. Thirty-nine stories must be found and screen plays written, thirty-nine casts assembled, thirty-nine combinations of scenery built, thirty-nine complete musical scores composed, and thirty-nine combinations of footage cut and assembled.

Financial considerations impose a limit of not more than twenty-five thousand dollars to be spent on each picture. Some may cost less, depending on the story; some must cost more. If the imperative demands of a weekly show and the necessary overheads are to be met, each has to be made in not more than five days. This places a degree of strain on directors, camera crews, set builders, studio carpenters, laboratory technicians, and all the essential members of a production group, which only the most rigid organization can overcome. Fairbanks has now made two such series (the second group having replaced N.B.C. with another set of backers), and has nearly completed a third, appearing in one film in four himself and supervising the over-all production. It is hardly surprising that over the last two years he has reduced himself to a state of near nervous exhaustion and has had to cut his outside activities to an absolute minimum.

He gives employment at the National Studios in Boreham Wood, near Elstree, the modern and superbly equipped group of stages he leases, to more than four hundred people. Two films are made at a time. Each series has been completed in about five months, and he is now trying to keep his highly trained group of technicians together by accepting outside contracts of a similar nature. Television reproduction rights in the second and third series of seventy-eight films have been sold for nearly two hundred thousand pounds to Associated Rediffusion Limited, the British commercial television giant due to commence operations in August 1955, and Fairbanks is being pressed to continue his activities on an expanding transatlantic basis.

Some of Douglas' friends in the commercial world are apt to describe him as a poor businessman. In fact, he has inherited a good share of his father's acumen. His judgment is perhaps more erratic and less dependable, and he tends to concentrate on problems as a whole and gloss over the details. However, he has the good sense to seek out and abide by loyal advice. His own desk is usually a disordered mess, but he insists on orderliness and precision in others. One trait he has inherited from Fairbanks Senior is his inability to fire anyone. He will do anything to avoid it, even to the extent of maintaining lame ducks on the payroll. He admits to being a moral coward, who hates scenes and has great trouble telling unpleasant truths. It is a fault with its compensations. He inspires, for the film world, an extraordinary degree of loyalty in those who work for him. There is a family-party atmosphere and a complete absence of backbiting at his studio, which must be almost unique in the industry.

The shows have a high professional polish and have the highest Nielsen and Hooper ratings for productions of their type in America, although *Time* magazine could not resist commenting that this "was overshadowed by the glossy commercials delivered in pear-shaped tones by Douglas Fairbanks, Jr., himself, including asides on the Magna Carta and the American Revolution, and the suggestion that the international set is rapidly abandoning pink champagne in favor of the more dizzying delights of Rheingold Beer." In the summer of 1954, the series won the *Billboard* magazine annual TV film-award election.

Only the experience of a lifetime could carry Fairbanks through the grueling schedule involved. The actual record of a day picked at random while engaged in the making of these films reads like the combined output of a whole office staff.

He left The Boltons at seven-thirty, as he does every morning, and during the forty-minute drive to the studios scanned a dozen newspapers, made notes for a speech he had been asked to make later in the week at a city dinner, marked correspondence for his secretary, and found time to exchange quips with his gigantic Irish chauffeur, Hogan.

This particular day was one of the five set aside for shooting a wartime story called *International Settlement,* in which he played the part of an American airman who crash-lands on an isolated Pacific atoll inhabited by a small polyglot community totally ignorant of the conflict in progress.

In the pauses between a full day's shooting schedule, wearing work for everyone else engaged, he found time for this kaleidoscope of activity:

Ten o'clock: Visited the adjoining stage to check on the progress of a simultaneous production, *Leave to Die,* with Yvonne Mitchell and Ram Gopal, stopping to speak a few words of encouragement to a very cold little Indian actress in a subordinate part, who was shivering in a sari amidst the wintry drafts.

Ten-fifteen: Called to the cutting room to give his advice on a synchronization problem in another completed production.

Ten-thirty: Viewed the rushes of the previous day's scenes in both current films, and, while sitting in the dark, took a telephone call from his London business office to settle a finance query.

Eleven o'clock: Called back to his own set for a further short scene.

Eleven-twenty: Returned to the studio cinema to pass judgment on the first rough version of another production, *Ship's Doctor*.

Twelve o'clock: Back for the last morning shot on his own set, after a delay of ten minutes while he dictated a cable in answer to a query about a business deal from "Chummy" MacDonald, his partner in Hollywood.

Twelve-thirty: Another glance at *Leave to Die*, interrupted by the arrival from the London office of his associates, Harold Huth and Peter Marriott.

During lunch, from one-fifteen to two-fifteen, at a side table in his office, telephone calls, production problems, casting difficulties, a lamb chop, and a glass of milk all competed for his attention.

Two-fifteen: Spent a quarter of an hour in the projection room to give an opinion on a new back-projection system evolved by one of his assistant cameramen.

Two-thirty: Sat through another completed film, *Second Wind*, to give final approval before air-freighting the print to New York.

Three-fifteen: Back on his own set to deal with a sheaf of correspondence brought by his secretary from London. This included a letter requesting him to perform further services as one of the fifteen original sponsors of the Cordell Hull Foundation Fund, reports from the American Relief for Korea, a request that he write an article on the Duke of Edinburgh for a group of American papers, and a personal letter of good wishes in her own handwriting from María de Borbón, Countess of Barcelona, wife of the Spanish Pretender.

Against the infernal racket of carpenters setting up the next scene, the director lining up the camera crew, and electricians remounting lights, Fairbanks, in full make-up, dictated the answers. These included a long memorandum on the fund proposals, intricate administrative directions to the Relief for Korea officials, and a flat negative to the request for an article.

Three-forty-five: Took part in a further scene, called away twice to the telephone to deal with laboratory and copyright problems.

Four-forty-five: Another check on the *Leave to Die* set.

Five o'clock: Last shot of the day. Retired with his leading lady,

Mary Parker, and one of the assistant directors to an office to rehearse dialogue for the next day.

Between six and seven o'clock, while slowly peeling off his costume and make-up, his dressing room was thronged with associates and directors. They had a problem with *Leave to Die,* which looked as if it would run three minutes short. After various solutions had been bandied about, Fairbanks himself came up with the unanimously agreed suggestion that Ram Gopal should insert one of his Indian dances at a pertinent point in the action.

At any time during the day his whooping guffaw could be heard enlivening the routine. When he was not cheerfully encouraging Mary Parker, whose first film this was, he was exchanging jokes with the property men, helping to make running revisions of the script, darting off to talk to visitors on the set or checking through the continuity girl's minutely recorded timetable of the day's activities. Through it all he himself never fluffed a line or caused a retake. When he finds time to learn his part no one knows, but sometimes his stand-in, Steve Donohue, has a blackboard ready to refresh his memory.

Something of the gifts of personality which make these protean activities possible can be detected even in such a single day: the ease and grace of manner, the mid-Atlantic tone of the quietly modulated voice, the invariable impression of undivided interest in what the person to whom he is speaking has to say, the spontaneous chaffing of clapper-boy and distinguished visitor, the felicity of expression and the amazing facility for pertinent comment on the bewildering variety of subjects which come his way. In contrast, there erupt a boyish enthusiasm and an almost disconcerting penchant for practical jokes and slapstick byplay.

The forty-minute drive home found him again poring over papers out of a six-inch-thick brief case, the contents of which often keep him up until the small hours. That night was an exception. The Duchess of Kent was coming in quietly to play Scrabble with the family.

In his attempt to build up the situation of financial independence which will enable him to devote his time more fully to his public

work, Fairbanks is associated with several other companies. The Fairbanks Company, which made *The Exile* and *The Fighting O'Flynn,*
went through a difficult period when these films were slow to earn
their outlay, but is now in a healthy position again. In order to keep
their financial obligations separate, another American company, the
Dougfair Corporation, was formed to make television films in America
and has produced a highly successful series based on the American
strip-cartoon characters known as *Terry and the Pirates.* Douglas has
also formed a partnership with the American film magnate, Sol Lesser,
called Odyssey Pictures, to synchronize and reissue for television and
the ordinary cinema market, the films of Douglas Fairbanks, Sr., to
which Douglas and Lesser now hold exclusive rights, having bought
out the interests of his stepmother, Sylvia, and the other beneficiaries of
the senior Fairbanks' will. Yet another organization called Cellini
Films, formed with Sol Lesser's brother, Irving, buys the distribution
rights in the United States of foreign-language films.

Fairbanks is also acquiring other business interests outside the film
world. He admits rather sheepishly to a substantial share in a highly
successful popcorn enterprise in Britain and is also connected with the
manufacture of prefabricated houses, clothing and shoes. Through
existing business associates he is proposing to enter the Middle East
oil industry, and a tour in that area during the autumn of 1954 included
a stay of a week in Turkey at the invitation of President Bayar, which
gave full play to his penchant for high-level discussions.

Professional ties have not abated the Fairbanks' appetite for extracurricular activities. His hospitality continues its welcoming though
more careful course. When Winthrop Aldrich arrived in London as
American Ambassador to the Court of St. James's, the Fairbankses
were still cowering from the furore caused by their entertainment of the
Queen. The new Ambassador, who had known Douglas with increasing intimacy since he was a young man, sent word that the first dinner
he would permit to be given in his honor after his official arrival in
London was to be at The Boltons. In his first contacts, Mr. Aldrich
did not want for suggestions that this might be an impolitic gesture in
view of the feeling about the Fairbankses at the time, especially in

America, but these he brushed aside with some asperity, saying that if that was the case there was all the more reason for his showing his confidence in an old friend. He and Mrs. Aldrich have been frequent guests since.

When Prince Bernhard of the Netherlands paid a recent visit to the United States, he spent several days inspecting U. S. Air Force and naval air units in the neighborhood of Los Angeles. It was never announced that he was staying, at Douglas' invitation, at Westridge, conveniently vacant between two tenants. It is a not unamusing comment on the abundance of American life that when the Prince arrived in a car provided by his service hosts, he saw three or four handsome coupés in the Fairbanks' drive and assumed that Douglas' usual hospitality included the provision of transport. It was only when he dismissed the official car that he discovered he was stranded. One of the coupés belonged to the cook, another to the colored charwoman, a third to the gardener-caretaker, and the fourth to the hired butler.

Fairbanks can arrange more small services for his highly placed friends over the telephone than most men could in a week of negotiations. When the carpet Queen Mary had embroidered was on its tour of North America, a sudden crisis arose when the local committee could find no place in Los Angeles in which to display this example of royal needlework. The ideal setting would have been the civic museum, but the trustees had decided that it would be against regulations to permit such an exhibition. The British Consul-General, Sir Robert Hadow, had only one recourse, to ring up Fairbanks. Within a couple of hours the necessary permission was forthcoming.

More recently the Fairbankses were fellow guests with the Winthrop Aldriches and David Bowes-Lyon, the Queen Mother's brother, at a house party given in Drumlanrig Castle by the Duke and Duchess of Buccleuch, at the time of the Edinburgh Festival. The Ambassador was extremely anxious to see the Scottish Command Tattoo held under the frowning crag of the castle. On the only evening he had free he was patron at a performance given by the American Ballet, and in spite of urgent inquiries through the American Consul in Edinburgh, the Duchess had found it impossible to obtain tickets for any but the first performance of the Tattoo, which clashed with the ballet. Learning of the difficulties, Douglas started manipulating the telephone. "Och, Duggie, don't worry, we'll fix it," was the answer reported by a witness in the Scottish Command offices. "The Ambassador shall have the royal box on the second performance on the night he wants to come."

The Coronation period found Douglas in his element. "Hallo, old cock, did you have a good rehearsal? Hope you didn't drop anything," a casual visitor to his house might have heard him say, somewhat cryptically, on the telephone one morning before the great event. Subsequent inquiry elicited the fact that he was talking to one of his close personal friends in the royal household who was going to be responsible for carrying part of the Queen's priceless regalia. "I saw some friends who talked to Jimmy the other day," the conversation went on. "The old boy's very put out at not hearing a word from anyone." The "Jimmy" referred to was the Duke of Alba (and of Berwick in the peerage of the United Kingdom) whose name had been overlooked in the Coronation invitations, an omission which was quickly put right.

This is the sort of thing that goes on all the time. No man in the world has such contacts, and his services are always at the disposal of any of them if he can thereby be of the slightest assistance; nor does he hesitate to elicit their help in any project he considers worth while. It should not be supposed that his help is confined to the great. Humbler acquaintances find him a constant friend in need, providing introductions to possible employers, and finding time to deal with a myriad casual inquiries.

Some of his campaigns are greeted with tolerant amusement by his friends. During an earlier visit to the Edinburgh Festival he had noticed that the famous Scots Greys were not back in full-dress uniform and still wore the drab wartime khaki. For a couple of years, whenever occasion offered, he badgered friends to do something about it, telling Sir Alexander Maxwell, head of the British Travel Association, that a possible tourist attraction was being disregarded, pestering friends in the Army, bringing up the subject with Cabinet ministers, and even mentioning it to King George VI, so that it became something of a private joke between them. For a long time he met with good reasons why their re-equipment was not possible—the expense involved, the shortage of red facecloth, the fact that the regiment was now mechanized, and the lack of trained horses and riders. He kept plugging away, found out exactly how many yards of red cloth were being turned out by the mills, inquiring of the officers how many horses were required to mount a ceremonial guard, getting the Lord Provost of Edinburgh and the Secretary of State for Scotland on his side.

During the second visit to Edinburgh, just described, he noticed that the detachment from the regiment was in its prewar glory. It had been just another typical Fairbanks' operation. The final decision had been taken by someone else, and quite where along the line his share of the responsibility could be pinned down, no one can say. But if he had not been prepared to act as gadfly, the whole subject might well have been dropped. The difficulty which any Fairbanks' biographer has to face is in assessing the value of the part he has played in scores of similar circumstances. He is seldom the determining agent, but times without number he has been the principal persuader.

For nearly two years now he has been the most active protagonist of shipping the whole personnel of London's Royal Tournament in an aircraft carrier to the United States to give their incomparable display to an American audience, feeling, and quite rightly, that it would be one more gesture likely to increase Anglo-American amity. As a director of the American branch of the English-Speaking Union, he participated in the original plan, and in a purely private capacity helped with advice and suggestions, concerning the visit of the Queen Mother to the United States in the autumn of 1954. He has become a governor of the Shakespeare Memorial Theatre at Stratford-on-Avon, treasurer of the Alexandra Rose Day, is an active patron of the American Legion and French, Belgian, and British veterans organizations, has been promoted captain in the U. S. Naval Reserve, is President of the British-America Alumni Association, composed of exchange students. . . . He has had three holidays in fifteen years.

20

DURING A RECENT VISIT to the United States, Douglas succumbed to a virus infection and was confined to bed in his suite at the St. Regis Hotel in New York. Dr. Mason Hicks was called on again to render his professional services. "Every time I went in to examine him I had to throw half a dozen people out of his bedroom," says the doctor. "No one made any effort to move. They were projecting a movie on the wall, the radio was blaring in the next room, the telephone bell pealed constantly, and visitors kept coming and going. If you don't mind, I'd like to see my patient, I had to tell them."

"Why don't you stick around and relax?" asked Douglas.

"Relax in this?" queried Dr. Hicks. "I don't know how you stand it."

"I can't," laughed Douglas.

Nothing seems to slow down the clatter of activity which makes up his life. He can look drawn, white, and pinched beyond his years, getting up at six one morning and going to bed at three the next, but he still possesses astonishing powers of recuperation. *"Il ne faut pas ramasser la fatigue,"* quotes his old friend Gilbert Miller. "But Douglas seems to be able to pick it up and live happily on sheer exhaustion. The secret of his energy is that he can sleep better than anyone I ever knew. When he has stayed with us for an occasional weekend's rest, God knows few and far between, he can put in eleven or twelve hours' sleep and come up full of spring and energy. He has been doing this for years."

One of the characteristics he has inherited from his father is his ability to take a cat nap at any time of day. He can also relax physically during tense business conferences or long hours of concentration on the set, shifting his weight from one foot to the other like a crane, slouching when he sits, and putting his feet up when circumstances permit. The only surviving male of a highly volatile family, he has always sought to maintain, by contrast, an equable temperament. He will sometimes make a note to have a showdown with someone and then forget all about it, a process highly disconcerting to Mary Lee, who will be suitably cool to the person in disfavor, only to see Douglas at his most effusive.

The publication of this book finds Fairbanks at the age of forty-five, barely on the threshold of middle age, with a bewildering record of experience and accomplishment already behind him. His principal energies at the time of writing are being devoted, with apparent success, to establishing finally the position of personal and financial independence which will leave him free to concentrate on the world problems which absorb his interest. Neither he nor his best friends can foretell in what manner the intangible influence he has so far learned to wield will be brought to bear.

His own temperament has always prevented him from surrendering the ubiquity he prefers for the more closely defined framework of life of diplomat, administrator, or politician, yet he possesses abundant qualifications for each or all. The trim, athletic figure and impeccable tailoring have become a hallmark. The fair hair, graying now and receding at the temples, adds dignity to the boyish charm he will never lose.

Charm is an elusive commodity and almost impossible to reduce to the terms of a printed page. A young woman who knows and likes him well gives this picture of him: "He is not at first glance overwhelmingly good-looking, although he is undoubtedly handsome of face and figure. His attraction lies in his very blue and twinkling eyes and his smile. He has a 'way with women' and you fall for it with your own eyes wide open. He conveys, directly but decorously, that you are looking your best and then pays you the ultimate compliment of talking intelligently to you and listening as if your words were important. He will manage to imply that you for him are the only person in the room. No woman could fail to be flattered, although she may know that by reputation he is an outrageous flirt, and by her own instinct the first place in his heart belongs to his wife and children."

It was James Barrie who said that if you have charm you do not need anything else; Fairbanks certainly has it, although he has much more as well. His good English friend, Constantine Benson, came very near the essence of it when he described Douglas in the terms Rudyard Kipling applied to his Elephant Child, as a man "full of 'satiable curtiosity." The Elephant Child, it will be recalled, asked ever so many questions, and so indeed does Fairbanks. But he asks them with such grace and avidity and interest that his immediate companion has the pleasant feeling that he or she is the only person worth Fairbanks' attention. It is a most endearing characteristic and one which few men of real worth have lacked.

He is always looking for the best in everyone he meets. "Rather like a dog that's always wagging its tail and simply can't believe it when someone hits it over the snout," as one of his friends has said. There is in him this almost pathological urge to heal differences wherever he finds them, allied with tremendous enthusiasm for any good causes that attract his attention. Friends who give him some impartial account of international difficulties they have encountered are liable to have Fairbanks turn on them and say: "Why don't you do something about it? Why don't you speak to so-and-so or write to so-and-so?"—oblivious of the fact that those with less personality than himself do not possess the same means to do so. He also has the saving trait of an unquenchable sense of humor, which enables him to stop dead and laugh at himself. It is a rare gift for people as intelligent and hard-working and serious-minded as he is to possess this lighter side as well.

At some time in the near future Fairbanks may have to take another decision about the geographical location and nature of his activities. His acceptance in Europe is based on the fact that he is an American. In the United States he is liable to attract the comment that he has become too European, and almost an expatriate, although his television film series keeps his name and personality before the general public, most of whom are ignorant of the fact that he has spent almost all the last two years out of the country. When he went back to the States a few months ago, after being away for ten or eleven months, the policemen and taxi drivers asked, "How are things in California?" Three people at the airport said, "How did you manage to go abroad and come back so quickly, we only saw you on the air four nights ago?"

There are others, more influential, who are apt to comment, "He's been so long in Europe, he doesn't know his own country." Douglas could probably stand for office, an idea that has been suggested at various times by various people, but his skin is not really thick enough for the abuse and rough and tumble of party politics. Nor does he wish to get bogged down in Washington in an administrative job, feeling that in the end it would really bore him and that he would not do it very well being bored. "I don't want to concentrate on any one country," he says. "I know the life ambassadors have to lead and what they have to do. I know how specialized and restricted their operations are. Far grander than anything I could aspire to, but still a restricted operation, restricted to one area. I would rather be a free-lance and hop around in my own way."

His whole life to date has been bedeviled by the necessity of earning enough money to do the things he wants. Not as a means of enjoying his leisure time, which is the sum of normal ambition, but to provide the sense of complete independence which would enable him to make some more positive contribution to the well-being of his fellow world citizens. American public life is still so organized that many positions of influence, outside the ranks of the professional politicians, can only be held by extremely rich men. Some of the most devoted, selfless, and effective administrators and ambassadors in America are men of immense private means, so that it sometimes seems almost a condition of their appointment.

There have been from time to time rumors that Fairbanks is thinking of taking out British citizenship. It is not an intention he has ever expressed himself. In fact, he has frequently been at some pains publicly to deny the suggestion, and all his friends agree that it would be a fatal error. The greatest service he can render, with his unique understanding of both the American and European points of view, is to help to interpret to the countries of the Old World the policies and position of the new giant who has become the arbiter in their affairs. At the same time he can represent in his own country some of the quirks and resentments they find so baffling in their allies, but this he can only do as an American. The next stage in the Fairbanks career is for him to decide exactly in what manner or appointment he can best bring this influence to bear.

For Fairbanks this is a period of transition, a pause to recharge his batteries, consolidating his personal economics as a springboard for whatever the next twenty years bring. He will talk of his own personal problems with perfect candor. The best time to foster reminiscence is late in the evening, when Mary Lee has left him to his papers and gone to bed, and he relaxes quietly over a weak whisky and soda in The Boltons study.

He acknowledges cheerfully that his career as a Hollywood star is probably over. "My withdrawal," as he calls it, "is due both to the desire to go into the business end more fully, but also to the fact that I've been at it thirty years now. I've been what is known as a 'star,' that is really technically a star, my name above the title, for twenty-five years, which is more than twice as long as you're expected to last in this profession. I don't mean to say that I'm bored with it, but actually I have very few fresh ideas. The more grandiose of my former ambitions in this direction have been for one reason or another frustrated. I have never, at least not since I was very young, really enjoyed acting at all. I like to create, I like to build a thing and have a finger in a lot of pies. The few enthusiasms I have left in terms of actually playing are relatively minor. I've had a good deal of the best of it, am not particularly awed by the results, enjoy the work and enjoy the medium enormously —I think it's a wonderful medium—but at the same time I'm obliged to be guided largely by economic considerations, as I have had to be all my life.

"The effect of being recognized wherever I go is something which I take in my stride now, having been born to it and not having known anything else ever since I was an infant. The fact that you are somebody whom people look at—they don't always turn around with either admiration, respect or anything other than curiosity, but at least they do—is something of which you become aware and accept as part of the pattern of your life. It wouldn't bother me for one moment if it were to disappear tomorrow, because it is not a thing for me like it would be for other people, for whom it might be new and exciting and glamorous and fun.

"On the other hand, I recognize it, cold-bloodedly, as a medium through which other things can be done. If I persist in my professional life, it is always with the idea of keeping the door open for the occasion when I want to go on the radio or stand up at a dinner and say something on a subject of importance. There is a fair guarantee that people will have enough curiosity to stop, look and listen. That opens up the persuasive role behind the scenes. Not being a political figure in the strictest sense of the word, nor even a diplomatic or literary figure, the opportunities for getting many public things done would, were this interest to lessen or disappear, be severely restricted.

"By nature I hate being the center of attention. I don't like public life as such, it embarrasses me to be on the stage, it embarrasses me to be on a platform or in public. I know that has been my whole life and that I seem to get away with it. I seem to be at ease on the surface, but that is no indication at all of what goes on inside. It's a question of training. I have certain things that I feel must be done, either professional or economic, other things which are ideals, and I've now disciplined myself not to let my nervousness or sense of insecurity be apparent, so that the job can be done as well as possible.

"I suppose that the desire to do or help do something is in itself a form of ambition. If you're born with a certain integrity and you're well trained in your profession, you don't do a thing only for its sensation value. If I'd been inclined in that direction I would have allowed myself to have signed a long-term contract many years ago and just followed the routine formula of the industry. I would have compromised my own ideas in favor of someone else's taste. I've preferred not to do it that way. I have stayed in the same business, but played according to my own personal rules.

"In a way my possible usefulness on a wide mass public scale must to a certain extent be diminished so long as I am not, as an individual, on the public scene as much. As my whole life has been a series of ups and downs and cycles, it doesn't particularly discourage me. You begin to judge your career rather like a stock market or your own bank account, and concentrate on what can you do about it and still be honest to your own objectives, without selling yourself down the river, and keeping to your own standards of behavior and integrity.

"I realize that many of the things I want to do, a lot of my ideas, are to a considerable extent dependent on what might be called my celebrity value. Not in the really close personal contacts I've made. To the friends who know me as a person, it would not make any difference if my name were Joe Blow, but it would make a difference to somebody else I had not yet met or to appealing to people on a wide scale.

"A great many of the people I see and talk to seek me out largely because they are curious about a celebrity. Sometimes they are people with axes to grind, who feel that possibly I can pass a word through to the right places. That undergoes seasonal fluctuation, almost a barometer of your status. There are others, the most important, who are sufficiently aware of what I may be useful at, or who share enough friendship to listen, to talk to me and pay attention to what I have to say, whatever my position may be at the time. They know from experience that I am not going to abuse that friendship, they know exactly where my sympathies lie and what my point of view is, always was and still continues to be, an attempt to translate certain ideas away from the rose-colored-glasses state of mind, into some form of practical working operation, and to apply them to what I know is the workaday world. As a result of the years in my profession I have a certain instinct as to how masses would react to certain sets of circumstances, what they would accept and when and how to approach them. I have a fairly professional attitude toward mass psychology, tinged with instinct as to the right or wrong time to present a case.

"I suppose that there are too many facets to what may be laughingly called my 'character.' I was born with too many vitamins and more energy than I have a right to have, at once a sort of romanticist and a cynical idealist. I believe in many things, but am quite prepared to be disillusioned and go on optimistically hoping. That is part of the American breed, always the optimist. The belief in the happy ending is a national rather than a personal trait.

"Although I have worked hard all my life, the difficult times tend to go out of my head. That's part of my own chemistry. I have loved every minute of what must be to most people the equivalent of ninety years of living, crowded into a relatively short time. I am still fascinated by the world and the people who inhabit it.

"That sounds as if I'm a person with one foot on a cloud and another on a banana peel—but I don't think I am. I do have certain objectives, certain things that I want to do. The very fact that they're not as clearly defined as other people's objectives are, is partly deliberate. I could clarify them if I wanted to, but I find the expression of their clarification almost impossible. I'm not quite as vague or quite as undecided as this might sound. Although the horizon is worth working toward, I'm not quite certain in my own mind that I shall ever quite achieve it. What one should do is aim toward it all the time, because it's beyond the power of any man to decide the goal of his lifetime or of his generation or his epoch. If I believe in the pot at the end of the rainbow, it really doesn't matter if I ever get there. The fun of chasing it is reward enough for me."